"To gain 1,000 ideas all at once and gain all the advantages, read this brilliant, illuminating book."

—Mark Victor Hansen
Co-author, *Chicken Soup for the Soul*

"The 'Guerrilla' approach to business and life has become a classic. I've learned from the entire series . . . but *this one* is the best! *Negotiating* gives you the specifics for gaining a *fair* advantage. I love it."

—Jim Cathcart
Author, *The Acorn Principle*

"Messrs. Smith, Wilson, and Levinson have done it again! A straightforward, deeply researched book . . . a bullseye hit . . . to help all of us interested . . . to *really* enhance our negotiating powers!"

—Nick Carter
Vice President, Nightingale-Conant

"The Guerrilla Group has done it again. Sit down at the feet of the masters and learn how to negotiate right. And while you're at it, pray that your competition doesn't read this book."

—Guy Kawasaki
Author, *Rules for Revolutionaries,* and CEO, garage.com

"There they go again, the 'Guerrilla Guys,' showing us how to beat the odds, use our smaller size to our advantage, and more than anything, win with class . . . and for the benefit of ALL concerned."

—Bob Burg
Author, *Endless Referrals: Network Your Everyday Contacts Into Sales*

"You guys are amazing! Ano ... ible ideas that can be put to wor ...

... CSP

Guerrilla Negotiating

UNCONVENTIONAL WEAPONS AND TACTICS TO GET WHAT YOU WANT

JAY CONRAD LEVINSON
MARK S. A. SMITH
ORVEL RAY WILSON, CSP

John Wiley & Sons, Inc.

New York ➤ Chichester ➤ Weinheim ➤ Brisbane ➤ Singapore ➤ Toronto

Copyright © 1999 by Jay Conrad Levinson, Mark S. A. Smith,
Orvel Ray Wilson, CSP. All rights reserved.
Published by John Wiley & Sons, Inc.

Published simultaneously in Canada.

This publication is designed to provide accurate and authoritative information in regard to the subject matter covered.
It is sold with the understanding that the publisher is not
engaged in rendering professional services. If professional
advice or other expert assistance is required, the services of
a competent professional person should be sought.

Library of Congress Cataloging-in-Publication Data:

Levinson, Jay Conrad.
    Guerrilla negotiating : unconventional weapons and
tactics to get what you want / Jay Conrad Levinson, Mark
S.A. Smith, Orvel Ray Wilson.
        p.   cm.
    Includes index.
    ISBN 0-471-33021-3 (pbk. : alk. paper)
    1. Negotiation in business.   I. Wilson, Orvel Ray.
II. Smith, Mark S. A.   III. Title.
    HD58.6.L48   1999
    658.4'052—dc21   98-48158
                                                  CIP

Printed in the United States of America.
10 9 8 7 6 5 4 3 2 1

This book is dedicated to our children,
who taught us what relentless negotiating means.
And we're still proud of how they've turned out.

Acknowledgments

To all of our audience members and clients. Their tough questions drive us to find new and innovative answers. They are the source of our stories. They are the reason we write books.

To our wives and families, who put up with our absences for months at a stretch while we tour the world collecting all these ideas.

To our literary agents, Mike Larsen and Elizabeth Pomada, who are so fond of saying, "There's a book in that!"

To our colleagues in the National Speakers Association, who keep cheering us on.

A special thanks to Mike Hamilton, our editor at John Wiley & Sons. This is the third book he's championed for us, and we're grateful.

Contents

Chapter 4 Guerrilla Negotiating Tactics   71

Chapter 5 Guerrilla Negotiating Power Words   103

Preface

■ WHAT DO WE MEAN BY "GUERRILLA"?

When it comes to negotiating, the sale of a condominium or computer or corporate jet is an obvious example. But the vast majority of negotiations are more subtle, more pernicious. You are negotiating constantly with almost everyone you meet, for time, for resources, for space on the subway. You negotiate with your spouse over which movie you'll watch, and with your teenagers over car keys and curfews. You negotiate with lenders and laundries, as well as with lawyers. We can tell you one thing for certain: These people do not have your best interests in mind.

No one today can survive in business without understanding two things: first, that negotiating is an integral part of living, and second, that the quality of your negotiating determines the quality of your life.

■ IT'S NOT FAIR

You are not paranoid. They really *are* out to get you. Vendors from Asia to Austria to Argentina are attacking your markets, competing on price, and claiming superiority. They use every possible trick to turn your customers, take your profits, and tear down your business.

Customers are more demanding than ever before. Consumers no longer settle for shoddy quality or unresponsive service. They have more choices than ever, and you have to be positively *exceptional* to maintain their loyalty. To win the business in today's brutal battlefield, you must become a guerrilla.

■ WHAT'S A GUERRILLA?

Just as a lightly armed, fast-moving band of ragtags can paralyze an army, the business guerrilla can rapidly deploy business weapons and psychological tactics to gain an unfair advantage over their counterpart. Just like freedom-fighting guerrillas, you rely on *information* and *surprise* to gain a tactical advantage.

Guerrilla Negotiating®[1] is not so much a collection of techniques as it is an attitude, an approach, a philosophy of doing business. Guerrillas build a constituency of dedicated followers by consistently maintaining the highest standards of quality, service, and business principles. The guerrilla looks beyond the commission to the greater good. They often do the very *last* thing their competitors, or even their *customers,* expect. They tell the truth at all times, at all costs.

Guerrillas rely on *time, energy,* and *imagination* instead of the brute force of a big-budget marketing campaign or an army of salespeople. These are the three arenas where no one can outspend you.

The most powerful weapon in your negotiating arsenal is your own *passion* about what you're doing. The guerrilla has a good word for everyone, and never complains.

■ SET HIGH STANDARDS

To ensure that decisions and dealings will stand the test of time, guerrilla managers apply the litmus test of *fair-care-share.* Is it *fair* to all concerned? Do I really *care* about these people, and have I demonstrated my caring? Have I done my *share,* and a little bit more? Remember the mountaineer's motto, "Leave the campsite cleaner than you found it, and always leave some wood for the next fire." Follow these principles consistently and you can't go wrong.

---

[1] Guerrilla Negotiating is a registered trademark of The Guerrilla Group, Inc.

Introduction

It's a jungle out there. Buyers are using dirty tricks to get you to lower your prices. Customers tell you that they can find what you're selling cheaper. You're getting pressure from your boss to increase profits. The bank wants to raise your interest rate. Your employees want more money. Governments keep changing the rules. Global competition nips at your heels—and they don't have to obey the same laws that you do. It's an unfair world. Scary thought, isn't it?

■ WANT TO LEVEL THE PLAYING FIELD?

What if you suddenly discovered that you could read minds? Imagine the advantage that would give you as an entrepreneur, manager, or salesperson. What if you could detect, in *advance,* how much they're willing to pay, how much they need to charge, or how much they're willing to settle for, before opening your negotiation? You would be dangerous.

> What advantage would you gain if you had written proof of their position before starting?

> What would happen if you could sell your products at prices *higher* than your competition?

> What could you do if you understood the unconscious motivations of the Generation X kids who work for you, or the Boomers you report to, or the Matures who hold the purse strings?

1

How astounded would they be if you could answer their objections before they're even raised?

What if you could determine the outcome and write the contract before you made your presentation?

How would you feel if you could eliminate the fear, frustration, and financial losses of a failed negotiation?

Think about it. Haven't you ever wished that you could eliminate the conflict with your spouse, your teenagers, or your IRS auditor?

What if, when the odds are against you, you could level the playing field?

You hold in your hands the ideas and tactics you need to gain a fair advantage in an unfair world. Read on and you'll do *more* than level the playing field.

■ IGNORANCE IS EXPENSIVE

When you don't understand how to negotiate, every transaction is a crapshoot, and you may be taken for all you've got. You might try a tactic you've seen used in the movies. You might experiment with an approach you've heard your grandfather talk about. You'll probably feel stressed and you may panic, making an unwise move.

When you use guerrilla negotiating, your technique becomes invisible. You're able to look beyond today and see the implications of your decisions over the long haul. You can focus on what you want and how to get it, without worrying about which tactic to use and if it will work or not. You'll come to agreement quickly and without panicking.

■ SUCCESSFUL NEGOTIATION MEANS PREPARATION

Going into a negotiation without full armament is begging to be taken. Two-thirds of this book is about filling your arsenal with unconventional weapons and advanced tactics. Knowing how to deal with conflict and discomfort is the key to your negotiating success. And in this book, we'll prepare you to do so. The actual negotiating process is covered in the last third.

■ BEWARE OF THE OUTRAGEOUS

In our seminars all around the world, we've talked to tens of thousands of salespeople, working with thousands of different companies representing hundreds of industries. We've collected their favorite tactics, ideas, and war stories, and compiled them for you here.

Some of the ideas in this book are revealed here for the first time. We haven't taught them to anyone outside of our clients who've paid tens of thousands of dollars to learn them. Some of these are ideas you already know, and we'll ask you to think about them in a new way. Some of these ideas are things you used to do, and we'll remind you of how powerful they once were. Many of these ideas are new, and when you choose to use them, they will make you as successful as you wish to be. Some of these ideas are elegantly simple, and their simplicity may make you suspicious. Don't be. Often the most obvious yields the most impact.

You may judge some of our suggestions outrageous, outlandish, or even out-of-bounds, but we never advocate anything dishonest, dishonorable, or dangerous. Here's the deal: We will accept the risk of being controversial if you'll accept responsibility for selecting what's appropriate for yourself, your industry, and your customers. What works for one situation may not work for another. Practices that are considered acceptable in real estate may be unsuitable for selling industrial chemicals. Never run the risk of tarnishing your reputation. It's up to you to choose the weapons and tactics that will work for you.

Guerrillas deploy as many of these weapons and tactics as possible. Our job is to help you discover ways to improve your negotiation skills. You may disagree with our advice, but either way we've made you think. If you think your way is better, you're probably right. There is no *one* right way to approach negotiation. What works for you, works for you.

■ KNOW THE FUTURE IN ADVANCE

Can you keep a secret? The authors' families have a long history of psychic ability, and we can assure you that it's not magic, or evil, or sinister, although some people may wish to make it appear so. It's a natural skill that anyone can develop. The only reason most people aren't psychic is that they don't practice enough. This book shows you how to develop your skills to out-think, outmaneuver, and outsell any adversary.

Decades of experience have taught us how to apply these skills to business, and whether you are selling goods or services, buying a house or car, big ticket or small, this book gives you an advantage. This book puts you in control.

There are actually three ways to be psychic. Having well-developed intuition helps. Or you can use language that makes you *appear* to read minds, or even foretell the future. Or you can use modern research techniques to gather information with the skill of a private detective. In this book you'll learn how to use all three to gain a fair advantage over your unfair opponents.

■ KNOW THE LAW

This book isn't written to give you legal advice. Rules and regulations may limit what you can say and do in a negotiation. Government antitrust laws prevent you from discussing certain items with certain competitors. State and local legislation may impose other restrictions. Your company may have another set of standards. Ask your legal counsel and your corporate leaders what's not acceptable in a negotiation. Get regular updates for your protection.

Chapter

1

Why Negotiate?

You negotiate all the time. It's unavoidable. Most things are negotiable, and when you don't have the tools and skills to negotiate, you're not maximizing your opportunities. Your negotiation ability determines your income, who works with you, and how you'll grow your company. How well you negotiate will determine what kind of car you drive, where you'll go on vacation, and which schools your children will attend. How surprised would you be to discover that you *can* get what you want *and* have the other party be happy, too?

Decide to become a skilled negotiator and practice constantly: at the market, in business, with your friends and colleagues.

■ 25 REASONS TO NEGOTIATE AND WHY SOME PEOPLE DON'T

Many people think that negotiation means dickering over some trinket at a flea market. They think that if they're haggling, they're being chintzy. These attitudes create a barrier to getting what they want, and what they deserve. Change your view of negotiating and you'll get more and can give more.

Here are 25 reasons to negotiate, and some of the most common mistakes people make when negotiating.[1]

---

[1] Rutherford, Dr. Robert D., *The 25 Most Common Mistakes Made in Negotiating . . . and What YOU Can Do About Them.* Boulder, CO: Rutherford Group, 1998.

5

1. You Can and Should Negotiate

Have you ever failed to negotiate even though it was likely that you could have gotten what you wanted? How often have you seen others do the same? Most people are intimidated by negotiation. Think about it. Perhaps you've never been trained in the basics of negotiation. Or if you have some training, perhaps you feel that you don't have enough experience. Possibly you don't feel comfortable with some of the tactics you've read about, so you avoid negotiating.

Looking back at those situations, ask yourself, "Who won as a result?" The likely answer is "nobody." Most negotiations are not won or lost at the bargaining table. They are lost before they start, because the parties never *get* to the bargaining table.

Guerrillas are always ready, willing, and able to negotiate. They know that their careers, their lifestyle, and the health of their business depend on it.

2. There Is a Bigger Pie

It's natural to assume that negotiating is a zero-sum game, that your gain is someone else's loss. But this is seldom the case. Too often, both parties enter a negotiation with preconceived notions about what is available to be divided. If you are willing to expand your thinking, explore options, and discuss alternatives, then you will discover greater possibilities for everyone.

Break through this barrier by asking, "On what basis am I making my assumptions?" and "What evidence do I have that there is a fixed pie, with nothing else available?"

In the negotiation, ask questions like, "Would you consider . . . ?" or "What would happen if we were to . . . ?" or "What would it be like if . . . ?"

Consider this. We often see something only after someone has pointed it out, then we're struck by the blinding flash of the obvious. This is particularly true in the negotiating arena. Guerrillas take the initiative to be observant and creative. They gain the advantage by looking for possibilities for *mutual* gain that have gone unexplored. They are always thinking, "How else could we do this?"

3. Don't Define Winning as Beating the Other Guy

This concept comes out of the war model of negotiating. Someone conquers, someone is conquered. In the new millenium, *coopetition* (cooperative competition) is king. In many situations, the only way you can get what you want is to give your counterpart what they want. That means a collaborative, cooperative effort at mutual problem solving.

By definition, a successful negotiation is one in which *both* parties are satisfied with the outcome. Unfortunately, we all know people who see negotiation as a contest that they *must* win. They cling to the preconception that negotiation requires a certain kind of toughness. They demonstrate their mettle by adopting a hard line and conceding little or nothing to their opponents. This adversarial approach starts arguments, elicits retaliation, and leaves ill feelings. In virtually every case, the aggrieved party will find ways to get even by whatever sabotage or subterfuge they can manage, even if they can't get ahead.

Although there are times when it may be perfectly appropriate to be uncompromising, if you're preoccupied with winning at all costs, you may lose the opportunity to create a more mutually satisfying outcome.

Guerrillas strive for an acceptable outcome for *both* parties, knowing that in this small world, what goes around, comes around.

4. The Other Party Will Give You What You Want

How many times have you thought to yourself, "Oh, they'd *never* agree to that . . ."? How do you know? Is your belief based on an understanding of the facts, or on your own limited expectations? Check out your assumptions. Ask for more. More time, more money, more space, more help. Ask someone else. Ask again. Ask, "What would have to happen in order to make this work for you?" Ask, "If you can't do that, what *can* you do?" If you are not willing to ask for more, then you must be willing to settle for less.

Guerrillas know what they want and they ask for it.

5. You Have Just as Much Power as the Other Guy

Power takes many forms. It can be positional, as in the case of an elected official, or it can be technical, based on special training or education, as in the case of an attorney. It can even be personal; some people are powerful simply by virtue of their charisma. Power ultimately means the ability to influence others. Too often, negotiators attribute more power to their counterpart than they actually have. The result is a weakening of your own position.

When it comes to power, what you *think* is what you *get*. You probably have far more power than you imagine. In fact, when you think you have power, you do—even if you actually don't. And when you have power, but don't think you do, then you don't.

Guerrillas evaluate the power of their counterpart. Here's how:

Do Your Homework

Gather information about your opponents, their strengths and weaknesses, their aims and goals, their styles of negotiating, and their options.

Understand Yourself

Give yourself full credit for your own strengths and weaknesses. Decide which alternative you'll choose if the negotiation doesn't go your way. Nothing gives you more power in a negotiation than having an array of well thought-out options.

Evaluate the Other Parties' Options

They may not be as attractive as you think. They wouldn't be negotiating with you unless they thought there was something to gain.

Consider the Alternative

What's your best alternative outside negotiating? You may have an attractive alternative available without giving up anything.

6. The Other Party Isn't the Enemy

Too often, people approach a negotiation with an adversarial attitude. They set out to beat their counterpart and may become more preoccupied with winning than with getting a favorable outcome. In some cases, this attitude may be appropriate, even necessary, but those situations are rare. It is almost impossible to gain a mutually acceptable agreement when an us-versus-them atmosphere prevails. This almost always leads to an escalation of emotions, hostility, and conflict. The result is almost certain deadlock.

Guerrillas approach the negotiation from another angle. Physically go over to their side. Instead of sitting across from them at the table, put your chairs in a semicircle facing a flip chart and brainstorm options. Schedule the next meeting at their offices instead of your own.

7. Negotiating Creates Confidence, a Positive Self-Image, a Sense of Self-Worth

A common mistake is to have low self-esteem concerning your ability to negotiate. Like anything else, negotiation is a learned skill that can be developed and improved with training and practice. Your confidence increases with every negotiation you conduct. Your counterpart's agreement increases your self-image and personal value. If you see yourself as a powerless victim, unworthy of respect, then it's likely you will behave as an unworthy negotiator.

You may be responding to past conditioning that taught it's rude to ask for things, that you're being selfish or greedy. Or you might believe that if you get what you want, that others will somehow be deprived. You might fall into the this-is-too-good-to-be-true trap. Perhaps you believe that negotiation is only for specialists like lawyers or union stewards. Or perhaps you believe that negotiating is for tough guys who sit in boardrooms and smoke cigars. All of these assumptions can undermine your self-image and destroy your confidence.

Guerrillas know that they can be just as good at negotiating as a sports agent. With the ideas in this book, you can be even more effective.

Shortly after he received his license, Orvel's 16-year-old son was involved in a minor traffic accident. There was a major snowstorm, and the streets were icy and slick. While making a turn, he lost control, skidded across traffic, and was struck by another car. The officer on the scene gave him a ticket for driving at a speed unsafe for the conditions.

When his day in court came, he decided to challenge the charge. He asked the city attorney for copies of the evidence, including the accident report, and the report from the investigating officer. Even though the report showed that the accident was clearly his fault, and without the help of an attorney, he successfully negotiated the charge down from unsafe speed (a four-point violation) to defective headlight (a one-point violation). And he's just a kid!

8. Don't Let Your Ego Get in the Way of a Successful Negotiation

Sometimes we are our own worst enemies. You put yourself at a disadvantage when you are overly concerned about what others will think about you. When negotiating, you're not only working to solve a problem, but you're also dealing with people's feelings, emotions, and fears. It's costly when one spends valuable time and energy attempting to save face or trying to look okay. It can happen when one party sees granting a concession as a personal attack.

The guerrilla's strategy is to separate the people from the problem. They are hard on the problem, but easy on the people. Be considerate and empathetic. Use qualifiers like, "I realize that this isn't your fault, but . . ." or, "This may be beyond the span of your control, but . . ."

A negotiation is no place to show off your cleverness. If you appear to win at someone else's expense, it's likely they'll sabotage you in the end.

9. Prepare Properly

Preparing for your negotiation will help you improve the quality of your planning. Even if you don't end up at the bargaining table, you'll have a complete plan of action for your project. To succeed, you must bring as many issues under your control as possible. There are already too many unknown quantities in a negotiation, so give yourself every possible advantage by controlling as many as you can.

Here's how guerrillas prepare:

Know Your Boundaries
Set limits on your most optimistic expectation and your most pessimistic acceptable settlement.

Know What You Intend to Get
This is particularly crucial when the matters to be negotiated are complex and cannot be reduced to a single price or goal.

Know Your Rationale
Be prepared to justify every request. If you offer a particular price or set of terms, why should your counterpart agree? Why is it beneficial? If you can't answer these questions, you have no basis for your position.

10. Set Priorities on Demands, Needs, and Wants

Negotiating is a give-and-take process. This exchange requires that you establish priorities about what you want to gain and what you are willing to give up. When you are clear about the purpose of the negotiation, you can develop a hierarchy of demands.

Guerrillas rank order their objectives before starting the negotiation. Your first list is your *must gets*. If these demands are not met, then you are better off saying "no." Your second list is your *intend to gets,* which are not quite as crucial, but will often determine your degree of satisfaction with the outcome. The third list is your *nice to gets,* and when all goes well, you'll get some or all of these. They have value, but are not really crucial to the negotiation. Putting your demands or goals into these categories enhances your negotiating power.

11. Establish the "Rules of the Game" in Advance

One of the most common mistakes is to assume that you are only negotiating the *agreement* (price, terms, or compensation) without consideration for the *process*.

Guerrillas establish the rules up front. How are you going to negotiate? Who speaks for which side? How much authority do the respective parties have? What happens if you become deadlocked? How binding are the terms? Where will the venue be?

On whose turf will the negotiation take place? How you negotiate the rules of the game may radically affect the outcome. Remember that the *process* is a negotiable item. Deal with it before it becomes a disadvantage for you.

12. Establish Enough Trust to Negotiate Successfully

Trust is critical to your success. Someone who doesn't trust you will act more negatively and more cautiously toward you. This creates a barrier that can impede or even derail your negotiation. When your counterpart doesn't trust you, it's virtually impossible to arrive at a mutually beneficial agreement. They will spend unproductive time and energy to protect themselves from being exploited.

Guerrillas build trust between the parties to effect mutual gain. Ask yourself, "Why would my counterpart mistrust me?" Can this mistrust be overcome to gain an acceptable agreement?

An atmosphere of trust can be built in several ways:

Past Performance
Do you have a reputation for doing what you say you will do? Bring proof in letters of agreement, testimonials, and referrals.

Flexibility
Flexibility demonstrates a willingness to be open and receptive to meet the needs of others. Illustrate flexibility in your availability. Explore options for the location of the discussion.

Disclosure
Negotiation requires a willingness to risk open, direct communication. When appropriate, take the chance that your counterpart will not take advantage of your frankness.

Negotiated Recourse
You may need to sign a nondisclosure agreement, a warranty contract, put up a bond, put money into escrow, or agree to a penalty clause if you don't perform. Offering such commitments early in the process facilitates a more trusting and more productive negotiation.

Ask

"What would I need to do to build enough trust for us to continue? How can I demonstrate my good faith?"

13. Set Negotiating Expectations and Aspirations

In the negotiations—and in life—you don't always get what you want, but you almost always get what you expect. Expectations play an influential role in any negotiation. Guerrillas set high expectations. When you're optimistic about the outcome, your counterpart will be optimistic as well. You'll substantially increase the odds that you both will be satisfied with the outcome.

14. Manage the Other Person's Expectations

You are responsible for managing *two* sets of expectations: yours, and your counterpart's. All disappointment is the result of violated expectations. If your counterpart is unhappy with the outcome, it's because of unmet expectations.

Guerrillas create an advantage by outlining what both parties can expect to achieve in the negotiation. Start by conveying a realistic picture of your expectations to your counterpart, and then outline a conservative picture of what they can expect to achieve. If the end result exceeds their expectations, they will be delighted, even astounded.

15. Defend and Value Concessions

Negotiation can be viewed as a series of trade-offs and compromises. You give and take concessions in order to reach an agreement. Make every concession count. What you have to offer has value, or you wouldn't be negotiating.

Create an advantage in any negotiation by following this fundamental guerrilla principle: Never concede *anything* without asking for *something, anything,* in return. Make every concession conditional, and obligate your counterpart to offer something in exchange. The condition *defends* the concession. If you do not require a reciprocal concession, then your concession will be perceived to have little or no value.

Guerrillas create a negotiating advantage by offering a small concession, then asking for a *large* concession in exchange. Although the likely response will be "no," it establishes value for you, and you are much more likely to reach a favorable outcome.

16. Require Reciprocal Concessions

Look at it this way: A concession is not a gift. The only reason to offer a concession is to get something in exchange. Perhaps your counterpart has nothing of apparent value to exchange. Guerrillas reserve the right to *withdraw* the concession, or to request an unspecified concession in the future.

17. Your Concessions Have Value

You might think your concession is mundane. To paraphrase the old saw, your trash is their treasure. An important strategy in guerrilla negotiating is to offer concessions that have little value to you, but have high value to your counterpart. Evaluate what you have to offer from your counterpart's point of view.

Let's say that you are interviewing a perspective employee, and negotiating the starting salary. Your firm has much more to offer than just a paycheck. This job may also be an opportunity for the candidate to gain experience, get special training, work with sophisticated equipment, work in a casual environment, or work flexible hours. You may be able to offer health insurance, day care, a company car, or the opportunity to travel. The entire *package* determines the true value of the job.

For example, that old reel mower that's been sitting in your garage for years may be useless to you, especially since you bought your new riding yard tractor. But for an urban homeowner who has only a tiny patch of lawn to maintain, it may be just the right tool for the job. No noise to bother the neighbors, no fumes, no engine repairs, no gas or oil, and it hangs up out of the way on the garage wall. All he has to do is *push* it.

18. Know What You Want in Exchange for a Concession

There will be times when you're not sure what they have to offer, or what they might be willing to give, or what you will need later on. Get a clear picture of why you are negotiating, and review your goals and objectives.

If necessary, call a time-out. Guerrillas gain the advantage by saying, "I will do this for you, *if* you will do this for me in return." At a minimum, be clear that your counterpart owes you one. This tactic can create problems. How *much* do they owe? When? These questions open the possibility for further negotiation, and may later erode your position. Fix the worth of the concession in advance to preempt these problems.

19. Manage Damaging Information

"We've got a bunch in stock," volunteers the sales rep. After that statement, the price is going down. If the rep had first established how many the customer wanted, then that information would be valuable. "Well, the good news is that we have enough in stock to meet your needs."

Information is one of the guerrilla's secret weapons, so be careful when and how much you disclose to your counterpart. Some legal proceedings require full disclosure by both sides, but most negotiations aren't that formal. To arrive at an outcome, both parties must exchange *enough* information to arrive at a settlement. But you're not required not tell the *whole* story. You are not under oath to tell the whole truth at the outset.

When shopping for a used piano, Orvel Ray answered a newspaper ad. The piano was a beautiful upright in a massive walnut cabinet. The seller was asking $1,000, and it would have been a bargain at that price, but Orvel had received a $700 tax refund, and had set this windfall as the limit that he could afford to invest. He searched for a negotiating advantage.

He was able to deduce several facts from the surroundings. The finished basement where the piano sat also contained a set of drums, and an upright acoustic bass stood in the corner. Obviously the seller was a serious musician, and probably played jazz. There had to be a compelling reason for selling such a beautiful instrument.

Orvel asked the first, obvious question, "Are you buying a new piano?"

The seller hesitated. "Well, I don't know yet. See, we're moving to North Carolina, and it would be very expensive to ship this piano clear across the country."

"Did they say how much extra it would cost?" Orvel queried.

"They said an extra $300 or so."

"When do you have to decide?"

"The packers are coming this afternoon."

Now Orvel knew where the seller was vulnerable. He could ship the piano cross-country, or sell it for $700 and still break even. Or he could hold out for his asking price and take his chances. "Here's what I can do: I can give you $700 in cash, right now," Orvel said as he took seven $100 bills out of his pocket and spread them on the keyboard. "And I can have a truck and three of my friends here to move it *out of your way* by noon today."

The seller hesitated, then picked up the money. "Well, I suppose that would work. I can always buy a new piano when we get settled."

Orvel left before the seller could reconsider. By the time the group returned with the truck, the seller had received three other offers at his asking price, but because he had accepted the cash, he had to tell them that the piano had already been sold.

If the seller had not *volunteered* the information about the packers coming that afternoon, Orvel may not have been able to negotiate the price.

20. Be Flexible in Your Negotiation Position

A common mistake is to take a position and then cast it in concrete. "I want $200,000 for this house, and I won't settle for a penny less." Insisting on a particular position precludes other, potentially advantageous options.

It's often said, "You can name your price if I can name my terms."

Guerrillas gain the advantage by exploring other possibilities that may be of value instead insisting on their price. You may make more profit on the financing than on the sale.

21. Confront the Other Party When Appropriate

Your counterpart in the negotiation may be less than honest, or may be using dirty tricks, or may simply have bad information. In these cases, a failure to confront these issues seriously jeopardizes the negotiation. You may feel uncomfortable confronting them because you've been taught that it's selfish or impolite to point out another person's mistake or unfair practice. But do not confuse your need to be liked with the need to be respected.

Here's how the guerrilla gains the advantage:

Do Your Homework
There's no substitute for knowing as much as possible in advance.

Accept the Inevitable
Negotiation is almost always a confrontational process. View this as a positive part of the challenge.

Rehearse Scenarios
What's the worst that could happen if you were to confront your counterpart? What would you do if that happened? Role-play possible outcomes.

Divide and Conquer
Take on only one part of the confrontation at a time. Use the Colombo approach: "Just one more thing . . . ?"

22. Avoid the "Sympathy Trap"

Of course you want to be seen as a good person—kind, generous, and sympathetic. But a negotiation is not social work; it is not charity. You are negotiating to reach a mutually advantageous outcome. It's your responsibility to look after your own best interests. Others in your organization are depending on you.

When guerrillas find themselves feeling sorry for their counterpart, they ask themselves, "Whose problem is this?" You will discover that although it may indeed be an unfortunate situation, it is not *your* problem. Ask yourself, "At what cost am I being sympathetic? Is it worth the price?"

23. Empathize with the Other Party

One of the most effective ways to understand *what* your counterpart wants, and *why* they want it, is to develop the skill of empathy. You gain an advantage in negotiating by putting yourself in their position. That doesn't necessarily mean that you *agree* with their position. Just that you *understand* and *appreciate* their situation.

Gain an advantage by using the guerrilla-negotiating phrase, *"I understand."* This phrase can have many meanings. It can mean "I agree," or it can mean, "I see what you mean," or it can mean, "Enough, already, you've made your point." It can even mean, "I think you're an idiot, but I'm not going to comment on that right now." You understand.

Use "I understand," instead of "I disagree," as in, "I understand that you feel your price is justified, *and* I can only pay . . ." then present your counteroffer.

You can also develop empathy by practicing *role reversal.* Outline the negotiating situation, then take the position of your counterpart. Rehearse with a colleague.

24. Develop Strong Rationales for Your Demands

The proper construction of demands is critical to the success of any negotiation. "That's what I want," while valid, is seldom a persuasive position.

Always state a *rationale* when making a request in a negotiation. It's easy to forget. Developing a rationale requires time, energy, understanding, and planning. You may feel that you're giving up your power when you defend, explain, and justify every demand you are making. Chances are your counterpart isn't thinking about your situation. They won't see things from your point of view unless you justify your position. The rationale is what defends the demand, and gives it weight and value.

Guerrillas use the magic word *because.* "This is important to me because . . ." This is particularly effective when combined with the word *need.* "I *need* a six-month lease *because* I'm going to school." Read more about creating influence in Chapter 4.

Never present your rationale from your counterpart's point of view. Present it from your own point of view. This protects the rationale from being sabotaged, or hijacked. If you build your rationale on what you *think* is important to your counterpart, and you're wrong, then the rationale loses much if not all of its value.

25. Search for Options

Guerrilla negotiators are often able to get what they want, while at the same time, meeting the needs of others. Seldom is there only one right answer. Although flexibility is often mistakenly equated with being indecisive, inconsistent, or weak, it is one of the guerrilla's most potent weapons.

Develop your flexibility by being open to testing a new idea, following through on a suggestion, or considering alternatives. To meet these various needs, the guerrilla often has to shift gears, and suspend or abandon a particular line of negotiation in favor of an entirely different strategy. Recognize when you and your counterpart are deadlocked on a particular issue; offer to "put that item aside for now" and continue. Often, when you revisit the issue later, it seems much less important in the larger scheme of things.

■ WHAT YOU CAN GIVE AND GET

Here is a list of things you can negotiate in your favor or concede to their favor.

➤ Price

- ➤ Shipping charges
- ➤ Guaranteed prices
- ➤ Partial shipments
- ➤ Delayed payment
- ➤ Financing terms
- ➤ Extended warranty
- ➤ Guaranteed upgrade
- ➤ Free upgrades
- ➤ Free trial period
- ➤ Return privileges
- ➤ Waived restocking charges

- ➤ Duties paid or waived
- ➤ Taxes paid or waived
- ➤ No setup charges
- ➤ Free installation
- ➤ Two for one
- ➤ Samples
- ➤ Free software
- ➤ Reduced interest rates
- ➤ Waived service fees
- ➤ Payment of a premium
- ➤ Future discounts
- ➤ Waived security deposit
- ➤ Trade-ins
- ➤ Free change orders

➤ Delivery

- ➤ Multiple release points
- ➤ On-site stocking
- ➤ Early delivery
- ➤ Loaners
- ➤ Customs clearance brokering
- ➤ Favorable positioning
- ➤ Extended deadline

➤ Quality

- ➤ Upgrades
- ➤ Guaranteed trade-in

➤ Consumables

- ➤ Paid utilities
- ➤ Spare parts
- ➤ Maintenance

➤ Fuel
➤ Supplies
➤ Raw materials

➤ Support

➤ Extra documentation
➤ User training
➤ On-site support
➤ Maintenance training
➤ Temporary help
➤ International support
➤ Toll-free support line

➤ Add-ons

➤ Accessories

➤ Comfort Factors

➤ Free accommodations
➤ Free meals
➤ Free drinks
➤ Free coffee
➤ Free cleaning
➤ Free transportation
➤ Free uniforms
➤ Free laundry service
➤ Free phone calls

➤ Business Help

➤ Marketing assistance
➤ Co-op advertising money
➤ Consulting

➤ Database exchange
➤ Free follow-up visits
➤ Personal benefits
➤ Referrals

➤ Intangibles

➤ Future favors
➤ Introductions
➤ More time
➤ Information
➤ Priority status

■ WHEN YOU SHOULDN'T NEGOTIATE

There are times when you should avoid negotiating. In these situations, stand your ground and you'll come out ahead.

➤ When You'd Lose the Farm

If you're in a situation where you could lose everything, choose other options rather than negotiate.

➤ When You're Sold Out

When you're running at capacity, don't deal. Raise your prices instead.

➤ When the Demands Are Unethical

Don't negotiate if your counterpart asks for something that you cannot support because it's illegal, unethical, or morally inappropriate. When your character or your reputation is compromised, you lose in the long run.

➤ When You Don't Care

If you have no stake in the outcome, don't negotiate. You have everything to lose and nothing to gain.

➤ When You Don't Have Time

When you're pressed for time, you may choose not to negotiate. If the time pressure works against you, you'll make mistakes, and you may fail to consider the implications of your concessions. When under the gun, you'll settle for less than you could otherwise get.

➤ When They Act in Bad Faith

Stop the negotiation when your counterpart shows signs of acting in bad faith. If you can't trust their negotiating, you can't trust their agreement. In this case, negotiation is of little or no value. Stick to your guns and cover your position, or discredit them.

➤ When Waiting Would Improve Your Position

Perhaps you'll have a new technology available soon. Maybe your financial situation will improve. Another opportunity may present itself. If the odds are good that you'll gain ground with a delay, wait.

➤ When You're Not Prepared

If you don't prepare, you'll think of all your best questions, responses, and concessions on the way home. Gathering your reconnaissance and rehearsing the negotiation will pay off handsomely. If you're not ready, just say "no."

➤ Better to Beg Forgiveness

A number of years ago, the Boulder Jaycees approached the city Parks Department to build a small playground next to the city-owned baseball diamonds. Many of these Jaycees played league softball, and were concerned about their children dodging traffic on the adjacent busy street. The Parks Department quickly agreed to their request. In fact, the city had already planned to build just such a playground—in five years.

The Jaycees asked the city planner for a copy of the site plan, and left the meeting feeling somewhat disappointed. At the next Jaycee meeting, they decided to adopt the playground as a project, and try to negotiate to accelerate the city's timetable. One member, who ran a landscape company, volunteered to do the excavation. Another, who managed a lumberyard, offered to donate the fencing. And so it went. Over the next four weeks, material, equipment, and manpower were quietly mobilized. In a single weekend, using all volunteer labor, these Jaycees built the playground, exactly to city spec, and on Monday morning, called the Parks office to come out and inspect it.

"That's impossible," they were told. "It will take several weeks just to get the necessary permits." When the laughter finally subsided, the Jaycee explained, "Of course it's possible. It's already been done—just five years ahead of schedule."

Negotiating Styles

The old model of negotiation was *win-lose*. You win, they lose. You would give up a concession and they would take an advantage. There was a fixed pie that you carved up among the participants and the pieces they took came out of your share.

■ EVERYONE KNOWS THE OLD TACTICS

You may have seen the movies, *Glengarry Glen Ross, Used Cars,* or *Tin Men*. If so, you know about the *shut up* tactic: make a statement and shut up, the next person who speaks, loses. You know about *the stall:* endless delay until one party caves. You know about *the higher authority:* "I'll have to check with my manager," common in car sales. You know about *take it or leave it:* where you have no choice. You know about the old-school negotiation tactics. And you won't be a victim of them anymore.

People now have more choices, more knowledge, and more power than ever before. They refuse to be blatantly manipulated, and will retreat in a hurry if they smell a rat. They know that there's another vendor that can help, and they know how to find them.

■ THE NEGOTIATION EVOLUTION

Win-lose has been around forever. It's based on a model of war, where an opponent is conquered and their property taken away. Negotiated settlements meant moving borders.

Win-win negotiating became popular in the 1970s. Although it has had followers all along, it became the widely accepted right thing to do. Often, too much was relinquished by both sides, making the win less palatable for both parties.

Guerrillas look for the bigger pie. The old belief of limited resources is fading.[1] Technology makes the pie bigger. We expand our oil supply by using it more efficiently. We create more real estate by building high-rise buildings. We replace transportation with telecommuting. We replace paper and ink with electronic publishing.

Imagine, in 1979, during the height of the gasoline shortage, if someone had told you, "Twenty years from now, all cars will have computers built into the engines, and they will go three times as far on a gallon of gas as they do today. At the same time, these cars will be more powerful, more responsive, and emit just a fraction of the air pollution." You would have carted them off to the funny farm.

■ THE GUERRILLA'S APPROACH

Because the world's an unfair place, guerrillas look to gain a fair advantage everywhere and in every possible way. Guerrillas gain an advantage when they find new unconventional ways to create valuable outcomes. How can we expand resources to give us more than we initially expected? How can we look at the situation in a new way to find unexpected gains? What innovation can we tap to get more?

➤ Why Is It Different?

The guerrilla constantly seeks *agreement*, because by definition, a successful outcome is one that both parties can accept. Agreement is what makes business work. It's what makes relationships work, and makes the world work.

Agree to agree. Begin the negotiation by agreeing that both parties will work toward a mutually satisfying outcome. This pre-frame focuses everyone on collaboration and problem solving rather than posturing and positioning.

---

[1] Toffler, Alvin and Heidi. *The Third Wave*. New York: Bantam Books, 1991.

Find, acknowledge, and document any points of agreement that might arise, no matter how small, then use these points as building blocks, rather than saying we disagree about this or that, consider them a *counterpart* rather than an *opponent*. Negotiation is not a contest, and this shift in perspective will free up creative energy you otherwise would have wasted on confrontation.

➤ Gain Share

We asked the kids to be more conscientious about turning off the lights around the house to save energy, then encouraged them by offering to split the resulting savings on the electric bill. This classic gain-share negotiation resulted in a $20 monthly savings, and a $10 increase in their allowance, while teaching appropriate energy conservation habits.

Guerrillas will look for similar opportunities to encourage their negotiation counterpart to comply or compromise, and then share in the resulting gain. For example, if employees need to work overtime to meet a deadline, let them share in the resulting savings over bringing in temporaries to complete the project. Because profit is often a function of sales volume, increase the commission by a share of the gross margin on orders turned in once the rep has exceeded a certain quota. Employee stock option plans (ESOPs) swept the nation in the 1980s as a new way to get everyone invested in the company's success.

➤ The Bigger Pie

In this guerrilla approach, everyone benefits from making the pie larger. Management agrees to specific wage increases on the condition that the union agrees to accept certain types of automation and delivers specific increases in productivity. Vacation time is extended for employees who do not use their sick days. "If you kids pick up your toys while I finish my work, we can leave earlier for the swimming pool."

➤ Win, Win, Win, Win, Win

Traditional negotiating usually ignores outside parties. Although some of your counterparts will follow the every-man-for-himself approach, and go after the best deal they can get for themselves, they often forget about all of the other people affected by the resulting agreement. Yet many of your counterparts will want more than just having their own way. They want all parties concerned to win. They want to win, they want you to win, they want their organization to win, they want the community to win, and they want the environment to win.

Guerrillas test their counterparts for these sensitivities with questions, then appeal to the greater good. You'll learn how later in this book.

➤ Almost Everything Is Negotiable

Keep an open mind during the negotiation. The conventional wisdom that "everything's negotiable" is misleading. In reality, everything is not negotiable, or to state it another way, not everything is always negotiable. Because people have certain values, beliefs, and principles that they will not compromise, the guerrilla tries to determine exactly what the true boundaries of negotiability really are. Once you've set aside those points that are indeed nonnegotiable, everything else is fair game. Now you're in a very powerful position.

■ STYLES OF NEGOTIATING

Your approach to the negotiation may be determined by the strategy of your counterpart. Most people have a particular strategy that they use in negotiations. These styles differ along a continuum ranging from *total indifference* to *adamant insistence*. In order to negotiate effectively, you must try to match the level of resistance you face. If you take a laissez-faire attitude toward your counterpart's hardball approach, you will lose. Recognize the style of negotiation being used by your opponent and adjust your counterstrategy accordingly.

➤ Whatever

This person offers no resistance at all, and virtually gives up the negotiation even before it's begun. They concede to "whatever you want." This "have-it-your-way" approach may be appropriate when you have little or no investment in the outcome. It may also be a smoke screen that conceals a more aggressive, covert attack. You may feel uncomfortable making even legitimate requests. You may also reciprocate by giving in without asking for what you really need.

The guerrilla response to this strategy is to ask for more than you really want, more than you even feel comfortable requesting. "Well, in that case, I'll take it *all*." You may gain a windfall, or at least stimulate a more substantive discussion of the issues.

Use this approach when dealing with customers who are dissatisfied and upset, and it really *was* your fault. Just ask, "What would you like me to do?" or "What would it take to make this right?" and *wait* for them to respond. Often the adjustment they ask for will be less than the one you would have offered.

An important point when using the whatever style: If customers ask for something you really can't do, avoid saying, "I can't do that." Instead simply counter, "I understand your request. What I *can* do is . . ."

➤ Whatever's Fair

These negotiators take the position that "as long as it's fair" they will accept the outcome. But beware. They are asking you to define what constitutes "fair." Because you will want to be seen in a favorable light, viewed as being a "fair" person, you may be overly generous, compromise needlessly, or concede more than you really should. On the other hand, they too wish to be viewed as equitable, and they may be more interested in how you view them. Or they may simply be using an appeal to fairness as a smoke screen to rationalize an otherwise unfair position.

A successful negotiation is not necessarily fair. The guerrilla response to this strategy is to weigh the scales of "fairness" so that they tip at least slightly in your favor. In fact, the guerrilla's objective is to gain a fair advantage whenever possible, and then use that advantage to negotiate an equitable settlement. Otherwise you don't get the bargaining chips you will need later to trade for what you really want.

Use the Whatever's Fair approach when building consensus among members of a group who may have conflicting interests or agendas. When they can all agree on what's "fair," you'll get buy-in from the whole group.

➤ Nice Guy

These negotiators will try to ingratiate themselves to you and try to become your "friend," and then appeal to the relationship. They may appear to be very generous in the beginning, offering many small concessions so as to curry favor. They will appeal to your need to be loved and appreciated. They might say, "That's not a very friendly thing to do," when calling in their favors.

This style is often used as a counterpart to the Hardball in the classic game of White Hat, Black Hat. The glad-handing car salesman offers you a substantial discount, a handful of optional equipment, and an overly generous trade-in, only to have the deal shot down by the Hardball sales manager. Not wanting your new friend to get in into trouble with his boss, you agree to pay a much higher price for the car.

The guerrilla response to the Nice Guy strategy is to maintain your perspective and keep your focus on the *outcome* you're seeking. Ask yourself, "How much history do I *really* have with this person? Is our relationship more valuable than what's at stake here?" In many negotiation situations, you'll never see this person again.

Use this approach when there is a long history of antagonism in an adversarial relationship. Your warm friendliness may thaw a frozen position out of deadlock.

➤ Whiner

This approach appeals to your sympathy. While they commiserate about the weather, the traffic, and their business or financial woes, you're put off balance. After listening to their whining for a while, you may find yourself granting concessions out of pure condolence.

The guerrilla response to this strategy is to ask yourself, "Who's problem is this?" and then ask yourself, "Is this problem germane to the settlement?" If it's not *your* problem, don't try to fix it, and if it's not relevant to the negotiation, ignore it.

Use the Whiner approach when confronted with frivolous or absurd requests. "Awww, geeee, but I have *kids* to feed. . . . You've got to do better than that." By attempting to elicit a guilt response, you may encourage more reasonable demands.

➤ Stonewall

You may recognize this tactic as the one your spouse uses when annoyed with you. In this case, your counterpart becomes withdrawn and sullen, and may even refuse to talk. But this apparent retreat is tactically intended to apply pressure. You may become so uncomfortable with the silence that you back off from your position just to restart the conversation.

The guerrilla response to this strategy is to let them be quiet, but fill the dead airtime with something else. "Okay, let's put that aside for the time being," and change the subject. Keep the conversation open, but defer further negotiation as long as they continue the silent treatment.

Use the Stonewall approach when they demand detailed explanations of every point of your position. "I'm not discussing it!" is a fair negotiating position.

➤ Guilt Trip

This counterpart will set you up to be wrong, then take advantage of your vulnerability when you're feeling guilty for being so demanding. This is a one-way ticket to being taken.

The guerrilla responds by remaining objective. Refuse to let your emotions control you. Do you really have a reason to feel culpable?

Use the Guilt Trip approach when your counterpart has injured you in some way, so as to escalate the stakes in your favor. Better still, offer forgiveness for the smallest slight or insult, especially if it was minor or unintentional. Unconditional forgiveness is the most effective way to induce guilt.

➤ The Nibbler

The Nibbler will work out the best deal they can, then ask for "just one more thing," and then a little something else, then one more tiny thing. Just when you think you have an agreement, they balk and ask, "but what about . . ." They have pen in hand, ready to sign, and they ask, "This *does* include the extended warranty, doesn't it?" They are like a small leak that sinks a large boat.

Because they will ask for more and more and more until you say, "no!" the guerrilla response to this strategy is to just say "no," or at least say, "I'm sorry, but I can't." (Learn 11 ways to say "no" in Chapter 8.) Or you can say, "I can do that, but *only* if you agree to write three recommendation letters and sign the contract now!" Asking for a substantial reciprocal concession usually stops the Nibbler.

Use the Nibble approach when you suspect that you have struck an agreement near the bottom of your acceptable settlement range. It never hurts for you to ask for "just one more thing . . ." They might say yes. Offer to act now if they do. "I could buy this car *right now* if you could just upgrade the radio."

➤ Tit-for-Tat

This negotiator uses a give-and-take approach, and will not offer a concession, not even a minor one, without demanding a reciprocal concession in exchange. They may be belligerent in their insistence.

The guerrilla response to this strategy is to keep your reciprocal concessions small, but be prepared to make a bunch of them. Brainstorm a long list of small concessions in advance so you'll be forearmed.

Use this approach when your counterpart is resistant to negotiating, or reluctant to budge from their original position. By offering some small compromise, you may be able to break the logjam. Also use this approach when confronted with the Nibbler.

➤ Rule Book

This negotiator will focus on the form and format of the negotiation, placing great importance on the place and time, the shape of the table, or the formatting of the documents. They will cry "foul" and bring the negotiations to a halt if they feel that the rules are being broken. This preoccupation with the process is a ploy to distract you from the actual outcome, and you may make the mistake of granting real concessions in exchange for mere exceptions to protocol. Beware, because they will often structure the process so as to create every possible endemic advantage for themselves.

The guerrilla response to this strategy is to mentally separate the form from the substance of the negotiation. Ask questions concerning their reasons, and request explanations of their position. "I'm confused. Can you help me understand how a different table will move us toward an agreement?" You should be just as adamant about procedural issues as your adversary, but do not let the rules of the game keep you from playing to win.

Use the Rule Book approach when you suspect that you are being hustled, rushed, or pressured into a decision. Insist on a particular timetable, or ask for an external review before making a binding commitment. Sleep on it. Insist that the contract be subject to the laws of your home state, or that future disputes be settled by binding arbitration. Impose your own set of technicalities.

➤ Hardball

Stubborn, uncompromising, and belligerent, this counterpart is a negotiator's nightmare, because they're not really interested in negotiating at all. They want their own way, and they are unwilling or unable to consider an alternative position.

The guerrilla response to this strategy is to look for ways to satisfy their core issues, without giving in yourself. They're playing for as much as they can get, often to stroke their ego or to show that they're a tough negotiator. Often what they really need is a lot less than what they're asking for.

Use the Hardball approach when you feel *very* strongly about the issues at hand, or when the requested concession runs counter to your moral or ethical values.

➤ Infantile

This party approaches the negotiation with the emotional maturity of a two-year-old. They want it all, and will scream, scratch, and throw a fit until they get what they think is theirs. Their approach is summarized in the following list:

Eight Laws of Toddler Property

   1. If I like it, it's mine.

   2. If it's in my hand, it's mine.

   3. If I can take it from you, it's mine.

   4. If I had it a little while ago, it's mine.

5. If it's mine, it must never appear to be yours in any way.

6. If I'm building something, all the pieces are mine.

7. If it looks just like mine, it's mine.

8. If I think it's mine, it's mine.

One approach to Infantile negotiators may be a reprimand. Better yet, find someone else to negotiate with. Move them along with, "I can't help you, you'll need to talk with someone else."

Forewarned is forearmed. By recognizing these old-school tactics, you can neutralize them before you give up your advantage.

■ YOUR NEGOTIATION SUCCESS FACTORS

Fifty percent of your success as a negotiator is dependent on the motivation of your counterpart, 40 percent of your success is based on the relationship you have with them, and only 10 percent of your success depends on the way the agreement is structured. (See Figure 2.1)

Most negotiators focus on the structure of the agreement and overlook the larger opportunity. Conversely, when guerrillas manage their counterpart's motivation and the focus on relationship, then the structure of the agreement comes together smoothly. In later chapters you'll learn how to manage their motivation and your relationship in order to gain an advantage.

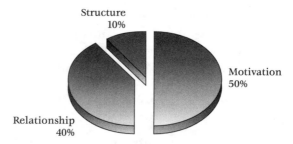

Figure 2.1 The success of your negotiation relies on these three factors. The least important is the way the deal is structured.

➤ Preferred Learning Style

Guerrillas gain an advantage by presenting proposals in the form and format that's easiest for their counterpart to understand. By supporting your position with forms of proof that are easy to understand and accept, you make it easier for your counterpart to agree to your proposals.

There are three ways people learn: by doing, by watching, and by listening. Different people have different preferences for processing information. When you can use all three of these learning modes, everyone on the negotiating team will process the proposal in the way that is best for them.

Physical Learners

Thirty-seven percent of the population are physical or kinesthetic learners.[2] They learn best by moving, touching, smelling, tasting, and experiencing. Demonstrate your ideas with samples, models, and trials. Give them the 50-cent tour.

They will respond to phrases like:

"That feels about right."

"Something here smells fishy."

"I've got it handled."

"Oh, the sweet smell of success."

"That left a bad taste in my mouth"

"I know what you mean."

"I don't get it."

Auditory Learners

Thirty-four percent of the population are auditory learners.[3] They learn by talking it over, discussing the issues, and brainstorming. They will often switch positions, debating one side of the question, then the other. By *talking* themselves through the issues, they arrive at a conclusion (which can be very confusing from your point of view.) When you hear these phrases, your counterpart is in auditory mode.

---

[2] Specific Diagnostic Studies, Rockville, MD; 5,300-person sample from the United States, Hong Kong, and Japan.

[3] Ibid.

They will respond to phrases like:

"Sounds great."

"Tell it like it is."

"That rings a bell."

"I hear you."

"We're in harmony."

"That's music to my ears."

Visual Learners

Twenty-nine percent of the population are visual learners.[4] They learn best by looking at objects, seeing pictures, or reading. Here are phrases that indicate your counterpart is in visual learning mode.

They will respond to phrases like:

"Looks good to me."

"Picture this."

"It seems unclear."

"I see what you mean."

"What's your point?"

"In a black mood."

"Things are looking up."

➤ How Adults Retain Information

People remember only 20 percent of what they hear. They forget 50 percent of a monologue within 30 minutes, and forget 80 percent within two weeks (see Figure 2.2). On the other hand, they remember 25 percent of what they write down. The reason why they don't remember more is because their notes are sketchy and incomplete. Always encourage your counterpart to discuss issues because people retain more than 75 percent of what they talk about. This will work to your advantage because they are more likely to remember the key points of discussion. Guerrillas also gain an advantage by maintaining an open dialogue during their presentation.

---

[4] Ibid.

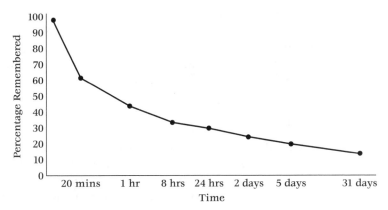

Figure 2.2 The Ebbinghouse curve of forgetting, based on experiments done between 1879 and 1885. Subjects forget two-thirds of what they hear within eight hours.

Seven Reasons to Take Notes

1. Taking notes helps focus your attention. You won't be able to think up a response while you're writing. When you're listening to them, you don't want to be considering your counteroffer, because you might miss something vital.

2. Your counterpart knows you're paying attention. You demonstrate that their opinions are important and you'll instill trust.

3. You don't have to look them in the eye the whole time; this can become uncomfortable. Occasionally, you may want to stare to create an advantage, but more often you'll want to make your counterpart feel as comfortable as possible.

4. Notes make it easy to resume the conversation. "Looking at the notes I took during our discussion . . ."

5. Your notes become a permanent record of the negotiation, encouraging your counterpart to speak with integrity. Later on they will be less likely to change their mind.

6. You can change the pace of the negotiation by putting down your pen and offering a comment in confidence: "Off the record . . ."

7. If negotiations are going badly and they keep changing their tune, crumple your notes and toss them aside. This guerrilla action graphically indicates that you consider

their side of the discussion to be worthless. Soften your action with an apology: "I'm sorry! I must have really missed something. Do you mind if we start over? I want to make sure that I understand what you want." You won't have to crumple another page.

➤ Feelings Count

Your counterpart will always remember how they felt about the negotiation. They'll remember if you made them feel anxious, angry, or happy. Manage their motivation by understanding what they want and need, and they'll remember the experience favorably.

➤ Smile

A warm, glowing smile is one of the most powerful weapons in your negotiating arsenal, because it makes a statement about the *relationship*. It's almost impossible to feel hostility toward someone who is smiling. Sounds simplistic, but when making an adamant demand, look your counterpart right in the eye and give them the warmest, friendliest smile you can muster. Then think to yourself, "I *really* like you!" The twinkle in your eyes will momentarily derail their rational mind, and they will be much more compliant. Ironically, this is especially effective if your counterpart is in a dark mood.

A few months ago, Mark special-ordered an expensive digital tape recorder from a local electronics firm. Later, while traveling on business, he found the same item in stock at another store, and bought it there. On his return, he went back to the first store to cancel the special order. The receipt was clearly marked, in bold type, **NO REFUNDS**. This policy was reinforced by a sign on the wall behind the register, **NO REFUNDS**. Mark smiled at the sales clerk and opened the negotiation, "I need to cancel this order and arrange for a refund," and handed over the receipt.

The clerk replied, "I can't do that."

Instead of getting angry or contentious, Mark smiled warmly, thought to himself, "Gee you're a really nice guy!" and responded, "I understand. Who do we need to talk to in order to *get this done?*" (Notice the use of an imbedded command at the end of his request.)

"We need to talk to the manager, but he's busy right now."

Mark smiled even bigger, now delighted to hear this good news. "Great! I'll be *happy* to wait."

After a 30-second conference, the manager came to the register and refunded all of the money, no questions asked.

■ NEGOTIATING WITH GENERATION X, BABY BOOMERS, AND MATURES

Your style of negotiating will also be influenced by the age of your counterpart, particularly if they are considerably younger or older than you are. Intergenerational negotiations can be tricky and confusing, because the values of the negotiators determine what's important, and ultimately what they'll agree to.[5] Values are created by major events in history and how opinion makers reacted to those events, and there are profound differences from generation to generation.

➤ Matures

Matures are those people born before 1946. Today they hold the wealth and the power. Living through the Great Depression has made them conservative by nature, so they protect their assets and resources. They were strongly influenced by World War II, and the promise of Social Security. Family is important to Matures because they grew up with extended families, where children, parents, and grandparents lived together in the same home or neighborhood. Matures were raised with an emphasis on family values. They probably attended church. They were raised to do the right thing, to work hard, to respect their duty to God and country and company, and respond to the values of sacrifice and thriftiness. The difference between right and wrong was clear. They saved money until they had enough, then they bought things. They separate social classes into *dos* and *do nots*.

When negotiating with Matures, focus on what's fair, and appeal to their sense of right and wrong. Show how you're making a sacrifice for them, and that you'll work hard on their

---

[5] For more information on this topic, contact Robert Wendover at Leadership Resources, Inc. (1-800-227-5510).

behalf. Stress loyalty and your willingness to work hard to gain an advantage.

➤ Baby Boomers

Boomers are those people who were born between 1946 and 1964. Growing up during a period of unprecedented economic prosperity made them more liberal. Their parents probably owned the house they lived in. They were the first generation to be exposed to television. Hollywood and the evening news influenced their values and perceptions. They lived through an age of political uncertainty, including the Kennedy assassination, Vietnam, and Watergate. It was an era of sex, drugs, and rock 'n' roll. No longer preoccupied with financial necessities, they set out on a quest for personal fulfillment. Raised during a period of optimism, they crusaded for causes. Institutions such as church, school, and work reinforced their beliefs. Money was easy, and confident in their future, Boomers bought things on the installment plan. They learned how to use technology to work more efficiently. They separate social classes into *haves* and *have nots*.

When negotiating with Boomers, show how your offer gives them personal fulfillment. You may have to include concessions that deliver a personal gain. Focus on the financial aspects of the deal, especially payment terms and conditions. Stress efficiency and show concern for everyone involved. Boomers tend to negotiate on behalf of what's best for their company.

➤ GenX

GenX (a term coined after the book *Generation X* by Douglas Coupland) are those people who were born between 1965 and 1980. The TV baby-sat this generation while their Boomer parents pursued dual careers. Tutored by Kermit the Frog and Big Bird, their attention span is set to MTV. They're masters of personal computers, cell phones, and pagers. Their view of the world is more pessimistic, strongly influenced by the threats of nuclear proliferation, high divorce rates, crack cocaine crazies, and AIDS. Cynical and mistrusting, they are resentful of their parents who had more. They tend to live for today, while looking for security and opportunity. They save more money than any other generation. They are also more entrepreneurial. Their ethics and standards are situational because they've been betrayed by their institutions. They'll judge what's right "in my context" and they continuously test the boundaries. They separate social classes into *knows* and *know nots*. Their goal is to use technology to eliminate work.

When negotiating with a GenX counterpart, show how you're increasing their personal security and expanding their options. Be aware that their sense of right and wrong may be different from your own. They'll laugh at most of the old methods of negotiating, and may play with the negotiating process just to see what happens. They respond to sincere recognition. They loathe meaningless tasks, petty politics, and revolt at the idea of "paying their dues." They won't be impressed by your war stories and they can't stand bureaucracy. They'll covet your contacts and your relationships with influential people. A promise of an introduction to someone powerful carries weight. They negotiate on behalf of their company and themselves.

➤ Millennials

Millennials are those people born after 1981. They live in an era of DVD and compact discs, Desert Storm, and Somalia. They're masters of cyberspace and the Internet. They simultaneously admire Dennis Rodman and Michael Jordan. They live in an environment where there is a general lack of adversity. Their goal is to have fun. Because of high demand for entry-level employment, they take jobs on their own terms. They know that all they have to do is show up, and they'll probably get what they want. Because their Boomer parents have money, they just ask for what they need. Being raised in an era of general mistrust of the government, they have no clear view of what's right.

Their vision of work is to watch someone else do it. They may have difficulty solving problems. Working with computers virtually from birth, they may exhibit "menu thinking." If it's not already right there in front of them on the screen, then it's not an option. They will work until they get stuck, then just stop, like a windup toy that has walked into a wall, awaiting redirection.

When negotiating with millennials, give them clear,

graphic, specific directions. If an option isn't spelled out, they may never consider it. They resist lectures about values. They rebel at comments about their clothing or appearance. They can't stand being compared with anyone else. They respond to choices and consequences. They don't care about protocol, just outcomes. And above all, they have to be constantly entertained and given a choice of fun things to do.

■ NEGOTIATING IN OTHER CULTURES

The cultural background of your counterpart will also influence your approach to negotiating. When working with other cultures, guerrillas take extra time to prepare and get advance coaching.[6] Other cultures have very different approaches to negotiating. For example, Asian cultures have a different view of what is true, basing their decisions on emotion and how they feel about you. Americans tend to be attached to numbers and logic, refusing to admit that emotion colors their view of the facts.

You can get great coaching from foreign exchange students at your local college or university. Check out http://www.profnet.org/intermar.html, http://www.geocities.com/Athens/Forum/8363/, and http://www.worldculture.com/index.html for more ideas.

---

[6] Morrison, Terri et al. *Kiss, Bow, or Shake Hands: How to Do Business in Sixty Countries.* Holbrook, MA: Bob Adams Publishing, 1994.

Chapter 3

Guerrilla Negotiating Weapons

Stock your arsenal with these guerrilla negotiating weapons. Each weapon gives you a fair advantage. Chose the weapons that will make the difference in your negotiation.

■ ACCESSORIES

Accessories usually have a much higher profit margin than the primary product. You can use accessories as high-value, low-cost bargaining chips. A tactic commonly used by new car dealers is to give you a deep discount on the price of the car, then charge you *full* price for the accessories. Because you've already committed to buying the car, you're in that impulse buying mode where another $1,100 for a sunroof doesn't seem all that expensive compared with the $30,000 commitment you've just made.

■ ADVERTISING

Offer to advertise on behalf of your counterpart, making funds conditional upon exclusivity, minimum quantities, or other criteria.

■ APPEARANCE

You can demand a higher price with a superior appearance. One of our client's rental units commands a 10-percent premium over other condos in the same complex because it is

43

always offered with a fresh coat of paint and immaculate carpet. Prospects remark, "This is the nicest looking place we've seen." He knows he has an advantage.

■ ATTIRE

You can gain an advantage with your clothing. If you want to give the air of authority, wear a uniform. For example, bankers and lawyers wear "power suits." Guerrillas will occasionally take the opposite stance. When you're facing a crowd in suits, you may opt to wear casual clothing. You gain an advantage by being different.

While in college, Mark would go to job interviews dressed in blue jeans. Sitting in the waiting room with everyone else in a suit, he stood out from the crowd. After his introduction, he would explain, "I came over here directly from work, and I'm going right back after we're done." That immediately opened the conversation about what he was doing now, and set him apart as a hard worker.

You can adjust your clothing to change the dynamics of the negotiation. When you want to get down to business, take off your jacket, and roll up your sleeves. Larry King has established his casual authority by wearing suspenders. You may wish to emulate his dress code.

■ AUTHORSHIP

"I wrote the book," creates incontrovertible authority. You can gain similar credibility when you write articles for publication in industry journals. Present your counterpart with copies of the article that you wrote to support your position. "I've written an article on the future of your industry. Would you like a copy?" You've just gained a fair advantage.

➤ Get Published

Here's how to get published. Next time you call a customer, ask them, "What's your favorite trade journal?" Get a copy from the library, look up the phone number on the masthead, and call the managing editor. This is the person responsible for getting the magazine out on time. Tell them, "I'm writing a *round-up article* on the *future* of our industry. (A round-up article consists of interviews of key industry leaders with their thoughts presented in a contrast-and-comparison format. Guerrillas write about the future, since it's *always* news.) Would you be interested in publishing it?" They'll readily agree, since they're always eager for good material. Now you have an assignment.

Call top officers you want to get to know. Say, "I'm writing an article *on assignment* for (trade journal) on the future of our industry. When may I have five or ten minutes to ask you a few questions?" They'll almost always grant an interview, because they want the free publicity.

Ask permission to tape-record the conversation for transcription. Ask questions like, "What do you think is the biggest challenge to the future success of our industry? What should the industry be doing now to eliminate those barriers? What do you think the industry will be like in 10 years?" Cut and paste together the interviews, writing introductory and closing phrases and transitions. This takes only a few hours. Ask the subject of your interview to send you a black-and-white glossy photo of themselves for inclusion, if possible.

Include *your* photo at the end and a small caption with the byline, "For more information, call to receive a free copy of our recommended list for . . ." and include a toll-free number, E-mail address, and Web site.

Oh, yes, it will get published. You interviewed the people the editors want quoted in their journal. Send a copy of the final printed article to the people you interviewed with their words highlighted. Enclose a note thanking them for making your article so powerful.

➤ Keep the Rights

When working with editors, always insist on a written agreement, that spells out what rights you are granting, even if you are not being paid for the article. Most publications automatically take *all* rights, so unless you spell out what rights you're granting, you lose control of your intellectual property. Grant *only* the rights necessary for the publication to run the article, but it is essential that you *reserve* all other rights. If the article is appearing for the first time, you can grant the publisher "First Rights." If the material has been published previously, you are granting "Reprint Rights only, one-time use." A client of ours in Romania ran several articles in a Romanian magazine, so we granted "Romanian language reprint rights only, one-time use."

You may want to publish the material again in another journal, magazine, pamphlet, or include it in a book. You may also want to develop audio or videotapes, CD-ROM, DVD, or other materials that would involve "Electronic" rights. You may want to publish in other languages. In any case, if you have inadvertently given up your rights to the material, it may create complications later on.

■ CASH

Cash has a magnetic, mystical quality. People will stare at a pile of cash as if they were the crown jewels. This is especially true when you bring out large bills. Be prepared to write a check, but walk into the negotiation with a briefcase full of small bills, put it on the table, and open it to demonstrate the size of your offer. Cash shows that you're serious.

■ CELL PHONE

When your counterpart says, "I've got to check with my boss," hand them your cell phone. When you need to take a break, say, "Call me on my cell phone when you're ready to move forward." Ask your assistant to call you at a specific time and to interrupt you if you expect trouble. You can excuse yourself to take the call or proceed—your choice.

Ask your counterpart, "Would you please turn off your cell phone and pager so that we can both work uninterrupted and arrive at a settlement?" Their agreement to turn off their phone also implies that they're willing to reach a settlement.

■ CHAT GROUPS

You can gain insider information by joining the appropriate Internet chat session and posing questions to the group about your counterpart. "Anybody have dealings with them? What was your experience? What advice would you have on doing business with them?" Use this type of background information carefully, since you don't know the accuracy or validity of the source.

■ COMPETING OFFER

"Hey, Paul, would you come on over to my place a little before three?" Orlo asked his neighbor during a phone call. "I've got someone coming over to look at the old Cadillac, and I need some competition. Just act interested."

When the prospect showed up, he saw two men poking around under the hood. Orlo greeted him, and introduced him to Paul who glanced up and grunted. After a quick tour of the car the prospect was obviously interested. "You mind if I take it for a spin?" he ventured.

Orlo looked at Paul. Paul shrugged his shoulders, "Sure. Remember, I was here first."

The prospect returned, impressed with the roominess and comfortable ride. "Okay, how much you want?"

Orlo quoted the price listed in the newspaper, and Paul objected, "Hey!"

The prospect stuck out his hand. "I'll take it!"

Orlo looked sheepishly at Paul and shook the now-buyer's hand.

After the new owner left, Paul said, "I can't believe he paid you that much for that old car!"

■ CONTRACTS

Good contracts are for well-meaning people with bad memories. Bring the contract to the negotiating table. Include clauses for exiting the agreement as well as for arbitrating disputes. When new players come on the scene, they have a written record of the ground rules. A potentially very valuable concession that you can almost always get for the asking is the option to *extend* the contract for a specified time, usually under the same terms.

■ CONVENIENCE

People will pay a premium for convenience. You've experienced this if you've ever been in one of these convenience stores, where you buy two loaves of bread and two gallons of milk, hand the clerk a 20-dollar bill, and get back four cents change.

■ CO-OP FUNDS

When negotiating with companies that advertise, explore the availability of co-op funds that can subsidize your media costs. Sometimes simply displaying a particular company's logo will earn you half the cost of the ad.

■ COSTUME

People in costume are given special consideration in any social situation. You can act up, act crazy, and act out a story in costume. They demand attention and compel people to listen. Your costume could be as elaborate as the Pillsbury Dough Boy, or as simple as a cowboy hat.

■ CREDIT CARD

Credit cards are a great way of offering financing. Guerrillas will offer to charge their counterpart's credit card for a portion of the deal over a period of months.

■ DEADLINES

A deadline is a commitment that your counterpart has made. They are motivated to keep that deadline. When you are the only person who can help them meet their deadline, you've got a strong advantage. When you know the cost of your counterpart missing their deadline, you'll have valuable insight into their settlement range.

■ DETAILS

"It has long been an axiom of mine that the little things are infinitely the most important."

SIR ARTHUR CONAN DOYLE, 1925

A board member of the Pepsi-Cola Company was in the market for a business jet. The Cessna dealer had the CitationJet clean, fueled, and catered, ready to take the prospect on a demonstration flight. The exec climbed on board and started poking around preflight, sitting on the seats, looking at the lavatory, working the window shades. He opened the galley and spotted cans of Coca-Cola. Without comment, he closed the cabinet and climbed out of the cabin. "Nice plane," was his only comment as he ducked into his limo and left.

The competing BeechJet salesman stocked the galley exclusively with Pepsi products, and won the sale of a $6 million dollar airplane.

■ E-MAIL

You may conduct your entire negotiation electronically. You can E-mail contracts for approval to various parties, speeding the agreement. Stay in contact with your counterpart, cut and paste information or news that supports your rationale. And back up all of your files; you may need them later to document the process.

■ EMOTION

A person who's crying can influence the outcome of a negotiation. More than one man has acquiesced to his girlfriend's request because of an emotional display.

■ ENTHUSIASM

Enthusiasm isn't negotiable, but it is contiguous. A young woman selling magazines door-to-door enthusiastically described publication after publication. Her presentation was so interesting and full of energy that Mark was compelled to listen and ended up buying three subscriptions—at a premium price.

■ EXPECTATION

When you raise your expectations, you'll get more. Sellers who start high get more. Buyers who ask for more get more. Sellers who make big concessions increase the expectations of their buyers, and vice versa.

Manage your expectations, keep them intact, and you gain an advantage.

■ FAIRNESS

Dean Akers owns a construction company. His secret to success is offering his customers a fair deal and providing excellent customer service, both woefully lacking in the trade. In a negotiation for a shopping mall project in Tampa, he met with a bevy of finance people. The lead buyer opens: "Dean, we want you to review your bid and make sure that everything is *fair*. Make any adjustments to your bid so you're offering us a fair price."

Dean replied, "What if I go home, review every line, and find that everything is already fair? If I made no changes, would you be mad at me?"

"No, of course not. But that's not how it works. We want you to rework your numbers to give us the fairest possible bid."

"Okay. Let me ask you a question. If all the prices were the same, whose bid would you pick?" said Dean, switching tactics.

"Well, we'd pick yours because of your reputation."

"So, you want to do business with me and the only hitch is that you want a fair deal. Is that right?"

"Yes. That's right," emphasized the buyer.

Dean jumped up. "I'll be back in five minutes," he said to the astonished buyer. Dean ran out to his pickup truck, reached behind the seat, and pulled out a box. He returned to the meeting room, opened the box, and took out an Ouija board.

"Okay, boys, I don't know what you call fair, so let's roll up our sleeves and use this all-seeing and all-knowing fortune-telling game to cut a fair deal."

The buyer laughed, and said, "Okay, Dean. I get your point. You play fair. You've got the contract."

■ FAX MACHINE

During telephone negotiations, take notes, either on your computer or by hand. Fax them the notes of your agreement. "I want you to review my notes to make sure that I'm not missing anything and I haven't misunderstood you." Ask them to initial the notes and fax them back. You'll cement your position and eliminate problems.

■ FOOD

Hunger is a very primal motivator. "As soon as we work out this point, we can go to lunch." In a sales contest, the losers take the winners out for dinner. The winners eat steak, the losers eat beans.

■ FURNITURE

You can turn discomfort to your advantage. Former commander of the U.S. nuclear submarine fleet, Admiral Hyman Rickover, sent out the side chairs from his office and had an inch cut off of each of the two front legs. Visitors found themselves sliding gradually off the front edge of the chairs.

You might remove some of the chairs from the negotiating table, limiting the number of delegates who can participate, or forcing spectators to stand. "Can you get us some more chairs?" becomes a concession.

In some circumstances, it may be to your advantage to create a comfortable environment, with cushy chairs that lull your counterpart. A conference center in California has a room equipped with a dozen wooden rocking chairs, just for this purpose. It's hard to be contentious when you're sitting in a rocking chair.

■ GENEROSITY

If you have established a reputation for being generous, you gain an advantage because your concessions will be perceived as being more substantive. If you are openly generous with your counterpart (especially during the early stages of the process), you mobilize the principle of *reciprocation* (see "How to Influence Your Prospect," in Chapter 4). When you pick up the check for lunch or dinner prior to beginning your discussions, they already owe you one.

■ GUARANTEE

Dealing with someone you don't know is risky business. Guarantees reduce the risk for your counterpart. It's the safety net that catches them if anything goes wrong. You can negotiate for a stronger or weaker guarantee. "Instead of your normal three-year guarantee, I'd like a five-year guarantee."

■ HIGHER CAUSE

Would you pay $4.00 for a dozen cookies if they weren't for the Girl Scouts? Let your counterpart know that what you're offering is supporting a higher cause. It's for the church, the widows and orphans, the Boy Scouts.

■ HOROSCOPE

You can use the common belief in astrology to your benefit. Check both your horoscope and that of your counterparts (http://www.astronet.com). If it's unfavorable for you and favorable for them, ignore it. But if it's favorable for you and unfavorable for them, you've got a weapon of possible psychological pressure. "You know, your horoscope isn't very promising today."

■ HOSPITALITY

Offering coffee and food to your counterpart creates a psychological debt, adding to your ability to gain concessions. Have refreshments catered in.

■ HUMOR

Guerrillas use humor to increase rapport. Use cartoons for a humor break (http://www.cartoons.com). Ask your counterpart to tell you the funniest thing that ever happened to them. Guerrillas avoid telling jokes that could offend their counterpart, and never use negative humor.

■ LAPTOP COMPUTER

Take your laptop computer and portable printer into the negotiation. Use it to present your multimedia presentation, show video clips, play audio clips, and play pre-meeting music to set the mood.

You can look up facts and go on-line to substantiate your position. Have a contract framework on your word processor, filling in the blanks as you go, and print the agreement on the spot.

■ LAWYERS

Have your attorney draft a letter summarizing your demands, perhaps even vaguely threatening legal action if an agreement cannot be reached. Knowing that counsel represents you gives you credibility and authority in any negotiation. The mere *threat* of a lawsuit may compel your counterpart into submission.

Make your final contract conditional upon *review by counsel.* If there are problems or loopholes, you can reopen the negotiations. Arrange to have your attorney available by telephone during the negotiation, so that you can call and ask questions if necessary. Call a recess to confer, or better yet, pick up your cell phone and say, "Let me check with my attorney on that."

Of course, the ultimate weapon is to take your attorney along to negotiate on your behalf. But beware. Many attorneys, while competent in the law, are not skilled negotiators. Ask around for referrals, and find a lawyer who has earned a reputation for being formidable. It's not how many cases they've won in court, but rather, how often they settle out of court that is a good test of their negotiation skills.

■ LIMOUSINES

Put your counterpart in a positive mood by picking them up in a limo. Many deals are made in the back of a limo. A limo can become your turf when you're traveling out of town. Or insist on being picked up by a limo at the airport.

■ MAGIC WAND

You can buy one at a magic shop for a couple of dollars, or in a pinch, just use a pen. "Imagine that this is a magic wand. Imagine if you could wave it and have anything you wish. Anything at all. What would you change about this deal?" This whimsical approach will let you discover attitudes that you'd otherwise miss.

■ MUSIC

Play soothing, upbeat music while your counterparts get settled. This creates a friendly, comfortable environment. We suggest light jazz because few people find it objectionable.

■ NEUTRAL TERRITORY

Suggest an off-site location to decrease your counterpart's position power if you're at a disadvantage. Many locations will naturally impose a time limit to the discussion. Here's a list of neutral locations.

Airline club room

Airplane

Bar

Church

Community hall

Country club

Hotel lobby

Hotel meeting room

Limousine

Local park

Museum

Restaurant

Sporting event

Sports facility

Train

Walking trail

Zoo

■ NEWS

If you can use a piece of video that has been in the news to support your position, check with your local television station. Network news departments keep everything in archive. If it's been on CNN, you can get a copy of it (for a fee of course) and use it in your presentation.

■ NEWS GROUPS

Post questions to Internet news groups asking for information and feedback on your counterpart. Search the archives for mentions and stories. Just be aware that the validity of this information can be suspect.

■ NEWSPAPERS

Most major newspapers have on-line archives that you can search by key word. You can also check for media releases from your counterpart on the Web. See the Appendix for a list of Internet URLs. Remember that stories written by a reporter may be more objective than the media releases written by your counterpart's PR firm.

■ NONDISCLOSURE AGREEMENTS

Parties agree in advance not to discuss the nature of the negotiation, the outcome of the negotiation, or even that the negotiation occurred. You may have good reasons to keep the terms of your final agreement private. You may choose to require your counterpart to execute a nondisclosure agreement prior to presenting a proposal. This reduces the risk of your competition getting their hands on your work.

Executing a nondisclosure agreement also creates an atmosphere of frankness for the negotiations. You are in effect saying, "This information is confidential, but I'm sharing it with you anyway."

■ ORIGINAL PACKAGING

When you're negotiating over used goods, having the original packaging increases the value. As any antique collector will tell you, saving the boxes and packaging can increase the valuation by 100 percent.

■ PAGER

Just like your cell phone, your pager can offer you relief from a negotiation. If you need to take a break, reach for your pager, look at it, and say, "I need to make a phone call." If you have an alphanumeric text pager, you can have a colleague send messages to you in the meeting if there's news you can use. "Pork bellies have just hit an all-time low. Bring home the bacon!"

■ PATTERN INTERRUPT

When your counterpart is stuck—they can't get past a certain behavior or demand, or when they're being uncooperative or disruptive, break their pattern by doing something completely out of character. Pull out a water gun and let them have it. Pick up your belongings and move to the other side of the table. Ask them to switch seats with you. Look at your watch and say, "It's time for my TV show." Stop and go out for ice cream. Take a walk.

■ PAY IN ADVANCE

Arrange in advance to pay for your counterpart's meal. Slip the maître d' your credit card before the meeting, tell him you do not want a bill presented, just add 20 percent as a gratuity, and that you'll stop by to sign the check before you leave. During dessert and coffee, excuse yourself (they'll assume you're going to the washroom) and take care of the paperwork. You'll gain an advantage with surprise and delight. Very guerrilla!

■ PAYMENT TERMS

Requesting or offering terms can mean the difference between a yes and a no deal. Terms could be as simple as 2 Net 30 (2 percent discount for paying early, full amount in 30 days), or possibly a more complex financing package.

■ POSTDATED CHECKS

Consider accepting a series of postdated checks to make terms simple. One of our colleagues increases her close rate with this tactic. When her counterpart says, "I can't afford it," she replies, "Can you afford one-third of it?" They'll say, "Sure." "Great," she says, "write me a check for a third. A second check for the second third payable in a month, and the third check payable the following month."

Beware, in some jurisdictions, a postdated check is considered a promissory note, and is subject to different collection rules than a check.

■ PHOTOS

Take pictures of your clients enjoying what you've done for them. No doubt you've walked into a car dealer and faced a board posted with hundreds of pictures of happy customers. The caption says, "We want your picture here." They're using the power of social proof. Prospects think, "This many people can't be wrong"

Couple photos with testimonial letters, and you have a powerful, double-whammy combination.

■ PRECEDENCE

This weapon has long been the basis of case law. In a negotiation for a lease of warehouse space, the landlord insisted on asking $5.80 a square foot, in a market where $5.00 a foot was the going rate, on the rationale that "I already have three other tenants who are paying $5.80."

■ PROFESSIONALISM

"I'm a professional," adds to your status. The difference between a professional and an amateur is that professionals never have a bad day. Granted, some days are better than others. Guerrillas operate with the utmost professionalism.

■ PROPS

Bring props to give your argument dramatic impact. Anything can become a prop: a map (helps find our way), a toy (boat, train, plane, ball, water gun), or a bottle of sludge.

■ PROVIDE AN ADVOCATE

During acquisition discussions between a big company buying a small company, the owner of the small company felt intimidated and deadlocked. To break the impasse, the larger company asked their counterpart to select a lawyer of his choice to be his advocate, and send them the bill. The generous offer of moral and legal support broke the stalemate.

■ PUBLIC OPINION

Poll your community on issues affecting your negotiating position. If the results are unfavorable, you can always discard them.

A car dealer had been petitioning the city for years for a zoning variance that would allow him to build a driveway into the service department that connected to a residential street. With microphone in hand and a video camera in tow, he asked each of the residents on the street how they felt about the potential increase in traffic, then compiled and edited the comments. This presentation dislodged the bureaucratic logjam and won him the variance.

■ PUBLICITY

The six most dreaded words in business are, "A crew from *Nightline* is here." For the guerrilla negotiator, there's no such thing as bad publicity. If your counterpart is doing well, send out press releases proclaiming their success. If they are uncooperative or acting contrary to the public interest, the threat of front-page coverage may motivate them to comply.

■ QUESTIONS

Knowing what questions to ask gives you an edge. Guerrillas consistently use two forms of questions: "How will you know . . ." and "Tell me about . . ." "How will you know who is best for this job?" or "How will you know I've done a good job?" "Tell me about your experience" or "Tell me about what you want." See Chapter 10 for more on constructing effective questions.

■ RACE

When negotiating with the government, you may have an advantage if your race is classified as a minority group. Often there are set-asides for minority-owned businesses. If they're available, ask for them.

■ REBATES

Offer to rebate your customer the difference when their purchases reach a certain threshold. "When you buy a total of

10,000 units, you will earn the 10K unit price, *and* we will rebate the difference on the units you've purchased to date." Now they have an incentive to buy more and more.

You can also offer to rebate the costs of freight, drayage, packaging, legal fees, travel, or any other item you choose, conditional upon your counterpart's compliance with some term or condition of your agreement. Move your inventory by making an offer such as, "Accept delivery by the 10th of this month and we will rebate the shipping."

■ REFERENCES

Compose a list of references that are willing to validate your position. If there's any doubt, pull out your reference sheets and suggest that they call anyone on this list for verification. Most often, just an impressive list with names and companies they recognize will give you an advantage. Update this list regularly to make sure that they're still in your camp and that their contact information is current.

■ REHEARSAL

Guerrilla negotiators choose from a set of well-rehearsed selections. Role-play likely negotiating scenarios. Take the side of your counterpart, evaluating likely rationales and concessions they'd accept. Explore the range of likely demands from the obvious to the ridiculous. Videotape your role-plays for analysis.

■ REPUTATION

When you have a solid reputation, you have an advantage going into a negotiation. The ground rules of how you behave are preestablished, and you don't have to prove yourself a worthy counterpart. Guerrillas do everything possible to create a solid reputation with consistent behavior. They prove it with testimonial letters and references.

■ REWARDS

Reward behavior during the negotiation. Send them a certificate of appreciation. Give them an engraved plaque proclaiming them Champion Negotiator—that disarms them. Send them a can of chocolate chip cookies with an attached note: "You're one tough cookie." Or emulate Senator William Proxmire's Golden Fleece Award, given to someone who wastes resources.

■ RIGHT OF RECISION

One of the first things guerrillas negotiate is the right to rescind the offer pending review of your legal counsel, the union membership, your CEO, or your spouse.

■ SCARCITY

Items that are in short supply are often in high demand, and thus command a higher price.

■ SERVICE AND MAINTENANCE

You can negotiate for service and maintenance agreements. Or you can bundle them in as part of the deal. The price of the product is negotiable, but the service agreement isn't. Many discount electronics companies will earn more profit on the service agreement than on the original product.

■ SERVICE HISTORY

If your product has a superior history of remaining in service or is easy to repair, you've got an advantage. Bring service records, mean time between failure (MTBF) and mean time to repair (MTTR) numbers.

■ SEX

It happens.

■ SMOKE

With the current popularity of cigars, you can use them as a negotiating weapon. Bring out a large cigar and matches. You'll get one of two reactions.

"You're not going to light that are you?" they may say with a shudder.

"Smoking helps me focus and concentrate. I'll make you a deal, as long as we're on track, I'll leave it unlit." You can use the unlit cigar as a concession or as a negative concession if you don't like their behavior.

Or they may respond with, "Wow. That's a good-looking cigar!"

You can reply, "Would you like one?" When they respond positively, offer, "I've got one for you when we're through for our victory smoke."

■ SOFTWARE

Software is expensive to develop, and very inexpensive to distribute. If you can make profits from the hardware, you may wish to use the software to gain a concession, making future profits on the upgrades. Or you may sell the software and offer a year of free upgrades. Offer spreadsheet templates and word processing templates that increase the value of your offering. They become bargaining chips that support your price.

■ SPARE PARTS

Availability of spare parts is a concern for anyone operating mechanical equipment, particularly if the equipment is highly specialized. Having a manufacturing line down can cost thousands of dollars an hour. Gain an advantage by offering to stock spare parts on site, and invoice your customer as they are consumed. Build the cost of financing that inventory into your price. You may actually save money because you don't have to warehouse the parts, or expedite them to the customer on order.

■ SPEAKERPHONE

A speakerphone allows others to listen in on the conversation. Because talking to another party on a speakerphone tends to be intimidating, do this with discretion.

■ SPIES

Look for insiders who, for reasons of their own, want you to succeed. The best spy is someone you've served previously who's changed positions, and wants you to serve them again. Guerrillas recruit spies from non-decision makers. Just tell them, "I value your opinion. What do you think we should do?"

■ STAND YOUR GROUND

Once you've stated your position, stand your ground. For example, you may be dealing with a buyer who keeps pressuring you to lower your price. Respond with, "We have no argument with those who sell for less. They know best what their product is worth."

■ STRATEGIC ALLIANCES

The people you normally do business with can be an asset when negotiating. Negotiate to have your product endorsed by prominent professional associations. We recently extended our line of credit with our bank on the strength of a strategic alliance with the American Management Association to sponsor our public seminars.

■ SUCCESS STORIES

Share your success stories with your counterpart. Be careful not to sound like you're bragging. Guerrillas add the strength of third-party testimonials to their presentation. Open with the preframe, "Our customers tell us . . ."

"Our customers tell us that we customize our training to a much higher level than other speakers that they've worked with."

■ TAPE RECORDER

Take a small tape recorder into the negotiation. Place it prominently in the middle of the table and ask, "Does anyone object to taping these proceedings, just *for the record?*" You'll find that the meeting will take less time, and that people will be less contentious and more forthright when they're being recorded.

Review your tapes to see how well you handled the negotiation, and to discover any missed opportunities or errors you may have made. There is no better way to learn from your experience and become a better negotiator.

■ TESTIMONIALS

Anytime a client compliments you, ask if they'd put that comment on a sheet of their letterhead, and send it to you as a testimonial letter. Make color copies of these letters so they look like the original. When you need to prove your point, bring out the stack of testimonial letters.

■ THIRD-PARTY EXPERT

Mahlone was facing tough competition in her aircraft negotiations. The buyer's chief pilot kept insisting that the competitor's jet would perform the mission profile. She knew otherwise.

She called the company that provides her with flight plans. She asked them to create a flight plan for her plane and one for the competitive jet as well, estimating fuel consumption and flight range based on cruise speed, winds, altitude, and payload. She presented this third-party proof that the competitor *could* make the trip, albeit with two fewer passengers than the pilot wished to carry. She won the sale.

■ TIME

There's little time to waste. When you can accomplish a task faster than your competitors, you've got an advantage. From one-hour photo finishing to express shipments, your counterpart already pays more for rapid service. Guerrillas charge more when they can do things fast.

■ TOOLS

If your product requires special tools for servicing or maintenance, you can offer or withdraw these as part of your negotiation. When you're on the buying side of the table, insist that they be included.

■ TRAINING

Negotiating for training can often be a valuable addition to a deal. Negotiate for additional people to be trained. Or negotiate for training to be at your location, thereby saving travel dollars. Untrained staff make costly mistakes, so by training your negotiating team in guerrilla tactics, you gain an advantage.[1]

■ TRANSPORTATION

Can they provide transportation? If not, will you provide transportation as part of the deal? Who's going to pay for the transportation? When do they take legal title and responsibility for the goods? Is the deal freight on board (FOB) or delivered?

■ UNUSUAL PACKAGING

A woman was in the supermarket purchasing raisins when a man approached her. He said that he was conducting a survey and asked *why* she was willing to pay six cents more for raisins in a round tub than those of the exact same quality and content in a square box. She giggled and admitted that she chose the round carton because it was *cute*.

We often buy things because they catch our attention with their unusual packaging. Guerrillas use this same concept in how they package their business. You might land a contract because you approach it from a unique angle. Instead of trying to fit your style and personality into a square box, guerrillas gain an advantage when they exploit their uniqueness.

■ USING GIFTS

When you give them a gift, make it personal. Better yet, have it monogrammed. Guerrillas refuse to use traditional advertising specialties such as coffee mugs or other run-of-the mill items as a gift. If it has *your* company name on it, it's a *chatchke,* not a gift.

People are suckers for kids, especially their kid. Send your counterpart an age-appropriate gift for their kid and they'll

---

[1] For a free information packet on the Guerrilla Negotiating Seminar, call toll free, 800-247-9145 or check out http://www.guerrillagroup.com.

remember you forever. Send them a coffee mug with a picture of their child on it. You can find a vendor at the local mall who will do it in 15 minutes.

■ VIDEO

The Rodney King case dramatically demonstrated to the world the power of video. Imagine how his day in court would have gone if the judge had only heard the testimony of the officers.

The Atlantis Hotel in Paradise Island recently launched a $400-million expansion, which includes a new water park, marina, and casino. The expansion even includes a 5,000-square-foot, $25,000-a-night suite, suspended 20 stories up between the two new towers. The marketing department sponsored the luncheon at a meeting of the American Society of Travel Agents, and used computer animation to take the agents on a video "fly through" of this new, 800-room hotel. The video encouraged travel agents to book the new facilities *months* before the construction was complete. The result, their occupancy rate is 99.9 percent, and they currently turn away three reservations for every available room.

■ VOICE MAIL

"Beeeeeep." You're expected to leave a message on voice mail. Guerrillas consider voice mail to be a golden opportunity to reach people they otherwise couldn't. You'll conduct some of your negotiations completely by voice mail. You'll never get a call back if they don't get your message, so guerrillas always leave a voice mail message, no matter what. Just create a message that is so compelling that people will call you back. Here's some guerrilla tactics that give you an advantage.

➤ Get Voice Mail

If your counterpart can't reach you, they may be forced to call your competitor. If you don't already have voice mail in your office, *and* at home, *get it.* Your customer should *never* hear a busy signal. The busy signal labels you as an amateur, and it says that you're too busy to take their call, or that you don't care enough to receive their message.

➤ A Three-Minute Commercial

Callers will listen to up to three minutes of your outbound recorded message before hanging up. When you get voice mail, hang up. Then script a three-minute radio-style commercial that lets your counterpart know who you are, what you offer, and why they should deal with you. Call them back and deliver a perfect phone presentation.

➤ Include Your Web Address

Tell your counterpart that you've placed the information they need in a private Web page, and give them the URL. You can include pictures, testimonials, references, and supporting information. They'll browse this at their leisure and will give you more time and consideration than they may otherwise.

➤ Make an Appointment

If your counterpart sits at their desk and lets the phone ring through to voice mail anyway, try setting an appointment for your callback. The script is, "I know you're very busy today, and I've got some great news for you! All I need is a few minutes and I can tell you all about it. I'll call back at 3:00. If you're at your desk, will you please pick up? Talk to you at three!" When 3:00 P.M. rolls around and their phone rings, they'll know it's you, and if they want to speak with you, they'll pick up the phone.

You can also make an appointment for them to call you. The script is, "I'm very busy today, and I've got some great news for you! All I need is a few minutes and I can tell you all about it. I'll be in the office this morning between 9:30 and 10:00, and available to receive your call again between 4:30 and 5:00 this afternoon." Of course you'll be in the office and available to receive their call *all day,* but because it *feels* like an appointment, they are more likely to call at the time you specify. By setting different appointments for different people, you'll greatly reduce phone tag.

➤ After Hours

When you're unable to return calls until late in the day, provide after-hours instructions. "I'll be traveling to New York today, and will not be available until 7:00 P.M. Eastern time. Leave a message, and please include your home number, and I can get back to you tonight. And please tell me when it would be too late to accept my call. Or you can reach me on my cell phone until 10:00 P.M."

➤ Alternate Access

Always include alternate access.

> "Press zero and an operator will come on the line and reroute your call to me."
> "My pager number is . . ."
> "My home phone number is . . ."
> "My cell phone number is . . ."
> "My assistant's extension is . . ."

➤ The Next to the Last Thing to Leave

The next to the last thing to leave is *your phone number. Write down the number as you dictate it* so that you know you're not going too fast. Repeat the phone number again at the end of the message so that your counterpart doesn't have to rewind the entire message to verify that they have transcribed it correctly. It's important to repeat your number if you're delivering a message by cell phone where there might be a signal dropout while you're leaving the number. Say it a different way the second time, using teens and hundreds. "One eight-hundred, two four seven, *ninety-one forty-five.*" People tend to remember the number better when grouped this way.

➤ The Last Thing They Should Hear

The *last* thing they should hear is *their name,* what Dale Carnegie called "the sweetest sound in any language."

So now your voice mail message sounds like this: "Hello, John. This is Orvel Ray Wilson, *calling from* The Guerrilla Group in Boulder, Colorado. I'd appreciate *the courtesy of a return call* at, one, . . . eight hundred, . . . two, four, seven, . . .

nine, one, four, five. *We're the people who* conduct the Guerrilla Selling and Guerrilla Negotiating seminars all over the world. *The reason I'm calling* is that I have some really *good news* I'd like to share with you. I'd like to send you some information about our new Guerrilla Negotiating program, and invite you to a special preview session we're conducting in your area. You can reach me at my office anytime today. That's one eight hundred, two four seven, *ninety-one forty-five.* I look forward to hearing from you then, *John.*"[2]

■ WHO'S WHO

You can gain amazing reconnaissance by looking up your counterpart in *Who's Who.* You'll learn about their education, their hobbies, and their business. Check out http://www.whoswho online.com.

■ WWW

Research your counterpart on the World Wide Web as part of your preparation. Do a name search. Run a check on their company with the search engines. See the Appendix for a list of research sites.

Chiat-Day, an advertising agency in Venice Beach, California, was preparing a presentation for a Fortune 100 client in Chicago. They were up against several candidates in a cattle call of presentations. They had 15 minutes to make or break the deal. One of the team members got on the Internet and looked up the prospect's Web site. While exploring the links, he stumbled onto the company's five-year marketing plan, which someone had posted presumably for internal distribution. He downloaded it and took it to the sales team, "Can you use this?" Here were the goals and objectives to which the company had already publicly committed. The team stayed up all night rewriting their presentation to align with the prospect's plan, point by point. They flew to Chicago, made their presentation, and won the contract.

---

[2] For more unconventional weapons to increase your effectiveness on the phone, read *Guerrilla TeleSelling* (Wiley, 1998).

■ YOUR BEST PRICE

Nigel Forrester was in final stages of a long and arduous negotiation. They had haggled long over price, and the offer was now at $3,973,000 down from $4,450,000. The prospect emphatically stated, "I want your best price and I want it now."

"If I offer you my best price, it will be my last and final offer," Nigel countered.

The prospect said, "I'll take it."

Fed up, Nigel picked up the contract, crossed out the price, and wrote $4,175,000. The prospect said, "Hey! That's higher than the last price you quoted. I thought you said that you'd give me your best price."

Nigel responded. "You asked me for *my* best price. That's the price that's best for *me!* Take it or leave it." The prospect signed.

■ YOUR INFLUENCE

You wield great personal power and influence.

➤ Power

If you are in a recognized position (CEO, CFO, CIO, EIEIO) in your company, you are granted certain powers because of that position. When necessary, bring in people of positional power to make your point.

You also have personal power. "I'll do that for you," carries a lot of weight.

➤ Information

Being an expert in your field gives you influence. Your experience and knowledge brings recognition and ability. Guerrillas neither sell themselves short nor overstate their abilities.

It's been said that it's not *what* you know but *who* you know. Guerrilla's know that the truth is, it's *who* you know that you *trust.* Knowing who to call to solve the problem or bring wisdom to the situation carries influence. People will ask you if they think you might know someone who knows.

➤ Time

How you use your time brings you influence. Being willing to accomplish a task outside of normal working hours creates an advantage. Guerrillas inventory their influence resources and bring them to bear wherever they can.

Chapter

4

Guerrilla Negotiating Tactics

These are approaches that you can use to help resolve certain situations. The more of these approaches you have in your arsenal, the more rapidly you can reach a successful conclusion.

■ DETERMINE YOUR POSITION

Before beginning any negotiation, determine your maximum justifiable position (MJP) and your minimum acceptable result (MAR). The MJP is the maximum that you can request and reasonably support. Your MAR is the least you are willing to settle for and remain viable. Conversely, your counterpart's MJP is the best they can ask for and defend. Their MAR is the most they are willing to pay you. If these two settlement ranges overlap, you'll be able to strike a deal. If there is no overlap, deadlock is certain.

For example, your list price is $1,500, and the lowest price you can accept without financial damage is $1,300. Your counterpart has found a source, albeit potentially inferior, at $1,100 and the most they can pay and still resell at a profit is $1,400. All else equal (see Figure 4.1), you'll settle at a price between $1,300 and $1,400.

Keep in mind that an agreement can be struck *anywhere* within the overlapping settlement ranges. Guerrillas present all possible rationale to support their position so that they can settle as close to the upper end of their settlement range as possible. If there is no overlap, look for ways to move up their MAR or lower your MAR. "You don't need on-site warranty because

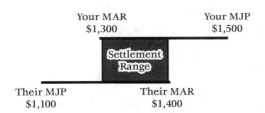

Figure 4.1 Maximum Justifiable Position (MJP) and Minimum Acceptable Result (MAR) of you and your counterpart. Where there is overlap, you can reach agreement.

you have a repair shop already? Well, we could delete that and I can offer you another $100 off."

Second tactic: Make the settlement ranges bigger. Add value to the potential agreement. "And not only will I let you have this car for $2,200, but I've got an extra set of studded snow tires and a car cover, and an extended warrantee. And I'll give you the snow tires for only another $200." Adding more enlarges the boundaries of the settlement range.

Guerrillas gain an advantage by knowing what they want and how much they can justify, and then some.

■ HOW TO WIN IN A DISAGREEABLE SITUATION

Here are some situations where you're facing a challenging situation.

➤ Hostile Negotiator

Start by confronting them. Call it the way you see it. "Your attitude toward this discussion is clearly antagonistic. You seem to be very angry about something. Would you please tell me what it is?" Often, they may be angry about something completely unrelated. Until they set aside their overt antagonism, little progress will be made.

Orvel Ray was asked to mediate a disputed right-of-way between his parents, who own a ranch in Colorado, and the county road department. From the very beginning of the meeting, his mother was openly sarcastic and rude to the county planner who was trying to explain exactly where they planned to widen the road. Orvel stopped the discussion, and confronted his mother. "Clearly you are angry with Mr. Jackson, here. What has he done or said that has made you so antagonistic?"

"Oh, nothin'!" she snapped.

"Well, then, you're obviously angry about *something*. Would you tell us exactly what has upset you, so that we can proceed with the business at hand?"

In fact, she and her husband had had a heated argument about a completely unrelated issue in the car on the way into town. We all agreed that they should work out that matter on their own another time. When she realized that she was projecting her animosity onto Mr. Johnson, we were able to review the blueprints, arrive at an agreement, and settle on an amount for the right-of-way.

Check Intentions
Ask, "Do you really want to settle?" You may be dealing with someone who really doesn't want to negotiate at all. Getting a "yes" response from them at this point lays the groundwork for continuing the discussion.

Walk Out
Warn them first, "I came here to settle this dispute and reach an agreement. I did not come here to be verbally abused. One more outburst like that and I will leave."

Change Players
Perhaps a different personality can defuse the situation. This is especially effective if the alternate player is of the opposite gender.

Call a Time-Out
Recess the deliberations for an hour or two, to give the players an opportunity to cool off. Spend the time apart. Walk. Eat. Review your position. Try opening the discussions on a different point.

Don't Get Hooked
You may find yourself in a situation where your counterpart is being difficult, emotional, or even abusive. Don't let them hook

you in. If you get entangled in their emotional outburst, you won't be able to think clearly. Remember the fish. What catches the fish? The hook? No. The bait? No. The *fish* catches itself when it takes the bait. Smart fish don't get hooked.

➤ No Common Ground

We recommend Bob Burg's excellent book *Endless Referrals* for a surefire method of making unforgettable impressions and finding common ground. He recommends asking these 10 questions when meeting someone for the first time:[1]

1. How did you get started?
2. What do you enjoy most about your profession?
3. What separates you from your competition?
4. What advice would you give someone going into this business?
5. What one thing would you do with your business if you knew you could not fail?
6. What significant changes have you seen take place in your profession through the years?
7. What's the strangest or funniest incident you've experienced in your business?
8. What strategies have you found to be the most effective in your business?
9. What one sentence would you like people to use in describing the way you do business?
10. How can I know if someone I'm talking to is a good prospect for you?

➤ Dirty Tricks

Forewarned is forearmed. Don't be fooled. Some are classics; others might be invented on the spot. If you feel you are being

---

[1] Burg, Bob. *Endless Referrals: Network Your Everyday Contacts into Sales*, New York: McGraw-Hill, 1998. Contact Bob at 1-800-726-3667.

manipulated in an unfair way, stop the proceedings and call them out. "Well, it looks to me like you two are playing the classic, 'white hat/black hat' game. Now, let's stop kidding around and negotiate in good faith, or the whole deal is off."

For a comprehensive review of negotiating dirty tricks, see Chapter 6.

➤ They Don't Really Want to Settle

Until they really do want to settle, there's no point in continuing negotiations. In fact, you may lose an advantage by revealing your position and your evidence prematurely.

Never enter into a negotiation without being just as willing to walk out of it. Find a different prospect, customer, or supplier. *No deal* is preferable to a bad deal.

What Do You Really Want?

Stop the conversation and ask them directly, "What do you *really* want here?" You may have to steer the conversation in a completely different direction. You may not be able to give them what they really want, but now, at least, you know where you stand.

Sell the Benefits of a Negotiated Settlement

Outline the alternatives to negotiation. Litigation is time-consuming and costly, and the outcome is still uncertain. By negotiating with you here and now, they save time, free themselves to deal with other matters, and may be able to create a win-win-win outcome that they hadn't yet envisioned.

Third-Party Story

Share an example of another situation where your counterpart didn't want to settle, and it was ultimately to their detriment. "I have a friend who restores cars. Several years ago, he made a generous offer to a farmer for an old Ford that had been sitting in his barn for decades. The farmer turned him down flat, and his asking price was nearly double what the car was really worth. Well, that farmer never did sell that old car, and last winter's snow collapsed the old barn, and now that farmer has nothing to show for his stubbornness."

➤ Threats of Lawsuits

Your counterpart may threaten to sue. Don't be too intimidated by this negotiation tactic. A lawsuit is costly and time-consuming for both parties. Nevertheless, this is a threat that you must take seriously, even if the law is on your side, because just defending yourself may be very expensive.

What Is the Best Option Outside of Negotiating?

Be clear about your options. It may in fact be to your advantage to take your case to the courts. Keep in mind that even though you may win, you may not settle. Getting a judgment is one thing; collecting it is another. Four out of five judgments are *never* collected.

Ask for Mediation

Hire a single attorney to advise *both* parties in the dispute. This allows you to consider the facts and the legal implications before proceeding.

Consider the Expense versus the Benefits

If you have the resources to put at risk, by all means, go to court. A jury just might grant you a generous award, plus punitive damages. The news is full of cases where someone burned themselves with a cup of coffee and walked away with millions. But these awards are rare, and are becoming even less common with the ongoing reform of tort law. You can reduce the risk by hiring an attorney on a contingency basis.

Is It a Matter of Pride or of Business?

Your counterpart may be enamored of the drama of going to court. Or they may simply be more interested in getting revenge than in reaching agreement. The courts frown on malicious prosecution, so if you can prove that you have tried to negotiate in good faith, and that vengeance is their primary motive, you may get the case dismissed. Don't be seduced into a battle of the briefcases unless you have exhausted all other options.

➤ Bad Past Experiences

Ask, "What's been your experience?" Giving them a chance to rehash the episode from their point of view may diffuse the situation. Take notes to indicate your interest and to keep them focused on the facts. You may discover causal factors that you were not aware of.

Ask them, "Will you forgive me?" This is a powerful way to move beyond a perceived wrong. For extra impact, get down on one knee. They'll get the point. When you're forgiven, they can't bring up that point again. It's tacky to renege on forgiveness.

➤ Deadlock

If the negotiation stalls, confront them. Ask your counterpart, "Does this mean we're through?" If they respond with, "Yes, we're through," you know that you're up against a solid impasse. You'll have to resort to other methods. If their reply is "No," you know that they're willing to soften their position.

Prioritize Your Outcomes
Set your goals in advance, so that you know what's really important to you, and what you may be willing to give up. Lobby hard for your top priorities, and offer concessions on your lower priorities.

Round Up Your Resources
Before going into the negotiation, notify your attorney, your banker, your technical expert, or even your shipping clerk that he or she may be called upon to answer questions. By putting your key resource people "on-call" you can reach them immediately.

Attack the Highest Payoff First
Secure your most valued points first, then move on to the minor points.

Attack the Highest Payoff Last
If both parties have strong feelings about a particular point, delay the discussion and move on to negotiate on minor points

first. Once a momentum of agreement has been established, return to the tough issues.

Call Time-Out
Call a recess, ranging from a restroom break to suspending discussion for several hours, days, or even weeks. Take a walk, eat a meal, sleep on it.

Refer to Your Notes
By taking a moment to refer to your notes, you can often defuse a tense situation, and reset the emotional climate to a calmer level. You might say, "I'm confused. Just let me take a moment here to review my notes."

Change the Venue
Move the negotiation to another location. Perhaps a more comfortable setting, or perhaps a less comfortable one. Often a change of scene will result in a change of heart.

Change the Players
Have someone else continue the negotiation. Switch genders. Someone who is abusive to a man will often become a gentleman when dealing with a woman.

Call in a Mediator
A good resource is your local Better Business Bureau. They have trained mediators on staff, and usually do not charge members. They do mediation and arbitration, and offer dispute resolution and mediation training.[2]

Bring in the Big Guns
Delegate the negotiation up to a higher level of authority by bringing in the president, CEO, attorney, or spouse.

What Do You Want to Avoid?
When setting priorities, you should also consider outcomes that you specifically want to avoid. Your partner today may become

---

[2] For more information contact the Better Business Bureau at http://www.betterbusinessbureau.com. (800-537-4600).

your competitor tomorrow, so anticipate the worst-case scenario and negotiate a noncompete clause in your original contract.

When setting up a national seminar tour, we asked that the sponsors avoid booking us in hotels of a particular chain, based on our negative experience with them in the past. This ensured that our clients enjoyed a certain minimum level of comfort and hospitality consistent with our own high standards.

What Do You Want Not Done?
When faced with multiple, competing tasks, return to your scorekeeper and explain the situation. Give them a choice. "Which of these five things do you want *not* done?"

Call in Your Favors
If you have given your counterpart a reprieve or a concession in the past, you can call in that favor in the current negotiation.

Ask for a Reprieve
It may be possible to simply suspend certain terms of a pre-existing contract or agreement. Financial institutions will often agree to let a borrower defer a payment, adding it back to the end of the term of the loan. Your counterpart may be willing to waive certain requirements, permits, or inspections. You may ask for deadlines to be extended.

■ HOW TO NEGOTIATE "NONNEGOTIABLE" ITEMS OR TERMS

Even items that may appear to be nonnegotiable may prove to be negotiable in the end. Almost all of the terms of the deal, including the terms of the negotiation process itself, are open to negotiation.

➤ Establish What's Truly Nonnegotiable

You need not automatically concede nonnegotiable points. To passively accept a point as nonnegotiable is, in itself, a concession. Instead, you can trade one of your counterpart's nonnegotiable items against one of your own. The form is: "If you have to have that, then I have to have this." You effectively agree not to challenge that term or condition. Never accept a point as being nonnegotiable without asking for a reciprocal nonnegotiable concession.

➤ Change the Rules

If the company policy is to never negotiate price, consider making an exception, making up the lost margin on accessories, service, or training. Look for a compelling reason to do things differently.

➤ Wait for a Change of Guard

Twenty percent of Americans change jobs every year, so odds are one-in-five that the person who's blocking you now will be replaced next year. The next election will change the board. Patience is a guerrilla virtue.

➤ Try Again with Someone Else

When you call to change an airline ticket, and the customer service agent says, "We'll have to charge you a $75 change fee," hang up and talk to a different agent. Keep trying until you find a CSR who will waive the fee.

➤ Move Up the Chain of Command

They'll see a bigger picture from higher up. Ask the front-line people: "I don't want to get you into trouble, but who could do this for me?" Or, "Under what circumstance could we do this?"

➤ Trade One of Your Nonnegotiable Items

Perhaps there's something on your list of "must haves" that you really could live without, assuming you could trade it for something *really* important. Rethink your own position.

■ GAIN AN ADVANTAGE ON YOUR OWN TURF

➤ Back to the Window, Facing the Door

Michael Korda, in his book, *Power: How to Get It, How to Use It,*[3] suggests that you sit with your back to the window, facing the door. Since you're framed with light from behind, you have an aura of power. Facing the door is a strategic position of control. Head for that chair when meeting in a restaurant or conference center and gain an advantage.

➤ Eliminate Barriers

Make it easy for them. Give them the VIP treatment. Pick them up at the airport. Have them checked into the hotel in advance: Just hand them the room key. At your office, have their name badge already printed and the guard alerted to their arrival. They'll know that you can deliver before the negotiation begins.

➤ Set the Tone

Send a welcome basket to their hotel room before they arrive. Fruit, cheese, perhaps a bottle of wine, always a welcome note. This demonstrates your ability to think ahead, plan ahead, and execute on ideas.

➤ Introduce Them to Your Family

Invite them to the homestead. Introduce them to the kids, the spouse, the new baby. Conduct the meeting in your own dining room, living room, or around the pool. When they get to know you person-to-person, it creates an atmosphere of trust, and you gain an advantage.

➤ Select Territory That Appears Neutral

Hold the meeting in a conference room instead of your office. Use the office of a coworker, or manager. Have the meeting at a

---

[3] Korda, Michael, *Power: How to Get It, How to Use It,* New York: Simon & Schuster, 1986.

local restaurant where you've scoped out the arrangements in advance. Select your own special table, and order a special meal in advance. Even though you're on neutral territory, now it's *your* favorite restaurant. Gain an additional advantage by meeting with the wait staff, and arranging for them to address you by name at every possible opportunity. "Thank you, Mr. Levinson. Is everything to your liking, Mr. Levinson? Is there anything else I can get for you right now, Mr. Levinson?" Wow! What power you have now!

Select a stress-reducing environment. Look for a location where there is running water. Embassy Suites hotels have dramatic water features in their lobbies. Buy a fountain for your meeting room or conference room. You can even play a recording of surf, rain, or birdsongs to create a relaxed atmosphere. Explain to your counterpart, "I want you to be relaxed and centered, so that we can be as productive as possible."

➤ Controlled Interruptions

Reroute your calls, and let them know it. "I've asked my staff to hold my calls during our meeting." Close the door to discourage drop-ins. Then have a member of your staff interrupt the negotiation with breaking news.

➤ Have Your Experts on the Scene

Provide seating for your attorney, quality control manager, purchasing agent, customer service manager, chief of engineering, marketing manager, consultant, partner, or executive assistant.

➤ Tours, Demonstrations, and Interviews

Prior to beginning the negotiation, take your counterpart on a tour of your facility. Demonstrate your newest product. Have them interview some of your key people. Just as introducing them to your family gives you an advantage, this familiarity with your operation helps them understand the context of the discussions to follow.

➤ Parade Them in Front of the Company

Schedule an all-hands meeting. Have everyone in the company, from the CEO to the forklift driver, show up to greet your counterpart. This show of force gives you enormous credibility.

➤ Rehearse in Advance

You can get all your equipment set up and tested. Brief your staff on the party line for tough questions

■ NEUTRALIZE THE DISADVANTAGE WHEN YOU'RE ON THEIR TURF

Here's how you can gain an unfair advantage when you have to go to them.

➤ Show Up the Day Before

The guerrilla arrived at the counterpart's office at 6:30 P.M., and spoke to the janitor: "I have an important meeting here tomorrow and I need to check the VCR in the conference room. Would you unlock it for me?"

"Sure," replied the janitor. The guerrilla opened the cabinets, and yes, there *was* a VCR available. He popped in his demo video, located the remote, turned on the system, and queued up the tape. While he was at it, he adjusted the blinds on the windows and counted the chairs. Now he knew exactly how many handouts to bring. He borrowed the remote and put it in his briefcase.

Imagine how astounded his prospect felt the next day when he reached into his briefcase, took out the remote control and, with a touch of a button, started his video.

➤ Call Ahead

Call from your cell phone to let your counterpart know that you're on your way, then ask, "I'm running about 15 minutes early. Is that okay?" You've alerted them to be prepared for your arrival, *and* you've just negotiated an extra 15 minutes. Then *ask a favor.* "Could you remind me again, which exit is that?

Where should I park, and would you let security know I'm coming and have a badge ready for me?" They'll meet you at the door and roll out the red carpet.

➤ Close the Door

"There are so many distractions, do you mind if I close the door?" You've already started to take control of the environment.

➤ Rearrange the Furniture

You may find that the facility your counterpart has provided is less than ideal. The more influence you can exert over the environment, the more power you will have in the negotiation.

Move the Chair

Before you sit down, move the chair. Even an inch or so. Even if it doesn't need to be moved. Move it. Now this chair is *yours*.

Move the Desk

As with the chair, moving the desk, even an inch or so, makes it yours.

Move the Stuff on the Desk

"Do you mind if I just set this aside? I need to make room for my laptop so you can see my presentation." Always ask permission. By persuading them to concede part of their space, you've improved your position.

Spread Yourself Out

Papers, reference materials, cell phone, notebook, computer, briefcase, jacket—the more space you can take up, the more you own.

Own the Space

Make yourself at home. The more relaxed you are, the more you can focus on your desired outcome.

Borrow Something

A good way to establish a connection with your counterpart is to borrow their pen or ask for a pad of paper to take notes. This is especially effective when the negotiation is impromptu. "I didn't expect for us to get started so soon. I left my pen and notebook in the car. May I borrow yours?" When they loan you a pen, they have started by making a concession to you.

When they hand you their pen, say, "Ooooh. Nice pen!" You complement them indirectly, building rapport.

You might think borrowing things shows that you're unprepared, and you would be right. If your counterpart perceives you to be unprepared, they'll relax and drop their guard, giving you a fair advantage.

Accidental Touch

The fastest way to create rapport is with nonthreatening touch. You can do this purposefully with handshakes (more about that in Chapter 8). And you can do it intentionally, but apparently accidentally, and achieve a similar level of connection. When you exchange something, such as a piece of paper, a pen, change, or a cup of coffee, reach just a little deeper into their space and brush your fingers against theirs. It has to seem accidental, so you may wish to practice this with someone you know well to get the hang of it.

We recommend practicing when you go shopping: accidental touch when you hand the clerk what you're buying, when you hand them your credit card, when you pick up the pen, when you receive your change. Notice the positive shift in their demeanor and behavior.

Go for a Walk

Reagan and Gorbachev changed the face of history when they took a break and went for a walk, alone, during the middle of difficult arms negotiations. During that stroll, they were able to explore personal motivation for moving forward.

■ SPECIAL CONSIDERATIONS FOR NEGOTIATION BY TELEPHONE

You face unique barriers when negotiating by phone. Here are some strategies for overcoming those barriers.[4]

---

[4] For a complete discussion of selling when you can't be there in person, see *Guerrilla TeleSelling* by Jay Conrad Levinson, Mark S. A. Smith, and Orvel Ray Wilson, CSP. John Wiley & Sons, 1998.

➤ Audio Only

People receive four times more information visually, so you're at a disadvantage. Only 34 percent of the population prefer audio as their dominant learning mode. If you're facing a complex situation, you have don't have visual aids to make your point. Because you can't see the other person, you can't read their body language cues, so you must request and rely on verbal feedback. Your conversation isn't always private because you never know who's listening in.

On the other hand, with the telephone you can conduct your negotiations in your bathrobe.

Guerrillas reserve telephone negotiations for minor details or for when both parties are already close to an agreement. Here's some ways to manage the lack of visuals.

Send in Advance

Send them your brochures, your white paper, the contract. "If you'll note on page 32, first paragraph: Are you there now? You'll see that . . ."

Fax

"What's your fax number? Let me send you a diagram that I think will help clear up the confusion." Don't be surprised if they are able to receive a fax at their home. Or ask where they can receive a fax, such as a Kinko's, at their church, or local coffee shop.

E-mail

Send them E-mail with an attachment, such as a photograph, a diagram, or the section from the operating manual.

WWW

"Do you have access to the Web right now? Great! Check out www.guerrillagroup.com. If you click on the . . ." You get the picture. And so do they!

➤ No Control over Distractions

You can control the distractions on your end by closing your office door, asking your staff to hold your calls, and clearing away the clutter on your desk.

If you hear distractions on the other end, ask your counterpart about them. "I hear another phone ringing. Do you need to get that?" Or, "It sounds like there's a lot going on there. With all that noise, I can't quite hear what you're saying. Is there some way that you could move to a quieter area?" Often they will comply.

Use a headset phone to decrease your distractions. You'll also keep your hands free so you can take notes or easily get reference materials while staying on the line.

➤ Imperfect Communication

Although telephone audio quality is much better now than in the past, it can be imperfect because of poor-quality telephone equipment or if your counterpart is using a speakerphone. Occasionally you'll get a bad connection, especially if your call is routed on a bargain long-distance carrier that's using old-technology long-distance lines.

If you can't hear well, try again. "I can't hear you clearly. Let me call you back on another line." If you're calling on a cellular phone in a fringe area, ask, "Let me call you back on a land line." Then call from the nearest pay phone.

➤ May Require Multiple Contacts

Often, you'll play phone tag. You may have to make multiple attempts, and contact multiple people to conclude your negotiation. The golden telephone hour is between 9:00 A.M. and 10:00 A.M., their local time. You are five times more likely to reach your counterpart during that hour than at any other time of day.

Set appointments with your counterparts, or ask them the best time to reach them. Make allowances for local time-zone issues.

Guerrillas use technology such as three-way calling or a phone bridge to bring together multiple parties for a phone conference. A phone bridge can connect from two to thousands of people on the same phone call. Call your local telephone company or check the yellow pages for more information on phone bridges.

Video conferencing is an excellent option when you can't meet face-to-face, but need to exchange visual information.

Kinko's offers public point-to-point videoconferencing at many of their locations. Call your local store or check out www.kinkos.com for details.

➤ E-mail or Fax Your Notes

At the end of your conversation, offer to E-mail or fax your notes to your counterpart. Ask them to review and initial them, then fax them back to ensure that there was no misunderstanding. This can preempt problems caused by miscommunication.

■ KEEPING YOUR ENERGY HIGH

An army travels on its stomach, so keep your troops combat ready by providing regular opportunities and healthy options.

➤ Food

To be at your best, eat light and eat right. If you're a road warrior, your choice of food is usually fast food. Think about it. When you eat a lunch of burgers, fries, and a soft drink, how do feel around 2:00 P.M.? Sluggish? Can you negotiate your best deal when you feel that way? If not, eat the right food when you need to be mentally acute.

Even if you don't normally like breakfast, during a negotiation you may not know when you'll get your next meal. You'll need all the stamina and energy you can get for the day ahead, and breakfast is the only surefire way to get it. We've found that the best breakfast is eggs and yogurt or other cultured dairy, such as buttermilk or cottage cheese. Your brain burns glucose (blood sugar) or galactose, which it prefers. Galactose comes primarily from cultured diary foods. And eggs contain sources of protein that can be converted to glucose over time, giving your body a time-release source of brain food.

A doughnut or other carbohydrate rapidly converts to glucose, which drives up insulin levels. Insulin decreases the amount of glucose available after about an hour, and you'll hit a slump as your brain craves food.

Coffee has a similar effect, but the glucose comes out of storage in the liver. A coffee and sweet roll breakfast will keep you going for about an hour, but then you'll crash.

Another benefit of eating breakfast is that it will keep you from having bad breath. If you don't eat breakfast, your body burns fat, which creates bad breath. This breath comes from your lungs, not your mouth, so breath mints or sprays will only mask it temporarily. Eating breakfast also keeps your stomach from rumbling in front of your counterpart.

Avoid heavy, greasy, protein-laden meals, and the exotic or spicy foods that could upset your stomach. This is especially true with a late-night meal. You need to sleep well, and heavy meals jeopardize your rest. Eat light, and you'll be way ahead of your counterpart in the morning.

Drink Up!
Before the meeting, stock up on low-calorie drinks, fruit juice, and bottled water. Drinking enough fluids is very important to feeling your best and preventing fatigue. Dehydration will make you feel more tired and make your negotiation less effective.

Limit Your Alcohol Consumption
It's better not to drink at all, and certainly *never* during the negotiation. Sixty percent of Americans drink at least occasionally, so some counterparts assume that it's acceptable to have a cocktail or beer as long as others are drinking. This is a fatal mistake. If you have alcohol on your breath from just a sip of beer or wine, you may alienate the 40 percent who don't drink. If you want to drink alcohol, wait until after the deal is done.

➤ Take Regular Breaks

Stop and take frequent 5 to 10-minute breaks, even when the negotiation is going well. Get up and take a walk outside, especially during the middle of the day. Regular breaks increase retention of ideas, allow you to start the discussion from a fresh viewpoint, and let you caucus regularly with your colleagues.

■ MAXIMIZE THE PERCEIVED VALUE

Add value to your low-value concessions. Give up things that are of little value to you and of high value to them. There is a tendency to give the low-value concessions as if they have low value. You have to position or justify it from your counterpart's viewpoint as if it was important, even vital to your issue. Don't complain. "As much as I hate to give up . . . I can see that it would be (useful, important, of value) to you . . ."

■ NO BUSINESS DISCUSSED DURING BREAKS

You can build rapport by insisting that no business be discussed during meals or break times. Your counterpart will relax and may be caught off guard. Guerrillas then listen intently to gather information about their counterpart's attitudes and personal tastes.

■ HIT AND RUN

If you think that a quick negotiation would work, schedule a hit-and-run visit. Fly into your counterpart's city, arrange the meeting in the Red Carpet Club at the airport, and await your outbound flight. You're meeting on neutral turf, the outbound flight sets a deadline, and if you have to reschedule your return to give them more time, you've granted a concession.

■ DON'T WEAR A WATCH

Consider leaving your watch in your pocket during the negotiation. Many people have a habit of frequently looking at their watch. When you look at your watch, they look at theirs, and you've created a distraction by focusing attention on the time. When your counterpart looks at their watch, it's possible that they're under time pressure, which is an advantage for you.

■ DON'T SWEAT THE SMALL STUFF

At a bicycle shop in Colorado, the policy is that if the item costs less than $1.00, it's free. If you need a nut for your front wheel, or if you need to replace a single broken spoke, they won't charge you. Why? Simple. It costs them more than $1.00 just to book the transaction. So for the price of a loose washer, they can buy a customer's loyalty and *still* be money ahead.

■ HOW TO GENERATE CREATIVITY

Handling difficult situations may require that you be creative in your solution finding. Here are some strategies that will give you the creative advantage.

➤ Attitude

Creativity begins with having a creative attitude. There are no problems, only solutions we haven't yet found.

Become aware of how you respond in a difficult situation. For example, you're on your way to an important appointment, and BANG! You have a flat tire. Your first response is likely to be the "oh *blank!*" response. (Some people say, "Oh darn!" Others use a different word.)

What's important is what happens next. Some people will sit behind the wheel and say, "Oh _____! Oh _____! Oh _____! Oh _____! Oh _____!"

The guerrilla says, Oh _____! I'm going to be delayed," then jumps out and changes the tire.

In any negotiation, when you find yourself exhibiting the "Oh _____!" response, stop, breathe, and focus on resolving the problem.

➤ History

What experience can you bring from the past that you can apply to this situation? You've solved the unsolvable before. Perhaps you've even worked a miracle or two. You can do it again. Take a look at some of the toughest problems you've solved, and consider the process you used to overcome them.

➤ Focus on the Possible

Your negotiating counterpart may ask for the impossible. When that happens, rather than getting stuck on, "That's impossible," divert the conversation to, "What we *would* be able to do is . . ." and suggest an alternative that actually *is* possible. Also consider alternatives that, although possible, may seem wildly impractical. Sometimes these over-the-top suggestions stimulate creative discussions that generate new, more practical options.

Once, when negotiating a speaking engagement, the client insisted that he was unable to pay travel expenses. Orvel Ray suggested, "Well, I suppose I could *hitchhike* from Chicago to Detroit." The client responded, "Actually, one of our reps will be driving in from Chicago; you could ride with him, and use the time to get acquainted with the company." This was a great suggestion, and solved several problems for both of us. The client saved the price of the airfare, and Orvel was able to use otherwise unproductive travel time to get to know the company and its issues. The extra preparation really helped customize the seminar, resulting in a standing ovation.

■ YOUR PROBLEM-SOLVING TEAM

Start by rounding up the brightest people you know. If you work with people who are creative, ask them to help even if they work outside your field.

➤ How to Find Them

Include people who are not in your industry. People with an outside perspective often ask naïve questions that lead to breakthrough answers.

➤ How to Brainstorm Creative Solutions

1. Bring together a group of five to seven people.
2. Assign someone to record a list.
3. Arrange seating so that everyone can see the list and each other.
4. Set a time limit. Ten minutes is acceptable for a first round.
5. Every idea gets recorded on the list.
6. No one is allowed to make any evaluative comment on any idea during the brainstorm. There are no bad ideas just now.
7. Moans and groans are prohibited as well.
8. Variations on ideas suggested by others are encouraged.
9. Everyone offers ideas until the time is up. Silence is okay.

10. Once you have built a substantial list of ideas, then and only then, open the floor to discussion.

11. Evaluate the best ideas for implementation.

➤ How to Make Them Work

Here are some ground rules for creating and managing ideas.

Every idea is a good idea. It may not be practical, or workable, or affordable, but can be a stepping stone to another idea that is.

Don't fall in love with any idea. When you become attached, it clouds your objectivity and blocks creativity.

Keep in mind that there's often more than one right answer. Remember, "there's more than one way to skin a cat."

Keep an idea log. Carry a small spiral notebook and use it to jot down your creative ideas. Try to put down at least one new idea every week. When you have a problem to solve or a new project to launch, you can review all your best creative thinking. Sometimes a solution will just jump off the page.

Combine ideas to create hybrids. What if you created a vending machine for money? That question created the ATM.

Execute on the ideas. Ideas are a dime a dozen; *action* is the only thing that really counts. Once you've thought your idea through, put it to the test.

➤ What You Can Expect

Expect to generate far more ideas than you can use. That's a natural consequence of the creative process. The more ideas you have to choose from, the better.

Expect support for your entire negotiation. Driven by imaginative ideas, your negotiation will have a creative edge.

Expect increased creativity over time. Being creative is a learned skill, and you'll improve with practice.

■ 21 WAYS TO CREATE CLEVER SOLUTIONS

1. Swipe File

Compile a set of file folders labeled by topic, and when you come across something in your reading that you can use, tear it out and file it. Scan through the files to swipe good ideas that work for you.

2. Reverse It

It's always a good idea to look both ways before crossing the street, even on a one-way street. While traveling in England, South Africa, and Australia, we've learned that Americans habitually tend to *look the wrong way*. Try looking at the problem from the opposite direction, and avoid being blindsided.

3. Change It 10 Percent

By widening the base of a coffee mug 10 percent, and narrowing the mouth 10 percent, the manufacturer was able to make it spill-proof. They now sell thousands to commuters who want to keep the coffee in the cup and off the dashboard.

4. Make It Larger or Smaller

Can we miniaturize it? Can we make it a giant family size? "You're asking me for $1.17 a pound price on a one-year contract. If you give me a five-year contract, I can do that." Or, "Buy a whole truckload and I can pay the freight."

5. Rearrange

Change the timing. "You're telling me you can't get started because of another project. If we could help you with that project, could you start our job sooner?"

Change the geography. "Can we start on the East Coast now, and then roll out on the West Coast when we have some experience?"

Change the space. "You can have the corner office, if I can have the office next to the conference room; I spend more time in there than you do."

6. Eliminate

What can you cut away or discard. "If you let me ship it to you in bulk, we can cut our packaging expense, and I'll pass those savings on to you."

7. Combine With . . .

The roll-aboard suitcase combines a hand trolley with an overnight bag, and bingo, a new class of luggage is invented.

8. Adapt

What would work even though it's not meant for that job? "We have a power switch in stock that could work for you. It has an extra pole that you don't need, but you could simply ignore it."

9. 360-Degree Point of View

Look at the problem from your angle, from the customer's angle, from the boss's angle, from the community's angle. Get the complete perspective.

10. Put to New Use

Baking soda sales were slow, since it was used sparingly in baking. Then it was advertised as an absorbent for refrigerator odors, and sales surged. Today it is a common ingredient in toothpaste. Who would have thought?

11. Break the Rules

This one is fun. Consider options that are blatantly unethical or even illegal, not because you would ever implement them, but because they may be stepping-stones to other solutions.

A construction company was having trouble getting the steel they needed to complete a project on time. Someone suggested, "What if we were to just go over there with a forklift and one of our trucks and *steal* it? The foreman replied, "That's not a bad idea." He called the fabricator and offered to send a truck, forklift, and crew over to pick up the materials, rather than waiting for the trucking firm to deliver. This solution eased the transportation bottleneck, and put the project back on schedule.

12. Everything Associated With . . .

Free-associate around a key word or point, and list everything you can possibly associate. If your negotiation involves intellectual property rights, prepare by developing a list of all associated rights, including copyrights, reprint rights, trademarks, service marks, derivative works, books, newspapers, first rights, sub-rights, foreign language rights, electronic rights, Orville Wrights. List *everything* you can think of to identify potential opportunities or points of conflict.

13. Stupidest Way

Think up the dumbest solution possible, and try to outdo each other. Sometimes the simple solution is the most elegant.

14. Substitute

- ➤ Credit for cash
- ➤ Barter for credit
- ➤ Services for goods
- ➤ Decaf for regular
- ➤ Regular for hi-test
- ➤ Blue for green
- ➤ Paper for plastic
- ➤ You get the idea

15. Rolestorming

Have a member of your team take on the identity of your potential counterpart. You might have them "become" the opposing CEO, and put themselves totally into that character. Then role-play possible scenarios.

16. For Quick Solutions . . .

Ask yourself, "If I were being paid $1,000 an hour for consulting, what questions should they ask me?" List the questions, then answer them.

17. List Your Contrary Ideas

If you're going up against a competitor whose product is of superior quality, make a list of 10 Reasons Why Quality Sucks:

1. It's more expensive to produce.
2. It takes longer to build.
3. Nobody really appreciates quality.
4. It lasts longer, but we want it to wear out so we can sell more.
5. It's going to be obsolete before it fails.
6. It requires better-quality components.
7. It requires better people to service it.
8. It requires fancier packaging.
9. It requires fancier collateral materials.
10. They're going to hammer you on price anyway.

18. List Your Hottest Ideas

Write down the ideas that you're afraid someone might steal, then share those ideas. It makes room in your brain for more new, and even hotter ideas. You can come up with new ideas faster than others can steal them.

19. What Can't You Do?

Make a promise you can't keep, then ask yourself, "What would I have to do to keep that promise?" List everything that you *could* possibly do, and get as close to keeping the promise as possible, then scale your promise back to one you can actually keep.

20. Sleep on It

Ask yourself the critical question before you go to sleep. Dreaming is your most creative state, and many great inventions have emerged from the mists of dreams.

21. Long-Term Solutions

The best solutions are an integration of all that you know. So the more you know about the problem, the more creative you will be.

Decide what you want to have happen. Know that you don't have to know how to make it happen in order to begin.

Converse. Consider other's opinions.

Feed your imagination with art, music, and literature. Read. Think. Play.

Then gather together what you already know. Review the facts, trends, and statistics.

Let go of the problem. Go for a walk, a business trip, or a vacation. Give it time.

Capture the solution when it comes to you. Carry a small "think pad" or 3-by-5 note cards, or a microcassette recorder. Pick up your cell phone and leave yourself a message on your voice mail. Don't let those flashes of inspiration slip away.

■ HOW TO INFLUENCE YOUR PROSPECT

Professor Robert Cialdini, in his book *Influence: The Psychology of Persuasion,* identifies six factors or influence agents that substantially influence people.[5] When you use any of these influence agents, you will increase your sales success. The more you use, the more impact you'll have.

➤ Consistency

Consistency is a highly valued trait in all cultures. Because people are rewarded for consistency and penalized for inconsistency, we tend to act in ways that are consistent with our public statements. For example, people who offer advice would be foolish to act contrary to their own counsel, especially when others follow the advice.

Get It in Writing
When your counterpart makes a comment or counteroffer, ask, "Would you put that in writing?" Putting things in writing represents commitment, and most people tend to act in ways that are consistent with their previous commitments, especially written ones.

---

[5] Cialdini, Robert, *Influence: The Psychology of Persuasion,* New York: William Morrow, 1993.

Record the Conversation

Carry a microcassette recorder into the meeting and ask, "Do you mind if I tape the conversation, just for the record, so that I don't miss any important details?" Give them some *rationale* for making the recording. If they resist, ask, "Is there some reason you don't want this conversation on the record?"

The sheer intimidation value of rolling a tape recorder will give you an advantage. People are much more careful about what they say when they're "on the record." This also creates an opportunity for you to stop the tape when you want to encourage a frank, "off-the-record" discussion.

Play It Back!

If there is any concern, any misunderstanding, offer to stop the tape, rewind, and play back the conversation. People tend to behave better when they know their comments can be replayed.

Assign a Scribe

Assign someone not directly involved in the conversation to take notes, documenting points of agreement as they are arranged.

Share Notes

At the end of the discussions, copy and circulate the master notes for all parties involved.

➤ Reciprocation

In every culture, *granting* a favor obligates the recipient to *return* a favor. So look for ways to *give* to your prospects *first,* then convert them to customers.

The customer handed the shopkeeper a $20 bill to pay for a $10.25 purchase. The shopkeeper returned a $10 bill in change, and said, "I didn't want to break your ten." For a mere 25 cents, this shopkeeper created a lasting impression that he may not have gotten from a more expensive marketing program.

➤ Social Proof

If everyone's doing it, it must be okay. The concept of precedence is grounded in social proof. Look for ways to show that what was accepted before should be accepted now.

Ask the Users
Get statements from the people who will be affected by the outcome of the negotiation. Opinion polls can sway your counterpart to your side.

Testimonial Letters
Testimonials harness the ultimate power of social proof. Always bring them with you to the negotiation.

➤ Authority

Most cultures are trained to respect certain authority figures, and to respond to their influence almost without question. Deadlines are created and followed. An official product is often more desirable than an unsanctioned one. If you are calling on behalf of their bank, or a well-known charitable organization, or some other authority, you'll gain an advantage.

The Outside Expert
Quoting a known authority or author can strengthen your case. Make sure they understand your viewpoint and can make their support clear.

Meet the Boss
Authority is often positional, and you gain an advantage by bringing in the boss, or quoting instructions you've been assigned by your management. Even better, bring them into the negotiation.

Documentation
You gain an advantage when you have authoritative records to support your case. Such documentation adds perceived value in the negotiation.

Service Records in a Folder
A car will command a higher price when the owner has kept the service records and receipts on file. The buyer can verify such things as when the engine was rebuilt, or the last time the tires were rotated.

All the Boxes and Manuals

Similarly, packaging attests to the age and condition of used equipment. You can ask a higher price for a used stereo if you have all the manuals, documentation, and packaging.

Blue Book

The Hearst Publications *Black Book* and the NADA *Blue Book* provide authoritative data on the current market value of cars and trucks. You can easily justify your asking price by showing its "blue book" value.

➤ Original Carton

Any item still sealed in its original carton will command a higher value in the negotiation, because the packaging attests to the mint condition of the contents.

➤ Liking

When a person likes you, they are more easily influenced by you. Sending a gift or valuable information in advance of your meeting increases your chance of success.

Bring Gifts

Bring pens for everyone, and legal pads too. And don't buy the cheap ones.

Bring Food

Bring snacks and fruit, coffee, or sandwiches. Host the meeting at a restaurant over lunch or dinner.

Guerrillas are careful about consuming meals high in sugar. After 45 to 90 minutes, the insulin rebound causes drowsiness. You may wish to turn this effect to your advantage by serving sweets, candy, sodas, or desserts. Your counterpart will lose their mental edge after 45 to 90 minutes, giving you a fair advantage, but only if you resist temptation.

➤ Scarcity

Anything that is perceived as being scarce is also perceived as being more valuable. If diamonds were as common as seashells they would be worthless, even though they would be no less beautiful. If what you offer is perceived to be scarce, you'll increase your success. Guerrillas use scarcity as a weapon in negotiations. If you have limited capacity or a one-of-a-kind item, say so.

Information that is considered exclusive, with limited distribution, has exceptional influence. For the greatest impact, let your counterpart know this in advance of delivering the information. "Please keep this between you and me, I won't tell this to anyone else . . ." You've got their undivided attention.

Chapter 5

Guerrilla Negotiating Power Words

You can change the way people think about your offer when you can get them to think in a new way. Magicians, mentalists, and even trial lawyers have been using these linguistic techniques for centuries to alter the way things appear. The sleight-of-hand artist makes the coin "disappear" by momentarily directing your attention elsewhere.

Mind readers make statements to which everyone agrees, or they make predictions that have a very high probability of being true for most people. "Let me see. You've *recently* traveled, and I get the *impression* that it was to a state *ending with the letter 'a'.*" You're currently in a *relationship* with someone who's name or nickname ends in *'y.'* "

They use open-ended statements and unqualified specifiers, "I *feel* you have some *unfinished* business to *deal* with" (and who doesn't?). Or they seem to know intimate details about you instantly, "You tend to be *overly hard on yourself"* (and who isn't?).

"Wow, that's *right!"* says the subject, amazed at the apparent psychic powers.

■ BEWARE OF HOW YOU USE THESE LINGUISTIC TECHNIQUES

Anyone can learn these techniques. Just imagine the advantage you gain when you walk into a negotiation armed with the same linguistic tools. In any negotiation, most people will benefit from some direction, because they're uncertain of what they really want. If you're going to ask them to think in a new way, they may need help.

The linguistic tools presented here are very powerful. They can be used to help a person see things from your viewpoint. They can move a difficult person to a more understanding position, and help you make your point. They can also be used to manipulate, steal, cheat, and make lies into truths and truths into lies. Just as any tool can be used for good or evil, how you use these linguistic tools is your responsibility. And we trust you to use them with discretion and for the good of your organization and your counterpart.

You needn't feel guilty about using these techniques. You'll never force someone to do something that's out of character, and your requests will never cause them to violate their values. These techniques are used every day by mass media and advertisers. You'll recognize these techniques when they are used on you and can decide whether to be influenced or not. Forewarned is forearmed.

Practice constructing your demands and supporting rationales using the words and phrases you'll learn in this chapter. You'll find yourself wielding powerful persuasive tools that can give you an extraordinary advantage.

■ GENERALITIES: WHAT'S TRUE FOR MOST PEOPLE

You can gain a substantial advantage in any negotiation by applying some simple psychology. People who have a positive self-concept, and perhaps even those who don't, will demonstrate a *self-serving bias*. That is, they will accept as true any *generality* that you might make about their negotiating skill, their personality, or their background if it reflects on them favorably.

Here are generalities that 90 percent of people agree with:[1]

➤ Most businesspeople consider themselves more ethical than the average person.

➤ Most people see themselves as less prejudiced than others in their community.

---

[1] Thanks to the late Herb Dewey for making us aware of this phenomenon.

➤ Most people see themselves as being healthier and more intelligent than average.

➤ The majority of stockbrokers and stock investors feel that their business intuition is better than average.

➤ Most landlords believe that their property is more desirable than other comparable units in the same market.

➤ Most tradesmen believe that they are more skilled at their craft than others.

➤ Most people prefer gold jewelry to silver.

➤ Most women feel that they are intuitive.

➤ Most people feel that they are resourceful, and could make it by themselves if stranded on a desert island.

➤ Most men have a broken watch at home. It was probably a gift.

➤ All purchasing agents are interested in getting a lower price (it's their job.)

The guerilla negotiator can put their counterparts into a receptive mood by making general observations:

➤ "You have a reputation for being a tough negotiator."

➤ "I see that you're an open-minded and tolerant individual."

➤ "You're a very intuitive and perceptive person."

➤ "You're not the sort who is easily impressed."

➤ "I understand that you have been a very successful entrepreneur."

➤ "You're obviously an expert in this field."

➤ "I'm sure that we can count on your complete honesty in these proceedings."

■ BUILD THEIR VALUE

Likewise, people will dismiss any derogatory comment about their property, products, or their company. Resist trying to discount the value of the items for which you are negotiating. Contrary to the traditional approach to negotiating, build up their value, and your counterpart will be *more* inclined to give you what you want.

When Orvel Ray was relocating to Boulder to take a new position with a training company there, he and Denise began looking for a house to rent. At the time, downtown Boulder was a bit out of their market, so they expanded their search to houses in the nearby mountains. The third house they looked at was a beautiful passive solar structure, newly built, with a large atrium and floor-to-ceiling windows with a spectacular view. Contrary to the traditional wisdom of negotiation, they got very excited about this house. "Wow, it's just *perfect!* This is just like the house we've always dreamed of building." They explained to the owner their ideas about solar architecture, and Denise's love of plants. The owner confided that he had designed the house himself, and built it to defend his master's degree thesis in Solar Design.

"Well, actually, I was trying to sell it," he explained, "but it's been on the market for a while, and I didn't want it to sit empty in such a remote location."

"Would you consider selling it to us?" Orvel asked, without even asking the price.

At the time, they were relatively broke, with two small children. Denise was between jobs, they had no savings, and the price was well beyond their means. But because they were so ecstatic about the house, the owner negotiated for them to lease it with an option, then applied the rent to the down payment, and offered to carry a second mortgage so that they could qualify for the financing.

In the midst of these negotiations, he actually *turned down* a cash offer for his full asking price. He wanted the house to be sold to someone who would really appreciate its unique design. For this builder, having an appreciative buyer was more important than having a cash buyer.

■ SELECTIVE PERCEPTION AND SELECTIVE RECALL

People tend to focus their awareness on aspects of information that fit with their existing circumstances. It's common for people to listen to the president's speech and get entirely different meanings from it.

You've experienced selective perception if you've ever bought a car; immediately after taking delivery, everywhere you drive, you see the *same* car. The sudden apparent popularity of the make and model you choose *reinforces* your belief that you made a sound choice.

The *base rate fallacy* refers to the tendency for people to ignore or under-use basic rates or statistical averages, and instead rely on immediate input in the negotiation. A potential used-car buyer may have looked up the current market value in the Blue Book, but will nevertheless agree with the statement, "This car is a very good buy at this price," even when the seller is asking *more* than the published value.

■ QUALIFIERS

Any statement preceded by a qualifier is left open to interpretation. Qualifiers weaken the statement that follows and can create the right level of generality for your statement or demand to be accepted. This group of adjectives opens up possibilities and permits multiple meanings. Your counterpart will come to the conclusion that matches their experience.

"*. . . can happen* frequently.

"At *times . . .*"

"*Hopefully,* we can resolve this issue."

"It *could be* that . . ."

"It *might* be *feasible* to . . ."

"It's *quite likely* that . . ."

"*Mainly* we need to . . ."

"*Mostly* you will . . ."

"*Occasionally* you can . . ."

"*Often . . .*"

"Only *rarely* does . . ."

"Our *primary* concern is . . ."

"*Possibly* we could . . ."

"The problem is *primarily . . .*"

"*Usually* people . . ."

"You are *likely* to . . ."

Use qualifiers whenever you are uncertain of their position, or when you want your counterpart to be uncertain of your position. By creating a degree of ambiguity in your communication, you encourage your counterpart to reveal details about their intention, goals, and acceptable settlement range. That will give you an advantage.

■ AMPLIFIERS

These phrases have the opposite impact of qualifiers, strengthening whatever statement follows with added weight and credibility. Use amplifiers to strengthen the rationales you offer for your requests.

"... is becoming *increasingly* ..."

"... is *doubly* ..."

"... is occurring *less and less.*"

"Isn't it *amazing* how that works!"

"It's *essential* to our success that ..."

"It's *imperative* that ..."

"It's *significant* to consider ..."

"*More and more* we're seeing ..."

"Of *substantial* value to you is ..."

"You might *already know* about ..."

"You might have *heard* that ..."

Exaggeration can also be used as an amplifier, but is effective only in moderation. Delivering it through an idiom can cushion it. "Isn't that incredible!"

■ SOFTENERS

A softener tones down a phrase that your counterpart may challenge. It softens your position. Any phrase that follows a softener becomes inarguable for the moment, so softeners open your counterpart's mind to consider your position more favorably. Since you're offering your opinion, and you're entitled to your opinion, softeners decrease the likelihood of argument.

If it is likely that your counterpart will be disappointed with the outcome, you can use a softener to preempt their objection. *"You might find that* the ABS braking system doesn't work as well on icy, snow-packed roads as you were led to believe."* Your counterpart may or may not *find* this to be true, but until they have further proof, they must accept your position.

"As *incredible* as it seems . . ."

"Do you think we *might* be able to . . . ?"

"I *don't know if this is possible,* but, . . ."

"It might be *impractical* to prove, but . . ."

"It *might* occur to you that . . ."

"It's *conceivable* that you'll discover . . ."

"It's *feasible* that . . ."

"You may *realize* . . ."

"It's *possible* that . . ."

"Perhaps you've heard . . ."

"Potentially, you might find . . ."

"While it's *impossible to predict,* still . . ."

"You *may be* delighted to discover . . ."

"You *might be* surprised to find . . ."

"You might *be under the impression* . . ."

The following phrases are softeners that can be combined with previous phrases to increase impact. "I *believe* that you *might be* surprised to find . . ."

"I *believe* that . . ."

"I *feel* that . . ."

"I have the *impression* . . ."

"I *think* . . ."

"I *thought* it was a bad idea the first time I heard it, too."

"I *trust* that . . ."

"I've *experienced* that . . ."

"In my *opinion* . . ."

"It's *not your fault,* but . . ."

"Since then I've learned . . ."

■ MINIMIZERS

Minimizers decrease the impact of a potentially negative statement. Minimizers can be used to preemptively undermine your opponent's counter position, because they tend to not disagree. To challenge you would be contentious.

> "I know that, *but . . .*"
> "I don't have a *problem* with that. Do you?"
> "That doesn't *bother* you, does it?"
> "This isn't a *big deal*, is it?"
> "You *don't care*, do you?"
> "You're *not annoyed*, are you?"

There's an old joke that goes, "How many union electricians does it take to change a lightbulb?"
"Six. Do you have a *problem* with that?"

■ AWARENESS DIRECTORS

These words and phrases direct your counterpart's attention to particular facts, feelings, and issues, and so redefine their scope of awareness. Until they are aware of your issues, you can't negotiate in your favor. You will often need to subtly direct their awareness if you wish to gain an advantage.

For example, when selling a piece of furniture, you might say, *"Observe* the *difference* between the finish on this piece and others you have *seen."*

> "Are you *alert* to . . . ?"
> "Are you *conscious* of . . . ?"
> *"Awake* to . . ."
> "Be *attentive* to . . ."
> "Can you *identify* . . . ?"
> "Can you *make out* . . . ?"
> "Can you *recognize* . . . ?
> "Can you *tell* . . ."
> *"Catch a glimpse* of . . ."

"*Check* this out."

"*Consider* this: . . ."

"Did you *detect* . . . ?"

"Did you *feel* . . . ?"

"Did you *note* that . . . ?"

"Did you *notice* that . . . ?"

"Did you *pay attention* to how . . . ?"

"Did you *realize* that . . . ?"

"Don't *feel* bad."

"Don't *miss* it!"

"Don't *worry*."

"For what it's *worth*."

"*Forewarned* is forearmed."

"*Forget* it."

"*Forgive* me."

"Have you *heard* about . . . ?"

"Here's *all* you have to do . . ."

"*Here's* the deal."

"*Hold* on!"

"I *see* that . . ."

"I *sense* that . . ."

"I'm certain that you *understand* . . ."

"Let's *see*."

"Let's *face* it."

"*Listen*. . . ."

"*Look*: . . ."

"*Notice* how . . ."

"Of course you *comprehend* . . ."

"Pay *attention*."

"*Remember*: . . ."

"When you *focus* on . . ."

"When you *identify* . . ."

"You might be able to *discern* . . ."

"You might be able to *distinguish* . . ."

"You might *experience* . . . for yourself."

"You probably *saw* . . ."

Create an advantage by constructing questions and phrases with awareness directors to draw attention to unique features and advantages that you offer.

➤ Use Their Name

Using your counterpart's *name* always grabs their attention. You gain a greater advantage when you use their name as a preamble to any attention redirect.

"*Bob,* when you *consider* the differences in our product . . ."

"Of course, *Lisa,* you may have *seen* . . ."

"Isn't that the case, *John?*"

■ AUTHORITY BUILDERS

These linguistic tools create authority and lend credibility to your argument.

➤ Unspecified References

Unspecified references draw their authority from some vague, but nevertheless authoritative source. When used as a preamble to any generalization, they add the weight of *authority* and *social proof* to whatever follows. Use them in the negotiation to supply outside support for your position.

"*Corporations* function . . ."

"Ever wonder why *people* . . . ?"

"*Everyone* knows . . ."

"*Many* think . . ."

"*Most* feel . . ."

"Our *culture* . . ."

"*People* often . . ."

"Positive minds bring . . ."
"Society says . . ."
"Some consider . . ."
"The *few* who . . ."
"The *public* . . ."
"Those who . . ."
"We are *all* . . ."
"When people listen to *others* they . . ."
"I was just reading a *book* that said . . ."
"There was a story in the *paper* about . . ."
"An item on *TV* about this said . . ."
"Our *customers* tell us . . ."

➤ The Power of *Only*

The word *only* has multiple effects on your counterpart. Every time you say *only*, it builds your authority.

Creates Bargains
"Only 50 cents" said the sign on the jar by the cash register. We didn't know what they were selling, but we knew we had to have one. Whenever you present your price, preface it with *only*. "And the best news is that it's *only* $10,000!" Gee, that feels like a *bargain*.

Reduces Complexity
"And you *only* have to dial one number." You can point out the simplicity or reduce the complexity of the situation by using *only*. This is especially powerful when your counterpart has objected. "Maintenance is scheduled *only* once a week. That's less often than you thought."

Or use it when you're trying to reduce complexity, "I *only* want one little concession!"

Builds Uniqueness
Brainstorm a list of features and capabilities that you can claim as your onlys. If you're the only company that can provide a service, you've gained the high ground.

■ TRANCE WORDS AND PHRASES

"Remember when you were a kid, and you would sometimes find yourself daydreaming?" That sentence contains three powerful trance words: *remember, find,* and *daydream.* Trance words direct a person *inward* to access experience, memory, or imagination.

Anytime you access memory, you temporarily check out, you leave the here-and-now reality. You are directing your attention inward, and therefore have a corresponding decrease of awareness of the outside world. You are in a trance, even if only for a fraction of a second.

People never argue with their own data. When you put your counterpart in a trance, they are automatically in a state of agreement; they're reviewing their own data.

This trance state can also be mobilized to gain cooperation in problem solving during a negotiation. When you ask your counterpart to access things differently, it's possible for them to find new options. When you can get them to consider their past history from a different viewpoint, you can change their mind.

The more trance words you use in a sentence the more compelling your request becomes. When used in combination they reinforce each other, and three in a short sequence become nearly irresistible.

➤ Rhetorical Questions

These questions ask your counterpart to answer a question in their mind. Use rhetorical questions when you think your counterpart is close to agreeing with your point.

"You did *know* that . . . ?"

"Get the *idea?* Of course you do."

"*Guess* what?"

"You have to *ask yourself . . .*"

➤ Past Experience

History has the power of precedence. You can use your counterpart's past experience as incontrovertible evidence that supports your position. *"Have you ever* paid more for something than you wanted, then *were glad that you did?"* Now they are predisposed to accept your rationale for your higher price.

"How did you *decide* . . . ?"

"How did you *determine* . . . ?"

"Ponder for a moment . . ."

"Recall when . . ."

"Recollect a time when . . ."

"Relive that experience . . ."

"Remember a time when . . ."

"Remember *what it was like* . . . ?"

"What caused you to decide on that price?"

"What led you to that conclusion?

"When was the last time . . . ?"

"When were you best able to . . . ?"

➤ Present Experience

Access your counterpart's present experience and you can discover the thought process they use to arrive at a decision. Direct the negotiation to follow the *same* process and your offer becomes readily acceptable. It's easy for them to follow a process that they find automatic and intuitive.

"Can you make a *rough guess?"*

"Help me understand . . . ?"

"How much are your other tenants paying?"

"Tell me about your situation."

"What are you *using* now?"

"What do you *like least* about it?"

"What do you *like most* about it?"

"What makes you believe . . . ?"

"What's it like *when* . . . ?"

"Where would that make sense?"

"Who else are you working with?"

"Why do you *think . . . ?"*

"Why is that important to you?"

➤ Future Experience

Have your counterpart project into the future how they might feel, think, or behave. Access their plans. When you can align with their future vision, your offer becomes increasingly compelling. "Imagine for a moment that we are one year in the future, looking back on today. What was it that we did that made us so successful?"

"Can you *foresee . . . ?"*

"How *would* you *decide . . . ?"*

"How *would* you *determine . . . ?"*

"This is a *preview* of . . ."

"This will *foreshadow . . ."*

"What *could* you do . . . ?"

"What if you could *foretell . . . ?"*

"What *will* it be like when . . . ?"

"What *would convince* you . . . ?"

"What would have to *happen . . . ?"*

"What would it *feel* like when . . . ?"

"What *would you do . . . ?"*

"When you *look ahead* to . . ."

"You'll *know by instinct . . ."*

The TV station manager had already decided to buy new Sony cameras. In a last-ditch effort, Jeff Rosica, the Philips BTS sales manager made a call.

He asked the station manager, *"Think* for a minute. *Have you ever* bought anything for yourself made by Philips?"

The station manager pondered. "Why, yes. I use a Philips shaver that I bought when I was in the military."

"How long ago was that?"

"Fifteen years!"

"We're the same people."

This station now uses Philips video cameras.

■ IMAGINATION TRIGGERS

These words and phrases allow your counterpart to examine alternate scenarios in a safe way. They test the water without obligation or commitment. You can say, *"Just imagine . . ."* and you'll switch on your counterpart's creative unconscious. The demands of the immediate situation are temporarily suspended, and anything's possible.

"Imagine how much fun it will be to drive this new car. *Who would* you take for a ride first?"

"Can you *conceive* of a situation where . . . ?"

"Consider this . . ."

"Do you ever *wonder* why . . . ?"

"Have you ever been *curious* about . . . ?"

"I know you can't, but *what would happen if* you did?"

"If the time were right, what would you need to move forward?"

"If you had unlimited funds, who would you choose?"

"If you were to agree to this, how would it work?"

"When you *anticipate* . . ."

"You have to *ask yourself '_____' "*

Imagination trigger words include:

Conjecture	Have the impression	Project
Detect	Hit upon	React
Discover	In some way	Remarkable
Dream	Magic	Reveal
Enchant	Miraculous	See ahead
Estimate	Mysterious	Sense
Extraordinary	Mystically	Somehow feel
Feel in your bones	Perceive	Strange
Forecast	Picture	Suppose
Get the impression	Ponder	Surprise
Guess	Predict	Suspect
Have a funny feeling	Premonition	Think
Have a hunch	Presume	Wish
Have a sixth sense	Pretend	Wonder

■ OPTIONS GENERATORS

These words and phrases trigger your counterpart to think about things in a new way, to examine their position in a new light, to use a new filter on what they already know. They adjust their current perceptions so they see things differently and they're willing to consider new options.

"Why are you throwing that lawn mower away?" asked Wayne.

"The engine's seized up. It don't run," explained his neighbor.

"Hmmm. *What if* you could take it to Goodwill? *You might* get a receipt for it that you can write off on your taxes."

"I hadn't thought of that. Good idea!"

Here are some examples of options generators:

"*Consider* what *might* happen if . . ."

"Did you *realize* that you can . . . ?"

"Did you *recognize* that you could . . . ?"

"*Even though* . . ."

"Have you ever *daydreamed,* only to *awaken,* and *realized* . . . ?"

"I think you can *see the truth* . . ."

"If you can *understand* . . ."

"*If* you listen, you can *think* about things *in a new way* . . ."

"What if you *allowed* . . . ?"

"What if you could *convince* yourself . . . ?"

"What if you could see *as it really is* . . . ?"

"What if you were to suddenly *find yourself* . . . ?"

"Would you *permit* . . . ?"

"You *might see it coming* . . ."

"You might *see the light* . . ."

➤ Thought Displacers

Any new option, thought, or idea you want your counterpart to accept, should be linked to a common stimulus that they will want to eliminate or that they're likely to be exposed to. This uses the linguistic technique of linking two otherwise unrelated issues in the mind of your counterpart. The general form is, "The more you _____ about X, the more you _____ about Y"

> "The more you think about your position, the more you will appreciate my offer."
>
> "The more you spend on repairs, the more you'll wish you had this product."
>
> "The more you search for an answer, the more sense this makes."
>
> "The more you listen to the traffic noise, the more you'll appreciate this location."
>
> "The more you listen to the radio, the more you'll recognize that print advertising works."
>
> "The more you hear your technicians complain, the more you'll want to invest in this diagnostic equipment."
>
> "The more you drive around looking for a parking space, the more you'll appreciate the on-site garage."
>
> "The more you bounce around in your old car, the more you'll want this new one."

You can use this technique to build your confidence and eliminate distractions. When writing this book, there was construction going on nearby. Orvel Ray complained, "That construction noise is driving me nuts." Mark said, "Orvel, *the more* you hear that construction noise, the more easy it will be for you to build this book." Magically the noise abated and his complaints stopped immediately.

> Tell yourself, "The more concessions my counterpart requests, the more I can negotiate for in exchange."
>
> "The more I'm distracted, the more I can concentrate."
>
> "The more I use these tactics, the more I improve my lifestyle."
>
> "The more I worry about the outcome, the more confident I feel about my negotiating abilities."
>
> "The more I apply these techniques, the more advantage I gain."

➤ Turns Words into a Magic Wand

Adding an "s" to any verb turns it into a magic wand that does the work for you. This creates other options that may not have been considered, and offers them with compelling ease. Instead of "You will make money with this," say, "This *makes* you money." The first version says that you will have to do the work to get the job done. The second version says that what's being discussed will do the work necessary to get the job done. Turning verbs into magic wands gives you a fair advantage:

Gives	Works	Creates
Makes	Returns	Becomes
Produces	Pays	Increases
Generates	Insures	Performs
Offers	Replaces	Changes

➤ Compensatory Benefit

A special category of option generators is the compensatory benefit. While conceding the objection, the negotiator offers an offsetting rationale.

"Some people consider the use of call waiting to be rude, but you can always ignore the beep, and it permits you to use the phone while waiting for another important call."

■ EMBEDDED COMMANDS

These phrases suggest and direct your counterpart to perform a specific task or to take a particular action. Often your counterpart will need a nudge to get going. Embedded commands allow you to gently give them that nudge.

Embedded commands are all around you. Next time you read, listen to, or watch commercials, be aware of imbedded commands. Because the command is embedded in an otherwise acceptable comment, the rate of compliance is very high.

"Can you review and sign these documents *quickly?*"

"Chances are when you do *decide,* the rest *will work out.*"

"Considering your busy schedule, it would be great if we could *move forward now.*"

"Hopefully, you will eventually be able to *see my point of view* before too long."

"I wonder if *you could . . . ?*"

"If you'll only _____, this might work."

"It's been a long day. Why don't *you relax* for a moment?"

"You can *get us copies* of these documents, can't you? Good!"

Pause momentarily just before the embedded command to set it off from the rest of the sentence. Just half a beat is enough. "If you could . . . *get us some coffee,* that would be great!"

You can also use the opposite tactic, by stripping away common preamble phrases, and making your request directly. A good example would be when you meet someone for the first time. Instead of asking, "What is your name?" use the *imperative* form, "Tell me your name."

Other examples:

"*Tell* me the price."

"*Sign* here."

"*Justify* that for me."

And the classic, "Just *do it.*"

➤ Spotlight Phrases

Often, an embedded command works even better when preceded by an amplifier phrase. Combine these amplifiers with your embedded commands.

"It would be *better* if you just *tell us* what you really need."

"It's *essential that . . .*"

"It's *imperative that* you get your facts straight"

"It's *material* that you . . ."

"It's very *important* that you . . ."

"It's your *duty* to *be* honest and fair."

"Now you'll *have to* make some *compromise* here."

"Of course you *must consider* the long-term consequences of . . ."

"The only *condition* is . . ."

"The only *demand* on you . . ."

"The only *necessity* is . . ."

"The only *requisite* is . . ."

"*Think* about it."

"To do this, it's *required that* you . . ."

"Understanding the *importance of* your role . . ."

"You probably *ought to* . . ."

"Your only *obligation* is to . . ."

■ TEMPORAL CONTROLLERS

A special subset of embedded commands, these magic words and phrases have the effect of subjectively altering the amount of time your counterpart will need to wait or think before making a decision. In cases where the time frame of the negotiation is critical, using these advanced tactics can be a lifesaver.

➤ Time Compressors

Use time compressors when you want to accelerate the negotiation process.

"Something came up *unexpectedly.*"

"All of a *sudden* . . ."

"If possible, we would like to resolve this issue *at once.*"

"*Right now,* it's *urgent* that you . . ."

"*Suddenly* this has become a *pressing issue.*"

"This price increase hit us *without warning.*"

"We can get that for you *in a flash.*"

"We'll take care of this *immediately.*"

"You can contact our customer service department *instantaneously* via our Web site."

"You will see results from this *instantly.*"

Now combine time compressors with trance words, softeners, and imagination triggers to build a self-fulfilling prediction that limits the amount of time they will take to make the decision.

"As you *think about* my offer, I *suspect* you may *find yourself coming up with* a *positive* response. I don't know when; *it may be* in an hour, it may be today, it may be the middle of the week. That's okay." They'll probably decide within the hour.

"*Remember,* the apartment that you look at *today* and *think about* until *tomorrow* is the same apartment that someone else looked at yesterday, and will *decide* upon *today.*"

➤ Time Expanders

These phrases have the opposite effect of time compressors, buying you more time when you need it.

"It's unlikely that we'll know *for a while.*"

". . . will *give you more time.*"

". . . may *take some time.*"

You can make the time expansion conditional by attaching a concession to the release of the time condition.

"That's *impossible* unless . . ."

"We *won't find that out* until . . ."

➤ History Generators

These phrases identify events or thoughts that your counterpart may not have been consciously aware of. By making a statement that your counterpart is likely to agree with, you can create or identify a past experience that they weren't aware of until you pointed it out.

"*As soon as* you toured the property, you *knew* that it was perfect for you."

"Of course you *knew in advance* that we *would not be able* to do that."

"You *expected* that we would come to a favorable conclusion *early on.*"

"You *guessed* that _____ *would be* the case."

"You *knew* it would *come to this.*"

"You *were suspicious* of _____ all along."

They now have history where there was no history before. History has the influential characteristic of precedence.

■ TRIGGER PHRASES

Trigger phrases can set a boundary that, when crossed, triggers a decision. Use trigger phrases when your counterpart isn't quite ready to make a decision. Help them by identifying for them a condition that means they should decide. Phrases such as *fed up, sick and tired, ready, time is ripe,* and *had enough,* trigger your counterpart to make a decision. Combine them to gain a fair advantage.

> "*Soon* (time compressor) when you've *had enough,* (trigger phrase), *give me a call.* (imbedded command).
>
> "You may find that you'll tolerate this service level *to the point* that you'll be *fed up* and then give me a call."
>
> "It's possible that you'll *find yourself tired* of the situation."
>
> "Soon, you'll be *ready* to decide."

■ EMOTIVE DIRECTORS

These trance phrases have the unique ability to attach a particular *feeling* or emotion to your statement, evidence, or rationale. Because your counterpart will access the specified emotion along with the evidence, whatever follows will be colored by the specified feeling. Use these with softeners when you're uncertain if they'll agree with your statement.

> "Isn't it *amazing* that . . . ?"
>
> "You might be *frightened* by outrageous claims."
>
> "You will feel *comfortable* with this agreement."
>
> "You would be *angry* . . ."
>
> "You would be *concerned* . . ."
>
> "You would be *disappointed* if . . ."
>
> "You would be *dismayed* . . ."
>
> "You would be *upset* . . ."
>
> "You would be *worried* . . ."

"You'll be *amazed* when . . ."

"You'll be *delighted* when . . ."

Emotive directors are especially powerful when used in combination with awareness directors. You are coupling awareness with emotions, as in the classic ad "Aren't you *glad* you *use* Dial?"

"I was *astounded* when I *found out* . . ."

"I'm *glad* I *thought* of that."

"Isn't it *surprising* to *see* . . . ?"

"Isn't that *curious?*"

"It may *startle* you when you *find out* . . ."

"You'll be *astonished* when you *hear* . . ."

"You'll be *satisfied to know* that . . ."

"You'll be *surprised* to *discover* . . ."

"*Scary thought,* isn't it?"

■ RESPONSIBILITY REDIRECTORS

Another special category of embedded commands is responsibility redirectors. These phrases turn the table on your counterpart, making them responsible for the next step.

For example, use the phrase, "I'm confused" (silence) when you wish to challenge a statement or rationale. The implication is that your counterpart has failed to communicate their message clearly, and it is now incumbent upon them to do whatever is required to help you understand their position. The redirect, "I'm confused," is much stronger than the often used, "I don't understand." If you failed to understand, it's *your* problem because you don't have the capacity to understand. If you're confused, it's *their* problem, because the message was faulty.

In these examples, the italicized responsibility redirector precedes the underlined embedded command.

"*You* know more about that than I do."

"*You're* better prepared to do that than I am."

"*You're* in a better position to know that than I am."

"*You* know who to ask about that."

"*You* have a meeting with them, don't you? *You* <u>ask them</u>!"

"*You* have their number; <u>call them</u>!"

"*You* have Excel on your laptop; <u>work up a spreadsheet</u> on that."

"Here's the book; *you* <u>look it up</u>."

"I'm stuck. Can *you* <u>help me</u> out with this?"

"<u>Help me</u> understand . . ."

"Please <u>explain</u> further."

"Can *you* <u>lead me</u> through this?"

"If I <u>understand</u> *you* correctly . . ."

➤ Silence

You can also redirect responsibility with silence. Just be quiet after your counterpart has asked a question. They may continue to volunteer more information, modify their stance, or change their mind. Guerrillas make sure their counterpart has finished what they're saying and have not just paused for a reaction.

■ CLAIMING TO KNOW

Now you're wondering, "Can this stuff really work?" I can tell.

That phrase is an example of *claiming to know*. When you demonstrate that you have an insight into what's in your counterpart's mind, you may get credit for being psychic.

Claiming to know what your counterpart is thinking or feeling can take the pressure off a difficult moment. Simply responding with, "Yes, I know," after any statement made by your counterpart, establishes a bond and makes you appear both knowledgeable and reasonable.

Use *claiming-to-know* statements in the negotiation when you feel that something important is being left unsaid. The most effective application of this weapon is to make a stronger connection with your counterpart. This can create incredible rapport. Taken together, these perceptions substantially strengthen your negotiation position.

When using claiming-to-know statements, remember that there is a continuum of certainty, ranging from "Yes, I had a *hunch* that . . ." to "Yes, that *matches* my experience," to "Yes, I *knew* that, and . . ." (fill in plausible details not yet revealed).

Claiming to know must be sincere and natural to be effective. It can't be a throwaway line like, "I knew you were going to say that."

Never follow a claiming-to-know statement with a reflexive close, like "don't you?" "aren't you?" "isn't it?" or "am I right?" These tag lines open the preceding statement to logical scrutiny and destroy your obvious certainty.

"And *I realize that you believe* that's a lot to ask."

"He *feels like* he's being taken advantage of."

"He's *wondering* if . . ."

"I don't blame you *for thinking* . . ."

"*I know* that you know about . . ."

"*I know* that you're busy, but . . ."

"*I know* this is a bad time to bring this up, but . . ."

"*I know,* you thought . . ."

"*I understand* why you feel . . ."

"Right now, *you're wondering* . . ."

"She *thinks* you're in on this with me"

"You *felt* . . ."

"You *honestly believe* that we're trying to take advantage of you?"

"*You might be thinking* . . ."

"*You probably think* . . ."

"You *question* . . ."

"You *simply won't* . . ."

"You're a professional; you've *experienced that* before."

"You're in this business; you *understand.*"

"You're *not buying it.*"

"You're not sure about . . . *I can tell.*"

"You're *not sure* . . ."

"*You're reconsidering* . . ."

You can combine *claiming to know* with *generalities* and *emotive directors* and *embedded commands* to make your case overwhelmingly irresistible.

You might say, "You *have* a broken watch at home, and I *sense* that it was a gift from someone special. And while it has no real intrinsic value, you hate to *part with it*. I *get the feeling* that this issue is just like that watch; you're hanging on to it purely for sentimental reasons. Perhaps you should *let this one go*, too."

When someone challenges you and asks, "How did you know that?" respond with, "I can tell."

■ INGRATIATORS

A special application of *claiming-to-know*, these phrases can allow you to safely make guesses about your counterpart's resources, abilities, and background. Even if you are not right, they will be flattered by the comment. This phrase will cause your counterpart to subconsciously search for a case where the statement could fit. Use these when you need to build rapport, trust, and liking. You can also use them to build up your counterpart's confidence in their own negotiating ability, and put them off guard. The guerrilla gains an advantage by making the counterpart believe that they are smarter than you are.

"Congratulations! . . ."

"I can't actually believe that *you could* . . ."

"Oooh, *good* tactic. Where did *you learn* that one?"

"*Where did you learn* to be such a good negotiator?"

"Where did *you study* psychology?"

"Wow, *you're quite* . . ."

"You *did it all yourself*, so you must . . ."

"You have an *incredible knowledge* of . . ."

"You *must actually be* . . ."

"*You really know* the market."

"*You're really good* at figuring this out."

"You've *done this before*, haven't you?"

■ PRESUPPOSITIONS

Presuppositions cause a temporary suspension of disbelief because linguistically they presuppose that what follows the phrase is fact. They can turn guesses into evidence and fantasy into fact. Whatever you choose to follow the phrase is presupposed to be true.

"Do you find it *curious* that . . . ?"

"How *lucky* that . . ."

"I *guess* you'd be startled that . . ."

"I was *wondering* how . . ."

"I'm *astonished* that . . ."

"I'm *devastated* that . . ."

"Isn't it *funny* how . . . ?"

"Isn't it *strange* that . . . ?"

"It might be *unnerving* . . ."

"It's a bit *bewildering* . . ."

"It's quite *peculiar* that . . ."

"What *bothers* me is . . ."

"What's so *astounding* is . . ."

Phrases following a word ending in -*ly* also become a presupposition.

"*Actually* . . ."

"This is *unbelievably* . . ."

"*Surely* . . ."

"*Naturally* . . ."

"*Virtually* . . ."

"*Evidently* . . ."

"*Eventually* . . ."

A simple way to construct presuppositions is to use the form: *As* _____ *as* _____ . Whatever follows is presumed to be true. *As* <u>simple</u> *as* <u>it seems</u>, this has a very powerful affect.

"*As* expensive *as* this is, you should get the extended warranty."

"*As* important *as* this discussion is, we should tape it."

"*As* skeptical *as* you are, you should check with my attorney."

"*As* uncertain *as* our business is, we will need an escape clause."

"*As* warm *as* it is, you should pay for the air-conditioning."

Link your *as* _____ *as* _____ presupposition with a softener to increase persuasion. "*I think* that you'll see that *as* complicated *as* this may seem, it's really very simple."

"As . . . as . . ." statements can also be used to substantiate what may not be obvious, or to draw attention away from weak points in your case.

"*As* crazy *as* this seems . . ."

"*As* dangerous *as* this appears, it's actually quite safe."

"*As* ridiculous *as* this sounds . . ."

"*As* troubling *as* this may be . . ."

■ COMPARATIVES

Sentences using words ending in *-est* can be used to create comparative presuppositions. In the following sentences, the superlative is presupposed

"But the *oddest* thing is . . ."

"Even the *sharpest* mind doesn't always see it."

"That's the *craziest* suggestion I've heard all day."

"The *easiest* way to get this done is . . ."

"The *scariest* part of this agreement for me is . . ."

"He is the *shrewdest* person I've ever met."

"This is probably the *clearest* . . ."

"This is the *cheapest* in . . ."

"This is the *hardest* . . ."

"This is the *newest* technology in the field."

"This may be the *smartest* thing you ever do."

"This product is the *best*."

You can combine a superlative (italicized) with a trance word (underlined) for extra persuasion.

". . . beyond your *wildest* <u>dreams</u>."

". . . granting you *grandest* <u>wish</u>."

". . . exceeding your *greatest* <u>expectations</u>."

■ UNSPECIFIED ATTRIBUTION

Your evidence gains credibility when credited to a third party, even when that party is unspecified or even fictional. This tactic takes advantage of the influence weapon of *social proof.* Position your statement within quotes for added persuasion.

This tactic is also useful for presenting ideas that may be unpopular or off-putting. You can get by with saying it because it's not really you who is saying it, it's someone else.

"*People* often think . . ."

"*A man* once told me, . . ."

"*Science* states that . . ."

"*Studies* show . . ."

"Our *survey* indicates . . ."

"*People* in our seminars tell us . . ."

"*Authorities* agree . . ."

"*Doctors* recommend . . ."

"*Those who study* _____ have found . . ."

"I heard on the *radio* that . . ."

"I read in a *book* . . ."

"I saw a *magazine article* that said . . ."

"Our *clients* tell us that we're different because . . ."

"My *mother* told me . . ."

"*I* always say, . . ."

■ *AND* LINKAGES

Use the linkage *and* to take the authority and factual nature of one idea and link it to another idea that you need to strengthen. "I've done it before *and* so I know."

"I know you're in a hurry *and* . . ."

"You could have chosen any vendor *and* . . ."

"I know you changed your mind, *and* yet I still have this feeling that . . ."

"_____ *and* _____ are obviously at work here."

"Times have changed *and* . . ."

"Anything is possible *and* . . ."

". . . *and* write that down."

". . . *and* play along for the moment."

". . . *and* that says something about you."

"You may doubt that right now, *and* . . ."

"Stranger things have happened, *and* . . ."

■ CREDIBILITY HELPERS

Idioms and similes are learned when we are young children before the age of reason. We accept these credibility helpers as true without question. Even as adults, when we hear them they elicit instant agreement. For example: *as easy as pie.* When we hear the phrase, we instantly assume that what's discussed is simple to do. Yet, how easy *is* pie, really? The words are linguistic nonsense, but the phrase creates a nonjudgmental response.

Similes take the form *as* _____ *as* _____ *(As dumb as they come)* or *Like* _____. *(Like a duck to water).*

Using idioms and similes in your discussion will help you gain credibility and establish instant rapport with your counterpart.

Chapter

Guerrilla Strategies That Fortify Your Position

Guerrillas prepare themselves to take the high ground in a negotiation. Here are some strategies you can use to strengthen your position.

■ WHO'S ON THEIR TEAM?

Few decisions are made in a vacuum without the negotiator consulting others. You've got to identify the players or you'll be left out in the cold. The following people are involved in the decision-making process, either directly or indirectly. Find them, and befriend them. They are invaluable sources of information and insight. Learn all you can from them.

➤ Gatekeeper

The gatekeeper is usually the first person you meet. The gatekeeper answers the phone and guards the door to the organization. Although they are trained to say "no," and have no authority to say "yes," gatekeepers are very influential during the negotiation process because they decide who gets consideration. They know the politics and will tell you things that no one else can. More than one gatekeeper has killed a deal by mentioning, "They're real jerks. Are you sure you want them working with our people?" They can interrupt your negotiations with phone calls or documents to sign.

Guerrillas gain an advantage by treating gatekeepers with deference and respect. Approach them as if they run the company . . . *because they do.* So, get them on your side first. Let them know what you can do for their organization, what problem that you can solve, and how you can make their life easier.

Ask them for a favor: "Will you help me? I know that you know who's the best person for me to speak with. What's the best way for me to approach them? What drives them crazy?" Ask them about the best time to call. Ask them to hold calls during the meeting. Ask them to interrupt you if an important document arrives.

➤ Influencer

The influencer has technical or financial knowledge about what is being negotiated. An influencer can be someone who has successfully used your product, or has read good reviews about your products, or is skilled at analyzing similar products. They have influence because of their recognized knowledge and wisdom. They could be your counterpart's attorney, accountant, or aunt.

Find influencers before opening negotiations by asking, "Who else, besides yourself, is involved in making this decision?" Even if you think you've found the decision maker, continue to ask everyone else this question. Be aware of outside consultants who can influence the outcome.

Once you've found the influencers, ask them, "What process do you use to make your decision?" or "How will you know who's the best vendor?" or "What criteria do you use to make your recommendation?" Once you know their decision-making process and criteria, you'll know exactly what to show, do, and say to gain a favorable outcome.

➤ Economic Buyer

The economic buyer places the order, sends out bids, or issues a purchase order. The economic buyer is charged with getting the best possible price for your product, so they may bid you against your competitors. All things being equal, the economic buyer chooses the lowest cost vendor. Guerrillas ensure that nothing is equal. Buyers will almost always choose reliable delivery over lowest price. Win them over by convincing them you'll deliver at a fair price.

➤ Decision Maker

This is the person who ultimately makes the final decision and is responsible for the choice made. They can say "no" when everyone else says "yes," and vice versa. Most salespeople are taught to find the decision maker and sell to them. Although most decision makers are not influenced by salespeople, they are influenced by their staff—willingly or otherwise. The decision maker will be most influenced by you when they regard you as a professional colleague.

Ask the staff to review your product and give you their commitment. Then approach the decision maker with a summary of what their staff suggests. "I've had your staff review this decision and here are their comments." When the staff is on your side, the decision maker will almost always give you the nod.

➤ User

The user is the ultimate decision maker, and users can sabotage the decision. Guerrillas invest time with users to understand their concerns. Work the graveyard shift, talk to users at off-hours when there are few visitors. Bring in 20 pizzas and treat them to lunch. Listen to their complaints in the lunchroom. Just by eavesdropping, you can gather information that will serve you well in your negotiation.

➤ Spy

The spy is someone who, for reasons of their own, wants you to win the negotiation. The best spies are people whom you have served well at one facility and have moved to a new location. They want you to serve them as you have in the past.

You can recruit a spy by seeking the advice of a non-decision maker. Look for people who are lower down on the organization chart than your counterparts, and invite them to lunch. "I want to get your opinion of what we should do." These people will be flattered by your attention, and will tell you things that no one else can or will.

■ AVOID TRAP QUESTIONS

You must control the discussion of certain dangerous topics. You need to know how to avoid these topics tactfully and how to answer sensitive questions consistently.

➤ How Much Does It Cost?

This is a common question, often asked early in the conversation. Even the least qualified, least trained negotiator can ask, "How much does it cost?"

If your counterpart doesn't understand *what* you offer and the *value* you give them, you'll *always* seem too expensive. So your first step is to build up the value of your offer.

Always control *when* the topic of price is discussed. If your counterpart asks it as the first question, put them off.

> "That depends on what you want. What do you need?"

> "I'll be glad to answer that. But first, what do you know about what we're offering?"

> "Before I quote a price, I need to understand your needs. That way, I can offer you just the right thing. What are you looking for?"

> "I'll be glad to quote you our prices, but unless I can meet your needs, the price I give you won't make any sense. Can we discuss what you need first?"

If your counterpart insists on a price, quote your least expensive product, saying, "Our entry-level product, which includes (list all of the important features), *only* costs X dollars. Is this within your budget?"

It's very important that your counterpart understands what is included in the price, and how much money they can save by buying your product. Summarize the product features and benefits before quoting the price.

➤ So, Why Are You Better Than Your Competition?

Questions about your competition should always be handled with care. Unless you know *who* the counterpart is, *why* he's asking the question, and what he's really looking for, any response could backfire. Many counterparts will feel uncomfortable about competition-bashing. One of the biggest credibility busters is for you to discuss something your competition has changed recently, or now does better than you. Guerrilla responses include:

> "Our competitor is a fine company. But our customers tell us that we are better able to meet their needs. Tell me what you're looking for specifically."

> "That's a hard question to answer. Obviously *their* customers think *they* do a good job, and *our* customers love *us*. What do they offer that you think is critical to you?"

> "I'm not an expert on our competitors. We have people in our company who study them extensively, but I'm focused on how my customers benefit from what we can do. What are you looking for?"

A well-known software company ran a magazine ad against its competition. In the same issue, the magazine editors who reviewed the respective products declared the competitor's to be superior. Yes, the ads made us think about and check out the situation, but in the process, the advertiser lost credibility.

➤ How to Handle Sensitive Topics

It's imperative that every member of your negotiation team have a single message when asked sensitive questions. These answers are your party line. This list will give you an overview of some of these topics. A pre-negotiation briefing on the company platform will help keep the message consistent, and help avoid problems. You may elect to discuss some of these topics under a nondisclosure agreement. Feel free to use this list of out-of-bounds topics for your company.

> ➤ *Financial projections.* Forecasts of orders, shipments, earnings and related internal data should never be disclosed. (When asked, "How's business?" the response should be, "Business is great!")

> ➤ *Operating results.* Don't divulge any sales or profit figures (past or projected) for the company, a product line, or a specific product.

➤ *Market share.* Don't estimate market share. Obvious generalizations are all right ("Our technology positions us as the leader in the marketplace . . ."), but avoid dollar estimates, percentages, or expressions such as "We dominate the market," unless you have irrefutable proof.

➤ *Marketing strategy.* This includes projected marketing plans and expenditures, sales force information, advertising plans, and other information that could aid competitors.

➤ *Legal matters.* Patent information, tax matters, and any other legal matters should not be discussed.

➤ *Impending changes.* This means changes in structure, expansion, staffing levels, and the like. It's often tempting to boost your ego by dropping hints or leaking information if you're in the know. It's better to play dumb and suggest that the person talk to a corporate officer. Your ego may suffer, but the company won't.

➤ *Products under development.* Until a product is officially introduced, it shouldn't be discussed—either directly or by implication. Any discussion should be covered by a written nondisclosure agreement, and then only with a bona fide customer or prospect. If necessary, keep copies of your nondisclosure agreement on hand.

Here are some deflecting replies to these questions:

➤ "I'm sorry, but I don't have the authority to discuss that with you." Refer the questioner to the right person in your organization.

➤ "That's a good question. What makes you ask?"

➤ "Our company considers that confidential. What makes you ask?"

➤ "Good question. Is that important to us doing business?"

■ MANAGING EXPECTATIONS

Your expectations of the outcome are a good indicator of how you'll do in a negotiation. Study after study shows that negotiators who expect more get more. Begin by determining your objective: What do you expect? What response do you want from your counterpart? What outcome would be acceptable? What outcome would be optimal?

Your expectations will vary with the situation and can change during the negotiation. Guerrillas monitor their expectations and refuse to adjust them unless there is a highly compelling reason to do otherwise.

■ BUILDING CREDIBILITY

One of the biggest challenges in negotiating is when your counterpart doesn't believe you. People are skeptical. They don't believe your position. They don't believe your claims. They don't believe that you are realistic. They don't believe you will keep your end of the deal. They don't believe you are honorable.

This is where credibility comes into play. The basis of credibility is the appearance of truth. It allows your counterpart to believe what you are telling them. If you tell them something that is outside of their experience, or if they've had a different outcome, they won't believe what you say.

■ HOW TO GET INSIDER INFORMATION

Information is the new currency of the twenty-first century. The Internet makes it easy to find, and it's often free for the asking. You might even resort to hiring a private detective, but first, do some guerrilla sleuthing on your own.

➤ The Iceberg Principle

In high school physics you learned that 90 percent of the mass of an iceberg floats *below* the waterline, which is why icebergs are so dangerous. The Iceberg Principle of Guerrilla Negotiating says, "It's never the tip of the iceberg that sinks you.

You may have direct access to only 10 percent of the information affecting the outcome of the negotiation. Fully 90 percent of the factors affecting their decision are issues that they will not reveal. If you sail on blindly through the fog, full steam ahead, you'll wind up like the *Titanic*.

➤ Get All the Facts

You can't even trust your counterpart to know the facts, so don't be too eager to accept the evidence they present at face value. It may be helpful to role-play in advance with a devil's advocate. By all means, research multiple sources. Confirm critical data. If it sounds too good to be true, it's probably not.

➤ The Boss Doesn't Know

You can't trust top officers to know the facts. A senior manager is only aware of a fraction of the problems in their operation, whereas a middle manager may be aware of more, and a supervisor, even more. The worker on the front line is aware of 100 percent of the problems affecting the organization. The lower you go on the organizational food chain, the more likely your source has complete information.

➤ Adjust Your Viewpoint

If you're negotiating with a competitor, you may have to adjust your viewpoint. Most people look at their competitors with disdain and contempt, possibly even hatred. These emotions create barriers to clear thinking and effective planning. Fear and loathing lead to negotiating myopia. View your competition as their customers do. Customers are curious, and open-minded, and probably excited. They're trying to solve a problem. We tend to be more critical than most customers and usually focus on things they're not concerned with, such as, "I can't stand the president," or "That's a bad location."

When you analyze your competition, do so as if you were someone with positive expectations. Take the "I've-got-money-to-spend" viewpoint. Or better yet, talk to actual customers about your competition to get an idea of what *they* think is important.

Then, look at what your competitors sell as if you were seeing it for the first time. Or ask someone who's unfamiliar with your competition to review their products. You'll be surprised at what you've missed. In the frenzied quest for dirt, more than one company has been baited by false information, or worse, has redirected marketing plans down dead-end paths. Savvy guerrillas don't let the competition blindly set their strategy. Objective intelligence leads to a pragmatic and successful negotiating attack.

➤ Get All the Relevant Literature

Call your counterpart and ask them to send you their catalog, samples, brochures, and literature. Tell them who you are, what you do, and that you'd like the literature so you can have a clear understanding of what the company tells your customers. If they refuse, call back, this time giving your home address, or ask one of your customers to request the information for you.

➤ Use Trade-Show Reconnaissance

A great source of competitive intelligence is a trade show. The exhibits are often staffed by those in the know who haven't been briefed on what topics are safe and which are out-of-bounds. Because of the unfamiliar show environment, these people are just insecure enough to feel that, by talking about "insider information," they'll command respect. It only takes a little prodding to get them started.

At trade shows, the unwritten rule is "seller beware." Walk up to their booth without your badge and start asking questions. Entire marketing plans have been unwittingly revealed at trade shows.

➤ Watch for Publicity

Have your entire staff search for news items about your competition. Watch the employment ad postings, which often reveal information about upcoming projects. You can determine a lot from staffing requirements, especially when you've been watching for a while.

➤ Build an Intelligence Network

Enlist all of your colleagues, associates, and vendors in your quest for information. Let them know that you're always interested in information, and reward those in your organization who become "industry experts." Make intelligence gathering part of your everyday awareness, and you'll never be blindsided.

➤ Search the Internet

Compile profiles that include online research from Dow Jones, Lexis, Nexis, DiaLog, and the World Wide Web. Go to news groups that customers are likely to frequent and post questions about competitors' products as well as your own. You'll find the responses pointed and pragmatic. Use search engines such as Yahoo.com, Infoseek.com, HotBot.com, and Lycos.com, to check facts on the Internet. You can also go to the Web site of any major daily newspaper and search for articles. For example, you can reach *The Boston Globe* at http://www.boston.com/dailyglobe. Search an on-line *Encyclopedia Britannica* at EB.com. Search www.amazon.com or www.barnesandnoble.com for books that provide authoritative information.

➤ Just the Fax

A drayage company in Chicago specializes in moving large, heavy objects in and out of McCormick Place for trade shows. The sales representative had been calling on a manufacturer of railroad cars who exhibited in Chicago every year, and was using the services of a competitor. The prospect kept urging her to lower her price, insisting that the competitor would do the same job for less. She was reluctant to negotiate because she *knew* her quote was competitive.

In an inspired moment, she called the competing drayage company and asked to speak to someone in Accounts Receivable. "I'm researching an invoice for XYZ Company. You moved some railroad cars for them last July, and I need to confirm the amount. Would you please look up that invoice?"

"Well, we're kinda' busy right now," came the reply. "Would it be okay if we just fax it to you?"

"Sure. That will be just fine. Here's my number . . ."

You guessed it. Her quote was already substantially lower than the amount charged by the competitor the previous year. Armed with a copy of the invoice, she got the account, and she got her price.

➤ Friends in High Places

Sometimes the easiest name to get is the owner or senior manager, so start at the top. Call and ask, "Mr. President, I realize that I'm talking to the wrong person, but who in your organization is responsible for providing advanced training for your sales team (insert your query here)?"

"That would be Mr. Sales Manager."

"Great. Would you please transfer my call?"

Their caller ID will identify the source of the call as the president's office. They'll take your call.

➤ Friends in Low Places

We spend a lot of time in hotels as we travel around the world leading seminars and training sessions, and one of the things we've learned is that in every hotel there is someone who has a set of keys that will open *every* door in the place: the custodian. Never underestimate who can give you useful information. The lower they are on the totem pole, the more reliable the source.

➤ Recruit a Spy

Your spy could be a friend, a neighbor, or a relative who works on the inside. The best spy is someone who, for reasons of their own, wants to see you succeed. Take them out for lunch, or for drinks after work. Ask them for the inside scoop.

Ask!

You'd be surprised what information you can get just by asking your competition. For example, Mike, who's the sales manager at a major hotel in New Orleans, had an association executive previewing the property for an upcoming conference. Mike asked, "Where was the best conference you've ever had?" The exec explained that the previous year's conference had been held at a high-profile hotel in Las Vegas.

After the meeting, Mike called the sales manager of the Las Vegas hotel. "Hello, I just had one of your guests in here raving about you. Would you do me a favor? Would you fax me a copy of their contract from last year?" Mike patterned his proposal after the Las Vegas contract and won the business.

Just because you wouldn't give your competition this information doesn't mean that they won't give it to you!

Go Where the Competition Hangs Out

Where do the employees go after work for a drink? Where do they go for lunch? You can pick up lots of interesting information just by sitting back and listening. Or encourage them with a round of drinks and then listen to their complaints. We've heard more than one industry secret revealed in an overheard conversation in a restaurant, bar, or airplane.

Interview Disgruntled Former Employees

Check the grapevine for someone who has just left your competitor. Invite this person out for dinner and drinks, and pick their brain by asking questions such as: "What do you think they do really well, better than us? Where are we falling down? What three things should we be doing that we're not?" Steer clear of asking them to violate any nondisclosure agreement that may have been signed. You may be liable for misuse of obviously confidential information.

Take Your Competitor's Customers to Lunch

If you want to understand your competitor's marketing strategy, ask your sales force about a deal that was recently lost to the competitor, and offer to take that buyer to lunch. Explain that you're only interested in finding out how to improve your service, so that next time around, you'll have a chance to earn their business.

Sure, this feels like eating humble pie, so you might be tempted to reject this idea. But you've already lost the sale, so swallow your pride and take advantage of the opportunity presented.

Listen objectively, without arguing, and ask questions such as: How did you find out about our competitor? What steps did you go through as you made your decision? What were the factors you based your decision on? Compared to the competition, what did we do well? What could have we done better?

Consider the lost deal an investment, perhaps an expensive investment, in planning the next battle. Focus on what the competitor does to win customers, not on how to save the deal. When customers are pushed to reconsider a decision, their natural reaction is to defend and exaggerate the deciding factors. Just ask questions and bite your tongue. You want the unvarnished truth.

Become the Competitor's Customer
Experience your competitors firsthand. Buy from them. When most companies buy from the competition, they dissect their purchase and look for the negative things to point out to their salespeople. This works in creating a traditional competitive analysis. But you still don't have an insight as to why others buy from them.

It is more illuminating to use your competitors' products just as their customers do. Most buyers gleefully bring their new acquisition into their lives. To truly understand the mind-set of your competitor's customer, you must (begrudgingly or otherwise) do the same.

When the competition orders from you, we suggest that you treat your competitor's orders as you would your most important customer. Astound them with your exceptional customer service. They'll assume that if you provide this level of attention to your competition, you must really go out of your way for customers.

➤ Read Their Trade Magazines

Subscribe to the trade magazines that serve your counterpart's industry. Here you'll find analysis and spot trends you won't see anywhere else.

➤ Read Their Press Kit

Call your counterpart's marketing department and ask them to send you a media kit. They probably have their media kit already on-line, ready for you to download. In publicly held companies, routine corporate reports tell the press what's new, and what's news. You can find them on-line, or request them by calling your counterpart's main phone number and asking for investor relations.

➤ Take Stock

Call a discount stockbroker and order one share of your counterpart's stock. You are now, in the truest sense of the word, a shareholder, and you'll automatically receive the quarterly stockholders report, which contains all kinds of insider information about the company, its departments and divisions, new product releases, and financial performance. You are also entitled to attend the shareholder meetings. If you really want to have fun, buy a share of stock for everyone in the company. Take a road trip to the annual shareholder's meeting, and sit in the front row. (Don't be disruptive!) Can you imagine the impact on your competitor's CEO when explaining how they will increase sales next year, and the competition is literally hearing it first? Notice the look on their face when you ask for a plant tour.

■ THE ELEMENT OF SURPRISE

Surprise is a secret weapon that guerrilla negotiators use to gain a fair advantage.

➤ The Last Thing Someone in Their Right Mind Would Do

One guerrilla in Dallas had been trying to get his counterpart to make a decision for well over a month. He barged into the office, brandishing a yellow plastic squirt gun. "Sir, I'm a desperate man. I need your answer today!"

His prospect looked at him, amused. "Son, is that thing loaded?"

"Uh, no, sir. I'm *really* desperate."

"Boy, you mean to tell me that you came in here to threaten me with a squirt gun and it isn't even loaded?"

"No, sir. You got any water?"

The prospect laughed and said, "Okay. Let's go." The guerrilla closed the deal that same day.

➤ Leak Your Intention

This is a popular tactic among Japanese businessmen. Have an intermediary leak your real concerns to your counterpart, or share sensitive facts that they otherwise wouldn't have access to.

➤ Call from the Plane

There are times when it's well worth the $3.00 a minute just to be able to say, "I'm on an airplane on my way to New York and I was just thinking . . ." They *will* take the call, and they will take whatever you say from the air phone *very* seriously.

➤ Contrary Stance

Take a position that you can support logically, then switch sides. When shopping for a late-model used car, our guerrilla started the conversation by saying, "Might as well just pay full sticker for this one. It's in great condition, low miles, and it's even the right color. On the other hand, I would feel like a fool if I didn't even *try* to negotiate the price, especially since I've seen the same car for less money at another dealership. What can you really sell it to me for."

■ GUERRILLA TACTICS TO COUNTER DIRTY TRICKS

Dirty negotiating tactics have been taught in classes and passed down within organizations. Inexperienced negotiators will fall for these tactics, not expecting them and not knowing how to counter them. Forewarned is forearmed.

➤ Throw a Fit

Some buyers use irrational behavior to lure you into concessions you don't wish to make. If they throw a tantrum, get up to leave. They'll always object to your impending departure. When they do, just say, "Are you through now? I know that you expect to be treated in a civil manner. So do I."

➤ Throw a Card

This is a variation of the throw-a-fit tactic. When you offer your proposal, they'll pick up your business card and with disgust, throw it into the trash can. Pick up your card from the trash and head for the door.

➤ Telephone Mistakes

When opening telephone negotiations, your counterpart may inflate their position or exaggerate your potential gains. They want you to get excited and reveal your best offer. When you meet, they'll take a substantially reduced position. They'll claim that you misunderstood them and insist that you stick to your original offer.

Combat this by accepting the blame. "I'm sorry, I misunderstood you. I quoted the discount that you would earn at 10,000 units. At 10 units you've not yet *earned* that discount."

Guerrillas preempt this sneaky tactic by announcing that calls are monitored for quality or by telling them that you're taking notes, insisting on faxing or E-mailing a copy for their review and approval.

➤ The Stall

"I have to think about it." Your counterpart uses this tactic when they know you're under time pressure. They're hoping you'll volunteer a concession in exchange for making an immediate decision.

Find out how long they need to consider. "When would you be done thinking about it? Do you need a few minutes or would you like to sleep on it and talk about it in the morning?"

Better yet, remove the time element from the decision. "If the *time is right* for you to make a decision, what would you need to move forward?" Often you'll flush out the obstacle that's stalling the decision.

➤ Hobson's Choice

"You can have any color you want, as long as it's black."

HENRY FORD

A Hobson's choice is an apparently free choice that offers no real alternative, named after Thomas Hobson, an English keeper of a livery stable who required that customers take either the horse nearest the stable door or none at all. When presented with a Hobson's choice, there is no negotiation.

One tactic is to present your own Hobson's choice. "I'll accept that *only* if you'll . . ."

➤ Split the Difference

When getting close to agreement, your counterpart may say, "Oh, heck, let's just split the difference." If this is acceptable, take the offer with a reciprocal concession: "If I do, will you sign the contract now?"

If it's not acceptable, say so. Splitting the difference isn't necessarily fair, and you shouldn't feel inclined to accept this common tactic. "Although that's tempting, I don't think so. What I *can* do is . . ."

➤ Lowballing

A tactic taught in negotiating classes is to make a ridiculously low offer to see how the counterpart will respond. It's a way to find their Minimum Acceptable Result.

One guerrilla countered this common tactic in his industry by carrying a novelty laughing box in his briefcase. When a counterpart would lowball, he'd pull out the box and turn it on. With maniacal mechanical laughter filling the room, he'd sit with a poker face and wait until *they* turned it off. Then he'd say, "Let's get serious, please."

➤ Itemizing

"Please give us an itemized quote!" And so begins the process of cherry picking and nitpicking, and you're open to negotiating from a position of weakness. Guerrillas counter with, "That's not the way we do business."

➤ The Lopez

General Motors created this form of negotiating to squeeze the last possible advantage out of their suppliers. The process starts with a request for detailed proposals from competing vendors. The documents were collected and copies distributed to all vendors, who were then asked to resubmit their proposals. Contact with the GM buying team was not permitted and buyers were routinely shuffled to ensure that a buyer–vendor relationship had no impact on the decision. A number of vendors have gone broke by underbidding the competition to the point of losses. GM didn't care; they knew that there would be other vendors to take their place.

Guerrillas refuse to play this game, knowing that if they can't make a profit, they won't be in business. They won't liquidate their company for the benefit of a customer. Guerrillas would rather sell their business and start a new company than play what is ultimately a losing game.

➤ The Crunch

Large buyers have used this tactic for many years. They'll approach a small vendor and offer them so much business that they must expand their operations to meet the demand. After expansion capital has been borrowed and invested, the buyer insists on a lower price or threatens to cancel the contract. The vendor has no choice but to capitulate, operating at a loss to service their new debt. Many go broke along the way. Guerrillas refuse to allow any one customer to dominate their capacity. Doing so invites abuse.

Another tactic is to find similar companies and subcontract to them, eliminating the need for increased financial commitment while still filling the order. Although some companies resist sharing business with competitors, guerrillas know that *coopetition* (cooperation with competition) makes them wealthy at reduced risk.

Chapter

7

How Guerrillas Win on Price

When you think about negotiating, haggling over price is probably the first thing that comes to mind. In many cultures, price haggling is a highly evolved ritual of exchanging insults and granting largess. When it comes to price negotiation, there are many psychological tactics your counterpart can use to drive down prices. Here are some tactics you can use to keep your prices up.

■ WHAT THEY WANT YOU TO BELIEVE

It's part of a buyer's job to ask for a discount. If they don't ask, they won't get a better price. They have nothing to lose and everything to gain by asking you for a price concession. Any buyer who's attended a negotiating seminar has been taught to ask for price concessions *at least twice* before settling.

You'll hear: "You're going to have to sharpen your pencil to do business with me." "That price is unacceptable." "You sure are proud of your products." "Guess again!" or other indications that they want a lower price.

It's always in the buyer's best interest for you to believe that price is the most important issue, otherwise, you would never lower your price. During negotiations, your counterpart will almost always respond negatively to your pricing. Remember that it's just part of their strategy to get you to lower your price.

Price is always more important to the seller than to the buyer. The result is that salespeople frequently offer discounts up front in order to head off this potentially negative discussion.

According to a 15-year study conducted by the VASS Training Group, 67 percent of salespeople will *volunteer* to cut their price, *without being asked*. That's not negotiating, that's *stupid!* When a salesperson needlessly cuts price, they're liquidating their company to benefit the customer.

Your counterpart is charged with getting the best possible price from you, and you're charged with selling your goods and services at maximum profit. Anyone can give products away. Sales professionals earn their commission when they sell at prices higher than their costs, at prices higher than their competition, and at prices higher than their counterpart initially wishes to pay.

■ WHY PRICE IS AN ISSUE

Even if your counterpart knows nothing about your offering, they can still ask about price. Or they habitually try to buy cheap, choosing only the lowest price. Or they could be going broke and want to take you with them into bankruptcy. They may not understand the difference between what you and your competitors offer. They may misunderstand the costs and paybacks of your offering. Most likely they're just negotiating for a better deal.

■ WHAT THEY REALLY WANT

A majority of your prospects won't buy on price alone. In a survey by the Forum Corporation, only 15 percent of industrial buyers change vendors when they find a lower price. The American Retailers Association found that only 14 percent of consumers base purchases solely on price. There's plenty of business out there where you don't have to be the lowest-cost supplier.

Guerrillas know how their customer really feels about price. When your counterpart understands the value of your offer, price is seldom the real issue. Your counterpart has a problem to solve and is willing to part with hard-earned cash to solve it. All things being equal, they will select the vendor who offers the lowest price. Guerrillas make sure that all things are *never* equal.

What keeps buyers awake at night is not that they've paid too much, but that that what they've bought won't do the job, or that the product won't be there when they need it. Your counterpart needs what you've got to run their business. If you don't perform, they *can't* perform. Your buyer doesn't fear overpaying; they fear nonperformance.

In a survey of 64 industrial buying agents, of those with more than two years' buying experience, 70 percent selected the vendor with the best delivery record, whereas 30 percent selected the vendor with the best quality.[1] Those who bought from the lowest-price vendor had fewer than two years' experience; they hadn't yet been burned.

Think about it. No one's ever been fired for buying from AT&T, Hewlett-Packard, IBM, Xerox, or Compaq. These companies are not the cheapest vendors; frequently they're the most expensive in their category. What they deliver is solid products that perform.

■ "BUT I CAN GET IT CHEAPER."

You'll always have competitors whose prices are lower. Look at it this way: There will always be someone smarter than you, who's figured out how to produce things a little cheaper than you can. And there will always be someone who's dumber than you, who doesn't know their real costs, and is willing to give away their margins by competing on price.

In a negotiation, your counterpart may try to use your competitor's lower prices to extract pricing concessions from you. They want *your* quality, *your* reputation, *your* delivery, *your* support, *your* guarantee, and *your* terms, but at the competitor's price. They'll compare your competitor's apples to your apple pie, and ask for the apple price.

You can counter this but-I-can-buy-it-cheaper tactic with the guerrilla negotiating phrase, "We have no argument with those who sell for less. They know best what their product is worth."

A woman in a butcher shop is looking for a deal. "I can get hamburger down the street for 79 cents a pound. Yours is 99 cents."

The butcher responds, "Well then, why don't you buy it from them?"

---

[1] Steinmetz, Lawrence L. *How to Sell at Prices Higher than Your Competitors.* Boulder, CO: Horizon Publications, 1994, p. 19.

"Because they're sold out," she replies.

"Well, when I'm sold out," the butcher responds, "my hamburger is only 59 cents a pound."

Guerrillas gain an advantage by expecting to be asked to lower the price, and having weapons deployed to defend their pricing.

■ WHY YOU DON'T WANT PRICE BUYERS

Think about the negotiations where you were hammered on price.

> Did your counterpart waste a lot of your time, making trivial and meaningless demands?

> Did they have silly complaints and insist that you take the problem off their hands?

> Did they insist on rock-bottom prices for your best? Second-quality products won't pass their QA test?

> Did they pay late? Or pay short? It wasn't enough to go after them in court.

> Did they brag about the deal they got? Did they blab to your clients till your credibility was shot?

> Did you notice that they have no loyalty? They'll switch vendors the next low price they see.

> Did they tell your competition about your plans? You're better off getting this customer off your hands.

➤ Three Ways to Dump Price Buyers

1. Increase delivery times. Or make yourself unavailable, "The next time I can see you is Monday. In three months."

2. Increase your prices. Or stand firm on your discount schedule, "You don't *earn* a discount until you purchase $10,000." Or make it more difficult for them to receive credit. "Our credit department has put your account on hold. Indefinitely."

3. Just tell them to go away. "I'm sorry, but at the price you're willing to pay, I can't give you the quality and service you truly deserve."

■ HOW TO AVOID PRICE-BUYER DIRTY TRICKS

Experienced price buyers use dirty tricks to get you to lower your price. Keep your prices intact with these guerrilla tactics.

➤ The Limbo

The buyer insists, "I won't pay any more than . . ." This is a game to see how low you can go. Guerrillas counter by asking, "Can you tell me how you arrived at that figure? What did you take into account?" Ask them to itemize their calculation.

➤ "They're the Same (or Better) . . ."

The buyer insists, "They're the same (or better) . . ." This is easy for them to say and difficult for you to corroborate. Counter by asking for specifics. Gain an advantage by asking, "In what way are they better for your application? What do you like most about them? What do you like least about them?" When you understand what your counterpart likes and doesn't like, you can build a case for your desired outcome.

➤ The First-Timer

The buyer insists that you should "Give me a good deal on the first one." Although this is tempting, it trains buyers to demand discounts. They'll want the same deal next time, or more. Guerrillas resist this ploy: "Although I could do that, I don't want to increase my delivery or cut my service on your first order, because when I cut price, I also have to cut somewhere else."

➤ Moving Up the Launch

"Now we need it tomorrow . . ." This is a typical tactic. Your counterpart negotiates for a favorable price based on future delivery, then demands immediate delivery. Guerrillas counter this tactic with a *rush charge*. "I can do that; I'm also committed to my other customers, and I will have to arrange for overtime shifts to meet their needs as well as yours. That necessitates that you pay a rush charge."

➤ Stopping the Countdown

Some buyers will do the opposite, appearing to be a hot prospect, then stalling while they deal with some internal glitch. "Now that we know you can ship today, we don't really need it until next month." Now they want you to reduce your price. Guerrillas counter this tactic with the *price increase*. "I can do that, but our price increase goes into effect next month."

➤ Excuse Me

"I'm sorry. I have to step out for a moment." A dirty trick from the old-timers: They'll leave a competitive quote out on their desk, and then arrange to be called out of their office so that you can "discover" it. They want you to proffer a discount, regardless of whether they're seriously considering the competition.

Guerrillas will refuse the bait. If your counterpart is going to use the competitor's prices, let them bring them to the table where you can do battle.

One grizzled buyer would place a soda can over the numbers of a competitive quote. Excusing himself for a moment, the curious sales rep would lift the can, and BBs would flood out from the hole in the bottom.

➤ False Quote

Fax machines, scanners, and computers make it easy for unscrupulous counterparts to falsify a competitive quotation. If you suspect that you're seeing a false quote, respond with, "That's interesting. I imagine that they must have a very good reason for selling at that price. But if prices were all the same, who would you choose?" If the buyer indicates that you'd be the choice, ignore the competitive document. If they insist on using the competitive quote, say, "I think there must be a typo here. May I call them and double check these numbers?"

➤ Quota Time

"How's your quota looking this month?" They're trying to trap you! If you flinch and admit that your numbers are down, they've got you. Guerrillas respond with, "Good question. How are your profit figures this month?" If they press you: "I'm sorry, that's not relevant to our discussion."

➤ **"Only Price Is Important . . ."**

"I don't care about anything but price. Give me your best price or get out." You might be tempted. Instead, call their bluff.

"Okay, here's the deal. Find the best price you can. I'll beat it by 10 percent, guaranteed! But I get to choose when I deliver."

"I don't think so," they'll retort.

"All right, I'll beat the best price you can find. But I get to select the quality that we ship."

"Uh . . . no!"

"Hmm. So I guess price isn't more important than on-time delivery or quality after all?" You've made your point.

■ WHEN YOU SHOULD DISCOUNT

There may be legitimate reasons to offer a discount. Perhaps you want to reward a loyal customer, or close a long-term contract. You may enjoy marginal increases in productivity at higher production levels, and choose to pass that economy of scale on to your customer. Or you may have excess capacity and fixed costs, and offering a discount brings in business that increases your overall profits.

You may wish to place a limit on the quantity you'll offer based on that discount, or limit the time-frame of its availability. A limited-time offer creates a deadline, motivating your counterpart to commit sooner rather than later.

In all businesses, a fraction of the price is reserved for marketing, research, development, and sales expenses. If your transaction doesn't require these costs, you may wish to offer that savings as a discount.

Guerrillas know exactly what they're giving away when they discount, and adamantly refuse to give away profit.

■ "MINE'S BETTER AND IT'S CHEAPER!"

A common position used to preempt price issues is, "We have a better product and it's cheaper, too." That argument isn't logically sound. Universal experience tells us that an apparently similar product at a higher price is *perceived* as being better. Higher quality = longer life = superior service.

When your counterpart observes, "You're expensive," the guerrilla will say, "Thank you!" And then proceed to help them understand the greater value.

When you *do* have a superior product for a lower price, you must offer a rationale for the lower price. "Because of our unique technology, we can offer you a better solution, and because of the way we do it, we've lowered our costs, and we pass those savings on to you."

■ TACTICS TO FIGHT PRICE NEGOTIATIONS

Guerrillas aggressively protect their price. Guerrillas gain an advantage by resisting pressure to grant discounts. When they do lower their price, they do so in exchange for a reciprocal concession.

Use these guerrilla negotiating tactics to combat price concessions.

➤ No Discounts

One tactic is to offer your price and stick to your guns. "This is the same price I charge everyone else. It wouldn't be *fair* if I charge you one price, and someone else pays a higher price. I can't do that to my other, loyal customers."

➤ Call Their Bluff

If your counterpart insists that you lower the price, call their bluff. Stand and ask, "Does that mean we're done?"

Although many are afraid to use this pointed question, the reply always reveals your counterpart's stance. If they say, "Yep, we're done," you know that price *is* the issue. If they say no, hang tough and keep your profits.

➤ Act Busy

A commonly held belief is that you've got to be *hungry* to get the deal. Guerrillas know otherwise. Busy people are obviously doing something right: They and their products are in demand. If you aren't busy, act busy.

➤ "We're Running Close to Capacity . . ."

Guerrillas use scarcity as a weapon in price negotiations. If you have limited capacity to deliver, say so. It may be more profitable for you to hold your line and find another, more accommodating customer.

➤ All Things Aren't Equal

Recapitulate how you'll satisfy their needs before you state your price. Build value by illustrating how your offering is superior to other opportunities. This tactic can backfire if you don't ensure that your proposition is valuable to your counterpart.

➤ Walk Away

If the deal isn't profitable, walk. The best way to drive your competitors out of business is to let them have all of the *unprofitable* business.

➤ We've Earned It

When discussing discounts, guerrillas avoid the phrase, "I can *give* you a discount of . . ." This phrase implies that you can give them more and opens the door to negotiation. It carries the implication that the discount is a gift, a gratuity, something that you can grant on your discretion.

Instead say, "At this quantity, you've *earned* a 7 percent discount." This tactic sets the ground rule that if they want a deeper discount, they have to earn it.

➤ No Round Numbers

If you normally offer a 10 percent discount, it's perceived that you've rounded the number, creating the opportunity for your counterpart to nibble at your price. When formulating discount percentages, if you use odd numbers and decimal fractions, such as 4.2 percent, 7.3 percent, or 9.9 percent, you'll create the impression that you've used a sharp pencil to arrive at your numbers.

➤ Take Ownership of the Price

When you relinquish the control of your price to a third party, such as your boss or your company, you open price to further negotiation. You create an advantage when you take personal ownership of the price. "My price is . . ." is a stronger position than "Our price is . . ." or "The price is . . ." Asking you to reduce your price becomes a *personal* issue. Guerrillas will make every discount a personal issue. When your counterpart requests a discount, let them know that the concession is coming out of your pocket. "If I do that, it comes out of my paycheck. Which of my two children should I *not* feed this week?"

➤ Cuts Both Ways

In some cases, you will have to negotiate your price in order to reach an agreement, but follow the rule of reciprocal concessions. Gain an advantage by explaining, "When I cut price, I also have to cut somewhere else." You can cut the price, but you have to withdraw the warranty. You can cut the price, but their order goes to the end of the shipping queue. You can cut the price, but you have to charge per call for technical support. You get the idea.

➤ What's Too Expensive?

When your counterpart objects, "Your price is too high," the guerrilla will then find out what *too high* means with an *about face*. "Too high? When you say 'too high' what exactly do you mean? Too high compared to what?" Find out if you're two cents too high, two dollars too high, or two hundred dollars too high.

➤ Memorize the Catalog

Chad Clay is the number-one salesman out of 16 for the Chicago-based, OilDry Corporation. They specialize in industrial spill clean-up materials, such as the material sprinkled on the garage floors to clean up an oil spill. Chad brought in 41 percent of the sales. Orvel tailed Chad around to learn his amazing secret.

While driving in his car, Chad receives a call on his cell phone. "Our price is too high? Do you have our catalog there? Great. Check page 7 . . . lower right corner. Yes. See we ship 48 to the bail. Do you have the competitor's catalog there? Perfect. Turn to page 31 . . . upper left . . . yes. Notice that they ship only 36 to the bail. Yes, that explains our price difference. You'd like to order two bails? Great! I'll call and expedite that for you."

Orvel Ray was amazed. "You've *memorized* your competitor's catalog?"

"We'll, it's a pretty brutal business," admitted Chad. "Actually, I've memorized all 16 of them."

Now Orvel is astounded. "What . . . are you, some kind of a *Rain Man* guy?"

"Oh, no! I just travel a lot and instead of watching TV in the hotel room, I study my competitors."

When you know more about your competitors than they know about you, they're dead.

■ COMBATING PRICE SHOPPING

You may get calls requesting a price quote. If a person knows exactly what they want, they'll shop around for the best price. Guerrillas choose how they want to handle these requests.

➤ "Call Me Last . . ."

When Mark decided to buy an electronic piano, he knew exactly what brand and model he wanted, so he called around for best price and delivery. One dealer refused to quote over the phone. "Call me last," he said, "and I'll see what I can do." Not only did this guerrilla match the best price Mark had found, but he threw in a free piano bench and delivery, locking down the deal.

➤ "We'll Be the Most Expensive . . ."

A housepainter was frequently asked to quote jobs. Although he put a lot of time into writing his estimates, very few of these inquiries actually brought results. Now this guerrilla prequalifies his prospects with, "I'll be glad to give you a quote on painting your house, but I want you to know in *advance* that it will probably be the *most expensive* quote you'll get." Half of the people hang up on him. He chuckles, knowing that he's saved a lot of time, and that he's creating a reputation for being the most expensive painter in town. When people stay on the line and ask, "Why?" he has an opportunity to explain his top-of-the-line approach.

➤ "I'd Prefer Not to Quote Until . . ."

Guerrillas never give price quotes without finding out about the customer's problem. A guerrilla who sells copy machines often gets requests for price quotes. She asks, "Who else are you considering?"

"We've decided on the model and our company policy is to get three quotes," they'll reply.

The guerrilla responds, "I'm in business to help you get the best possible copier at the best possible price, and offer you the best possible service. I'm *not* in business to help you get a better price from my competitor. Instead of giving you a blind quote, I'd prefer to see how I can serve you best. May I stop by to review your decision?"

■ WHAT'S THEIR BUDGET?

When you discuss your counterpart's budget, priorities, and expected payback, price issues will usually fade away. Budgeting includes more than just money. Here's a checklist of other items to discuss.

➤ Personal Agenda

What else do they have to take care of? Are there other issues that are more pressing, limiting the time that they have to get this job done? How can you help? Assist with their personal agenda and you'll score extra points.

➤ Politics

Has their superior barred them from doing business with your competitor? Are you the preferred vendor for political reasons? Use your spies to get this information in advance.

➤ Deadlines

Your counterpart faces a deadline and is motivated to keep the commitment, or suffer the consequences. Impending deadlines increase demand for your product and reduce the pressure for you to cut prices. If you can deliver when no other vendor can, the deal is yours, at almost any price.

➤ Special Occasions

If your counterpart is commemorating a special occasion, they may be motivated to spend more to celebrate. A couple who normally drives a Ford Escort will rent a limo for their wedding. A firm that customarily orders catering from the local deli will call the best caterer in town for a board meeting. A limited-edition production run requires highest-quality materials. Guerrillas ask, "Are you celebrating something special?"

➤ Cost to Buy

Negotiations incur some costs: the cost of time, the cost of research, the cost of lawyers, the cost of travel. Guerrillas ask their counterparts to examine the costs of acquisition. Guerrillas ask, "How can we reduce your requisition expenses?"

➤ Tax Implications

Gain a negotiation advantage by researching the depreciation schedules and tax implications of the deal. Guerrillas will point out any favorable impact on the overall budget.

➤ Shipping Costs

What will it cost to get the products delivered? If you are a regional supplier, you may be able to gain a geographical advantage. You may get a better break on your shipping costs than they can. If your counterpart needs the product immediately, guerrillas will include the additional charges for couriers.

➤ Budget Distribution

Are there other pots of money that you can tap? If you need to charge a fee for training, you may find the money in the human resources department. If there are installation costs, find out if there are funds in the facilities maintenance budget. If your proposal pares energy costs, prospect for cash in the utility budget.

➤ Other Priorities and Opportunities

Can you kill two birds with one stone? When you can help your counterpart complete other commitments and exploit other opportunities, you'll come off with flying colors.

➤ Financing

Can you offer financing? Can you help arrange financing? Can you work with a bank to set up a customer line of credit? Because financing is a cost of purchase, demonstrate how your favorable financing offsets your higher price. Or offer a discount when they take your more profitable financing package.

➤ Space Considerations

When your counterpart's space is at a premium, your smaller installation may save them the cost of expanding their facility.

➤ Utility Considerations

If your counterpart has limited access to power, water, gas, or sewage services, your solution may be a better fit than the competitors'.

➤ Training Costs

What procedures have to change? Does your counterpart have to retrain their people? Training is expensive, especially when the participants are pulled out of production and trained on company time.

➤ Operating Costs

How about costs to operate? What are the costs of raw materials, supplies, utilities, scrap, and quality control? Guerrillas will have these numbers on hand when they go into the negotiation.

➤ Downtime

What does it cost for your counterpart to be out of service? The price difference between the lowest-cost vender and the highest-priced vender is often less than the cost of workers standing idle waiting for repairs for an hour. Guerrillas will guarantee uptime and charge a premium for it.

➤ Maintenance

What about the cost of spare parts? Will they be available when needed? Can you stock spare parts on site at no charge, sending an invoice when they're used? Calculate your lower costs of maintenance and have the figures available to justify your higher price.

■ 22 REASONS WHY PEOPLE ARE WILLING TO PAY MORE

Your counterpart will make decisions for their reasons, and those reasons may be different than you think, and are often the very reasons that you don't take seriously. Here are some of the reasons your counterpart will be willing to pay you more than your competitor. Use this as a checklist as you prepare to support your higher price.

1. *Company Stability.* Savvy customers will select a technically and financially sound vendor over one that's obsolete or on the brink of failure.
2. *Fewer Headaches.* "Easy to do business with" is a guerrilla credo. Your counterpart will pay more to eliminate and avoid headaches.
3. *Knowledgeable Sales Force.* Buyers worry when a company rep doesn't know the product. It gets worse if your counterpart thinks you may have incorrect information. Gain an advantage by being an expert on your products.
4. *Reputation.* When your counterpart is uncertain of the market, they tend to select the vendor with the best reputation.

5. *Partnership.* Savvy buyers know that the best vendor becomes a partner in their mutual success. How can you create a partnership with your counterpart to create a larger opportunity?

6. *Consistency.* Consistent quality, delivery, service, and constant innovation create exceptional value in a negotiation. When your counterpart trusts and knows what to expect from you, you gain an advantage.

7. *Authority.* If you're the leader, the inventor, or the authority in the industry, you have additional power and influence. Gain an advantage by becoming a published author, and thus an authority. See Chapter 3 to learn how.

8. *Popularity.* Many people are influenced by what's fashionable. They decide, "If it's so popular, I can't go wrong." They want to be part of the in crowd, so they choose the standard.

9. *Exclusive Features.* Guerrillas seek exclusivity as a negotiating advantage. What is the one thing that *only* you can do?

10. *Higher Quality.* Guerrillas translate higher quality to higher value. This justifies your higher price. "When you care enough to send the very best!"

11. *Scarcity.* Anything that is considered scarce is considered more valuable, even if not more functional. A prime example is the Beanie Baby craze. Small stuffed animals that sold for $7.00 retail will resell for hundreds, even thousands of dollars after they are "retired" and no longer available. The waiting list for a Harley-Davidson motorcycle is now more than a year, and their used bikes are more expensive today than when they were new.

12. *Intrinsic Value.* Your counterpart will pay more if what you offer has value at the end of its life span. This could be the scrap value, or the secondary market demand, or your offer to take it back with a guaranteed trade-in price when they upgrade.

13. *Good Dollar Buy.* Your counterpart may be swayed by your increased value over other alternatives. A sit-down

meal served for the same price as take-out could be considered a good dollar buy. Better food and better service at the same price. We'll take that.

14. *Short Delivery Times.* Remember, when you buy things for yourself, you want the best possible quality for the lowest possible prices, and you want it delivered *yesterday.* Isn't your counterpart the same? Ask your counterpart if the competitor has ever short-shipped, or back-ordered the product. When you shorten delivery times you gain an advantage.

15. *Arrives in Perfect Condition.* If your competitor's product has ever arrived dented, dirty, or damaged, you've gained an advantage. When you can demonstrate that your products are guaranteed to arrive in perfect condition, you increase your value.

16. *Problems Fixed Quickly.* It's not product failure that causes problems. It's repair delays that are costly. A survey by Technical Assistance Research Programs[2] (TARP) found that when a customer *perceives* that an organization responds *instantly* to their request, the customer will do business with that organization again 95 percent of the time. Rapid reaction reaps rich rewards.

17. *Operating Cost Savings.* Your product may cost less for operator training, a lower cost to run, and reduced cost to repair than a competitive offering. These savings increase the price you can charge.

18. *Their Boss Gives Points for Value.* Perhaps your counterpart's superior recognizes value and quality, and supports those attributes in purchase decisions. This political influence adds power to your negotiation.

19. *Their Customers Don't Buy on Price.* Question your customer: "Tell me about your competition." If they respond with, "No one beats us on price," then you know they buy the cheapest possible components. If they reply, "We're the leader in quality and value," then you know that they respect these same characteristics in their suppliers, and they'll pay more to get it.

---

[2] http://www.tarp.com

20. *Environmentally Friendly.* As companies become more sensitive to environmental issues, they tend to select vendors that conserve natural resources. Your counterpart may give you points for your environmentally responsible behavior.

21. *Socially, Morally, Ethically Superior.* Many people select vendors who are socially, morally, and ethically responsible. Showing good intentions backed by positive actions creates advantages for these negotiators.

22. *Third-Party Beneficiary.* Will some third party benefit from your negotiation? Perhaps they're interested in you getting the business because their family owns stock in your company.

■ WHY PRICE BUYERS DON'T MAKE GOOD NEGOTIATORS

People who have a habit of buying the cheapest possible product don't fare well in price negotiations. They don't understand or appreciate value. They apologize for their product's prices. They'll say things like, "I don't know how they can get away charging this much." Because of this, they'll give the product away. They figure that they'll make it up in service charges or on change orders. And of course, they never do.

Guerrilla managers observe the lifestyle of their negotiators. They don't want people negotiating for profits who buy the cheapest possible products. Here's a test: Ask your candidate to go out and get "the best deal" on some item. If they bring back the cheapest possible product, don't use them on the negotiating team. If they got the best possible quality at a great price, include them on your team.

■ SPEAKING OF PRICE . . .

Most salespeople won't say the price. They'll offer, "Let me get you a quote . . ." or they'll write the price on a piece of paper and slide it across the table. This behavior signals a lack of personal commitment to the price quoted, opening up the price negotiation.

Guerrillas never hesitate to discuss price. Practice saying your price out loud until it rolls right off of your tongue. Deliver it with the same conviction and tonal inflection that you would use to give someone your phone number.

"What's your phone number?"

"800-247-9145"

"What's your price?"

"One-hundred-seventy-five-thousand dollars." Same inflection. You try it.

■ "GO AHEAD, NEGOTIATE WITH ME ON PRICE!"

Novice negotiators tip off their counterparts when price is negotiable. The most obvious mistake is offering to be negotiable. Saying, "And of course, that's negotiable" is stupid. You're going to take a hit. Guerrillas avoid these phrases, and maintain their advantage. When you hear any of these phrases, ask for a discount.

➤ Price Qualifiers

Avoid any phrase that indicates hesitation, lack of personal commitment to the price, or room to negotiate. "Get ready for this . . ." or "Are you sitting down?" or "The best we can do is . . ." These giveaway phrases scream, "Let's dicker."

➤ Acknowledge Status

Even acknowledging your counterpart's status will throw up a white flag. "Since you're one of our better customers . . ." Acknowledging your competitor does the same thing. "If you compare our price to our competitor . . ." invites haggling.

➤ Eager Beaver

Any statement which indicates that your counterpart's offer is extraordinary opens up price negotiations. Avoid such phrases as, "That's quite an order!" or "Wow, you're really serious!" or "I didn't expect anything that big!"

Any indication that you're not busy will invite your counterpart to ask for price concessions. Tell them, "I've cleared my afternoon for you . . ." and they know your price is going down.

➤ Volunteering Discount Opportunity

Neophyte negotiators prematurely disclose discount opportunities by blabbing, "And of course, there's a discount schedule." Guerrillas gain an advantage by letting their counterpart *request* a discount schedule. You'll retain your bargaining power because when they ask for the discount schedule, you can reciprocate with a "yes."

■ WHY PEOPLE ARE AFRAID OF HIGHER PRICES

Salespeople fear higher prices because it makes them work harder. They know that a small commission on a lower-priced sale is better than no commission on a higher-priced sale. They make excuses for discounting: "If I don't discount, I'll lose the deal" or "We're priced out of the market." Guerrillas respond, "Well, how do you know?"

Some people are afraid of damaging the relationship. "I want to be liked, and offering a discount is how I show my customers that I like them." Negotiations aren't a popularity contest. They're about ensuring a solid future for your company and yourself. Others are afraid of the work. "They make us justify higher prices." Well, that's your *job*. Or they believe that getting the deal will make everything all right. They claim, "We'll make it up in volume." Guerrillas know better.

■ WHY YOU'LL NEVER MAKE IT UP IN VOLUME

The only indicator of success is profit. Do the math. With a typical 30 percent operating margin, if you cut your price by 10 percent, you have to *double* your unit sales to make the same profit dollars. Will you double your sales with a 10 percent price decrease? Not likely! Your competitors won't stand for it. They'll immediately cut their price to match. If you *do* double your sales and fill your production to capacity, where will you get the money to expand?

■ HOW TO BE COMFORTABLE DEMANDING A HIGHER PRICE

Look at it this way. In the same margin scenario, if you raise your price by 10 percent you'll have to lose *40 percent* of your business before you give up profits. That's right, you can *lose* up to 40 percent of your business and take home more profit at the end of the day. Informal polls of our audiences show that most salespeople believe that they aren't charging enough. Most people would rather work less and earn more.

Here's some tactics that will make you feel comfortable in supporting your higher price.

➤ Know that not everyone is going to like you. Some people will become downright nasty when they hear a higher price. That's okay. Ultimately, you're the winner.

➤ Profit is not a dirty word. Some people think that high profits aren't justified. Guerrillas know otherwise. Just because your counterpart settles for a 7 percent net profit doesn't mean that you can't demand and get 17 percent.

➤ Be patient—deals come apart. Some you can patch up, others you can't. You won't reach agreement in every negotiation. Guerrillas choose whom they'll do business with.

➤ Review the list of 22 reasons why people are willing to pay more. Look at it before you go into any negotiation and you'll have the confidence to demand higher prices and profits.

➤ Say no to problem customers. People who are disrespectful and delinquent don't deserve your consideration. They require too much time, money, and energy to manage. Southwest Airlines routinely fires disruptive passengers. "Please don't fly with us again. We work hard to find good people to work here. They don't deserve your abusive treatment."

➤ Remember that higher price means higher value. Your higher price is a point of pride.

➤ Use your competition as a platform to move higher. Guerrillas respond to requests about their competitors with, "We have great competitors. They make me lie awake at night thinking about how I can serve you better. And my customers tell me they prefer us because . . ." Now you can brag with more credibility.

➤ Here's a warm-up exercise for your next price negotiation. Double your price. Go ahead, *double* it. Now list every rationale you can think of for why that new price is justified. Brainstorm every possible—reason, trivial and substantial. Next, return to your original price. Now does it feel like a bargain? You might consider raising your prices.

■ WHAT IF YOU LOSE THE DEAL BECAUSE OF PRICE?

If you do lose a deal because of price, know for sure. Perhaps your counterpart decided not to act. Maybe there were other reasons for moving forward with your competitor. When you know for certain, you'll be better prepared for your next negotiation. If they did choose your competitor, show up on the scheduled day of delivery. More than one deal was closed because the competitor didn't deliver on time, delivered the wrong thing, or delivered a defective item.

Nick Schneider of Raytheon Aircraft describes his approach. "Being pilots, we love new airplanes. We routinely show up for a competitor's delivery to congratulate the buyer, and occasionally we pirate a sale from the competition when they can't deliver, and we can."

If your overall sales are still good, well, that's one that got away. Move on to the next deal. If your overall sales are down, do some market research. Are your competitors' sales down as well? If so, it's a market issue. If not, you'll need to work on your market position.

■ HOW TO GET YOUR COUNTERPART OFF THE DISCOUNT SCHEDULE

When offering discounts, guerrillas are willing to change the rules. Do so and you'll keep more profits.

➤ Change the Sales Incentive

Most companies compensate salespeople based on gross *sales*. This motivates salespeople to discount, because a relatively large discount reduces the commission by only a small fraction. They can give away the profit margin and still get paid.

Guerrilla managers calculate commissions on the gross *margin* instead, and create incentive plans that take the first discount from the salesperson's commission check. When the salesperson has to part with their own money, they will defend their price.

One of our clients forgave an average discount of 9.3 percent on their industrial equipment. In their new plan, the sales commission was doubled from 3 percent to 6 percent of gross sales. But the first 3 percent of the discount now came from the salesperson. There's an incentive to hold firm on price! Even after the inevitable discounts, the sales force increased their take-home pay by nearly 50 percent, and the company added another one-third to their bottom line, even in a year of flat sales.

➤ New Sales Contests

Sales contests are designed to increase sales. The problem with most sales incentives is that they reward behaviors that people are already supposed to exhibit: selling things. Often the increase in sales is accompanied by an increase in the average discount rate. This increased cost-of-sales often reduces profits.

Guerrilla sales managers reward behavior that goes *beyond* the job description. For example, for your next sales contest, reward *competitive knowledge.* Have your salespeople learn about your competitors, their products, and their customers. Have pop quizzes, and hand out prizes on the spot for correct answers. You reward behavior that is proven to improve sales and protect your prices. There's no better way to increase confidence in your product, and your salespeople will be more aware of the competition long after the contest ends.

➤ Offer Soft-Dollar Bonuses versus Discounts

Estee Lauder beauty products never go on sale. But you'll often be offered "A $25.00 value gift when you buy today," and the gift is more of their products. The gift turns a sample into a reward that drives sales.

Guerrillas look for ways of offering value versus volunteering discounts. Buyers are rewarded by how much they *save,* not the level of discount they get. So offer them a larger savings when they *don't* accept your discount, but instead take your bonus package. "Based on this $100,000 order, you've earned a 7 percent discount, which saves you $7,000, or you can take the accessories package worth $10,000."

Select bonus items that have a high margin, such as financing, shipping (you probably get a better deal on shipping than your counterpart), accessories, supplies, training, spare parts, extended warrantee, and maintenance. Get your buyer accustomed to ordering these profitable items from you. Hook them on the initial agreement and set them up on an automatic reorder schedule.

➤ Put a Value on What You're Doing for Free

Many companies give away things that they should be charging for. Even if you elect to give them to your counterpart, put a value on them, increasing your guerrilla negotiating advantage.

Consider charging for loaners, training, and demonstrations when there is a clear advantage to your counterpart. You may choose to offer credit toward a future purchase, locking in your counterpart's business.

Send them a bill for your proposal. Submit an invoice for your time invested in responding to them. For example, you might want to charge them $125.00 an hour for a proposal that required four hours to create, and send them a bill for $500.00 with a *professional courtesy credit* of $500.00 for a total due of zero. They'll know what you've invested and will place a higher value on your effort.

Guerrillas send a zero balance invoice for everything they give away, making the invisible visible.

Chapter 8

Opening Maneuvers

■ GET READY

Are you ready? Have you reviewed the guerrilla weapons and tactics? Do you have a selection of tactics that you can use without second thought? Have you reviewed why your counterpart may be willing to give you more? Have you created a list of concessions and understand the value of those concessions to your counterpart? Have you set your expectations high? Are you fueled, ready to go?

Let's go!

➤ Control the Agenda

Guerrillas take control of every aspect of the negotiation, leaving nothing to chance.

Who

Exert control over who will participate in the negotiation. Be careful not to allow yourself to become outgunned.

What

Limit the scope of the negotiation, and what will or will not be decided. If the scope is not limited, the conversation can deteriorate into a free-for-all.

When

Strive to schedule the negotiation on your terms. Select a time when you are at your best, when you've had adequate time to rest and prepare, and when you're the most alert.

Where

Select a venue for the negotiation that is neutral, comfortable, and free from distractions.

How Long

Limit the term of the negotiation. Set a deadline for reaching an agreement. "I have to catch a plane. That gives us three hours to reach an agreement."

■ START THE EXCHANGE

You can gain a fair advantage when you lead off the exchange.

➤ Handshakes

Guerrillas reach out to their counterparts and offer a welcoming handshake. The act of touching a stranger does more to establish a relationship in a few seconds than anything else you can do. It formalizes the introduction and starts building rapport. In Western culture, and particularly in the business world, it's appropriate for either a man or woman to initiate a handshake. If they don't respond, gently drop your hand to your side, and realize you may have to do some icebreaking.

Handshakes telegraph a tremendous amount of information about the personality and intent of your counterpart. People have been greeting one another by shaking hands since the dawn of man, and no doubt, it originally meant, "See, I'm unarmed, you can trust me." But over thousands of years it's evolved, and today it conveys a number of subtle messages, each communicated by slight differences in touch, pressure, and force. These subliminal signals are easy to decipher *if* you know the secret code. Used carefully, these microgestures can send subtle messages that will put your counterpart at ease and help to neutralize differences in age, status, physical size, or gender.

Web-to-Web

A wimpy, fingertip handshake is sure to make an impression— a bad one. Make sure that you get hold of the counterpart's hand correctly. Most four-finger handshakes happen accidentally, because you're looking the counterpart in the eye, walking, talking, and not paying attention to how you're clasping the counterpart's outstretched hand. Extend your open hand with the palm rotated slightly counterclockwise, and then, at the moment of contact, push away gently against the fleshy part at the base of the thumb until it's made a good web-to-web contact. Then fold your fingers gently around the other person's hand. This slight delay communicates confidence, and avoids the accidental dead-fish slip-grip. Shake hands only for as long as it takes to exchange names, and then let go. An overextended handshake is uncomfortable for most people—they feel as though they've lost control.

Grip

One of the most frequent questions we're asked in our seminars is, "How hard should I squeeze the prospect's hand?" The answer: Match the pressure offered by your counterparts. They may grip your hand lightly or firmly. A firm grip is asserting dominance, and this counterpart wants to ask the questions and control the interview. A light grip communicates passivity, and this counterpart will appreciate your taking the initiative to guide the negotiation. Excessive pressure communicates insecurity. This is the exception to matching pressure; never reciprocate an excessive grip, but strive to relax and make the counterpart feel more comfortable.

Tilt

Differences in status are communicated by tilting the handshake. Some counterparts will rotate their elbow out slightly and roll their hand over, putting their hand on top, taking the one-up position. You may feel them press the top of your hand slightly with their thumb. This tilts the handshake down slightly on your side, tipping you a tad off balance, and creating the impression of them being taller. Subconsciously they are literally putting you down, elevating their own status at your expense.

We've observed that younger men often do this with when shaking hands with older men, and high-status managers may shake hands this way with subordinates. Men usually take the one-up position when shaking hands with a woman, and a well-dressed sales rep may do this with a counterpart dressed in a T-shirt and jeans.

You might think that an aggressive, assertive greeting communicates confidence, but this is really a kiss of death. The customer *always* has higher status, regardless of age, gender, or position. Whoever signs the check has the status.

Guerrillas do the opposite of what feels natural, reversing the tilt of the handshake and creating an advantage by relaxing their arm, gently rotating their hand underneath, and lifting their fingers slightly, tilting the handshake down on their side, and up on the counterpart's side. This sends the signal, "I acknowledge your higher status and I am here to serve you!"

Push Pull

A handshake quickly sets limits of personal territory. Most people will settle into comfortable distance during the handshake. This distance can vary from person to person. Some counterparts will literally push you away when they shake hands, whereas while others will gently draw you in as they step up to you. This indicates the counterpart's comfort with intimacy, and tells the guerrilla where to start the conversation.

The pusher is subliminally saying "Keep your distance." This person doesn't want to become overly friendly, and the conversation should focus strictly on business issues. Ask straightforward questions like, "What do you know about us? What has been your experience?" Never compliment clothes, hair, or jewelry with this person, and do not inquire about their family or personal matters, at least not right away.

The puller is literally inviting you into their inner circle of personal space. They want to get to know you person-to-person, and if you connect on a personal level, then they'll feel comfortable talking business. With this counterpart, it is essential to *establish common ground*. You might open with, "I see you're from San Diego. My wife went to school at UCSD. Maybe you know her?"

Ancillary Touch

A simultaneous touch with the left hand on their wrist or forearm denotes familiarity and acknowledges history. The most common form of ancillary touch is the two-handed handshake, which communicates intimacy. The degree of intimacy is communicated by moving the touch farther up the wrist. With someone you have known for a long time, you would touch higher up the forearm, at the elbow or even on the shoulder. Guerrillas never use ancillary touch with strangers because there is no history to acknowledge. They know it will be interpreted as insincere—the politician's handshake.

Ancillary touch can be helpful when being introduced by a mutual third party to create an atmosphere of immediate intimacy. You're bringing the history of their relationship into yours. And the farther up the arm you touch, the more familiar the message. Just a brush on the elbow is all it takes.

Stance

How you stand during your handshake is also significant. Stepping forward with the right foot is the most common form; it communicates parity, or equality with the prospect, mirroring the forward motion of their approach. This is good, but for a change, try stepping into the handshake with the *left* foot. Practice on a friend and you'll feel the subtle difference it makes. It makes the other person reach into your personal space with the outstretched hand, and communicates a degree of warmth, acceptance, and trust, which is even better.

Special Considerations

A colleague of ours, W. Mitchell, is an effervescent fellow who always wants to shake hands, and he often offers his hand first. The problem is that Mitchell is confined to a wheelchair, and his hands are severely disfigured, with most of his fingers missing as a result of severe burns. What should you do? When shaking hands with people who are missing fingers or wearing a prosthesis, clasp the hand as best you can and respond as you normally would. If they offer you their hook, treat it as if it were their hand; for them, it *is*. And most important, *maintain your eye contact*, resisting the temptation to stare at the disfigurement. These people really appreciate being treated as if fully functional. The more you treat them as if they are just like you, the more likely they are to like you, and to want to do business with you.

➤ Create Connection

Common experiences create connection. Look for every possible way to establish common ground.

Point Out Common Experiences
Perhaps you've held similar positions, or had similar training. Maybe you've worked for the same company, or traveled to the same cities.

Shared Risks and Rewards
Summarize the stakes involved in the negotiation, emphasizing areas where you can both benefit from a successful outcome.

Act As If
An extended care facility in Chicago prepares an engraved nameplate with the potential resident's name in advance of their tour. "Here's your nameplate. Now all you have to do is decide which door to put it on." Fill out the credit application in advance, "If we come to an agreement, this will save time later on."

➤ Initiate a Series of Exchanges

The exchange can be as simple as giving them a cup of coffee, offering a copy of an article that you thought they might enjoy, or even delivering a compliment. "You have a reputation for putting together creative deals." Although many negotiation trainers suggest resisting initial offers of hospitality and gifts, guerrillas understand that this creates momentum and gets your counterpart used to giving and taking from you.

➤ How to Negotiate with Angry Counterparts

You might have an angry counterpart for a variety of reasons. Some people may have had a bad experience your product, your service, or your company. Some people may object to what you sell based on their beliefs. And there are a few people who are in a foul mood because of something completely unrelated.

Don't Get Hooked
A person who's angry is temporarily insane. A sane person would never put their fist through a wall. The fist costs $10,000 to repair and six weeks to heal; the wall gets fixed for $50 in an hour.

People who are temporarily insane will do things to try to make you irrational, too. Insane people feel normal when they're around others like them.

The first step is to move them back to a rational state. As long as they are irrational, you'll never make progress. Avoid patronizing phrases like, "Calm down," or "I'm sorry." These just increase their anger.

Listen Carefully

Immediately begin taking notes. Tell them, "What you're saying is important. I need to take notes, would you please slow down?" This gives them a chance to take a breath, and they'll begin to calm down. Taking notes demonstrates that you're willing to listen and that at least you're trying to resolve the problem.

Assume Nothing

Behave as if you are completely ignorant of the situation. Sometimes your counterpart's account will be different from your knowledge of the same events. Allow for that difference. Say, "I want to understand the problem from your viewpoint. Please start at the beginning, and tell me what happened." Ask lots of questions to clarify points you may not understand.

Adopt Their Point of View

Listen to what your counterpart says, and paraphrase their account back to them for verification and clarification, even though you may disagree with it. This isn't the time to get into an argument. Who's right or wrong isn't the point. Right now you want to get them calmed down and thinking rationally again.

Stay Positive

Don't respond negatively to emotional language. A counterpart's anger usually isn't personal. They probably don't even know you that well.

Empathize

Do your best to understand your counterpart's feelings. What if you were in their situation? "Oh, I understand. That would make me unhappy, too."

Agree to Agree

Make a commitment to work toward an agreeable solution. Say, "I'm sure we can work something out here."

Ask for Suggestions

Instead of offering your position first, ask, "What would you like *us* to do?" This moves them to consider a resolution of the issue. Don't say, "What do you want *me* to do about it?" That sounds like you don't care.

Never Dextify

Do not attempt to *de*fend, *ex*plain, or jus*tify* what has happened. People don't want to hear you defend yourself. They want to be heard and to have their feelings recognized and acknowledged, even if you think they are wrong and irrational.

Never Say "I'm Sorry."

Don't apologize until your counterpart is prepared to accept your apology. Instead say, "I apologize." "I'm sorry," is what you say when you accidentally bump into someone.

Work Toward Solutions

Focus on what you can do, rather than what you can't. If your counterpart asks for something impossible, instead of saying, "I can't do that," make a counteroffer: "I understand your request. What I *can* do is . . ."

Call in Higher Authority

If your counterpart continues to be abusive, end the conversation. "I'm afraid that I can't help you any further. May I find someone who can?"

When you're negotiating by phone, brief your colleague before handing off the call, and introduce this person to the caller with a formal title. "Mr. Olson, this is Jane. I have Mr. Stephens on the line. He'll be working with you now." The change in status often breaks their abuse pattern. This is especially effective if the handoff is to someone of the opposite gender. A counterpart who feels justified being abusive to another man will often become a gentleman when dealing with a woman.

Let Go of Your Anger

If you hang on to the smallest bit of anger, you'll immediately have an impact on the rest of the negotiation, possibly causing you to lose the deal. Call for a break. Calm yourself after encountering an angry counterpart. Take four quick deep breaths, flooding your brain with oxygen. Next, inhale while you count slowly to seven, and then exhale while you continue the count to 15. Anger changes your breathing pattern and this exercise resets it to normal.

➤ Just Say No

One of the guerrilla's most powerful weapons is the ability to say "no." Several forms are available, depending on the circumstances. In negotiations, your counterpart will ask for more and more from you until you say no. Here's 11 ways to say no.

1. Flat "No."

Just that. No emotional content. Use when no justification is required, so do not offer one. Use sparingly and with care or you may risk being seen as uncooperative. When you hear a flat no, respond with, "I'm confused . . ." or ask for an explanation.

2. "I'd love to, but . . . no."

You're softening the no with "I'd love to, but . . ." Provide a reason or excuse why you can't accept their demand at this time. "I'd love to, but it wouldn't be fair to my other customers who already do business with me. So, no."

When you hear this, ask, "What would change that situation?" or "Well, under what circumstances would you love to say yes?"

3. "Let me get back to you on that."

A tactic for avoiding saying yes right away, without saying no. In the intervening time, the demand may be taken elsewhere. When this is used on you, counter with, "When will you get back to me on that?" Or, "If the timing was right, what would you need to say yes?"

4. No Time "No."

Make yourself unavailable for a while. "Let me check my schedule. Let's see, the earliest I could get to it would be next Wednesday." If you hear this, say, "Okay. What can I do to open up some time on your schedule?"

5. Considered "No."

A gentle refusal made after some lapse of time. "After considering the parameters of your request, the answer is no." You can respond with, "What elements of that proposal are causing you to take that position?"

6. Apologetic "No."

This is the soft letdown. "I'm really sorry, but I have a previous commitment that I can't break." You can say, "I'm sorry, too. I was counting on you to help me meet my commitments. What can we do so that we can both meet our obligations?"

7. Feeling "No."

This is an appeal to conscience. "I really wouldn't feel right about doing this." Very effective, because feelings are nonnegotiable. You can counter with, "I respect your feelings on this. What would help you feel more comfortable?"

8. Conditional "No."

This appears to be a "yes." "I'll agree *if* you will do . . . , and you will provide . . . , and if, and if," ad nauseam. You can respond with your own list of conditions.

9. Deflective "No."

Suggest options or alternatives. Recommend someone more qualified who could do a better job. "Joe is a real whiz when it comes to pulling together those numbers. I recommend that you ask him." When faced with this tactic, ask, "I could do that, but that would delay our progress. Because of that, please do it for me."

10. I Can't Do Everything "No."

"Which of these three things do you *not* want me to do?" Get them to prioritize their demands. You can counter with, "Each of these is necessary because . . ."

11. Play Dumb "No."

If there's any doubt, say that you don't know, or don't remember. "Have you looked in the manual? It's been so long since I've worked on that kind of thing . . ."

➤ Five Steps to Renegotiation

When you have developed a relationship, and have some experience dealing with a counterpart, your success is almost certain. Use this approach to your meeting and you can rapidly move forward.[1]

1. What Are We Doing Well?

Although many meetings start with a gripe session, start your meeting by finding out what's *working*. Write it down. If there is tension in the room, it may be a moment before people start volunteering information, because they'll have to change gears mentally. You can prime the pump by reminding them of a positive comment they made. "Please tell me more about that," gets them going. This tactic builds positive energy and creates agreement. It's easier to move from agreement to agreement than from disagreement to agreement. When your counterpart wants to complain, say, "There is plenty of time to resolve that later. First, let's find what we have to work with to move forward."

2. Why Does It Work?

Next, find out *why* what's working is working. Look for the people, relationships, technology, and systems that support the success so far. Make a list. This tactic builds resources. These are the things you can use to take the relationship to a new, more profitable level.

It's much easier to launch the new negotiation from a platform of past performance than to dig out from a deep hole of dissatisfaction. You and your counterpart might be surprised to learn that you're not so far apart after all.

3. What Do We Want to Change?

Now you're ready to consider their requests. Your counterpart is in a more positive frame of mind and it's possible that the magnitude of their complaints has diminished. You've won the negotiation before they've even begun. Listen to their requests, taking notes along the way. You're not ready to find solutions, just list their desires.

---

[1] Oakley, Ed and Doug Krug. *Enlightened Leadership*. New York: Simon & Schuster, 1991. Reach them at 303-694-4644.

4. Why Do We Want to Change?

This step examines the rationale for each request. Explore their motivation. Say, "Sell me on that idea," or "Help me understand your position," or ask, "What does that mean to us?" You'll discover their priorities and criteria for satisfaction and understand their motivation for their requests.

5. How Will We Do This?

Now that you have resources from steps one and two, direction and motivation from steps three and four, all that's left is to make a decision on the implementation plan. Expect a positive outcome that satisfied both parties.

➤ Managing Stress

The pressure and stress of any negotiation can severely reduce your effectiveness. Continuously monitor and manage your own stress levels. When they start running high, call for a time-out and use one or more of these seven strategies:

Music

What's the best type of music to listen to for reducing stress? Some people say classical, others say mellow jazz. The experts say, "whatever you like," Bach, Beatles, or Garth Brooks. You may consider playing music of your choice during your negotiation.

Moisture

Water has healing qualities. During your break, sit for a while by a fountain or stream. Watch an aquarium. Walk on the beach or around the lake. Go for a swim. Take a hot bath, shower, or steam. If you don't have access to such facilities during your negotiation, go to the washroom and wash your hands and face. Moisten and comb your hair. And drink lots of water—six to eight glasses a day. You'll need it to maximize your stamina.

Movement

Take regular breaks from the negotiation. Walk, run, dance, stretch, just move! Stress builds up muscle tension, particularly in the neck, shoulders, and lower back. Light exercise restores your mental alertness, giving you a guerrilla advantage.

Massage

Get a massage the day before you begin negotiations. You'll be relaxed and clearheaded, giving you an advantage. Trade shoulder rubs with a colleague, or even your counterpart. "Okay, what if I throw in a neck massage, right now?" This is a great way to break an impasse.

Meditation

Get away, mentally. Take your mind off the negotiation and recharge your spirit. Imagine a favorite beach or mountain meadow. Sit quietly by yourself and ponder what you've gained, and what you may have given up so far. Close the door, redirect the calls, and take a catnap. A rest as short as 10 or 15 minutes can be very refreshing. Check in and observe your emotional state; how are you feeling? What else do you want?

Menu

There is a reason why they call it junk food. You can't negotiate effectively if you're running on empty. If your meeting is taking place over a meal, be very selective about what you eat. Avoid fats. Avoid caffeine that could make you edgy or irritable. Avoid alcohol. Eat protein for breakfast, carbohydrates for dinner. Eggs and yogurt are brain foods.

Mirth

Read the comics in today's paper. Have fun. Bring cartoons to pass around the table. Do a magic trick. Put on a red rubber nose. Bring props and gag gifts. Laugh. It releases powerful brain chemicals that stimulate creativity, relaxation, and regeneration.

■ 100 WAYS YOU IMPACT YOUR COUNTERPART'S OPINION OF YOU

The devil is in the details. Here's a list of 100 personal details that will have an impact on your counterpart. Review them and decide how each could affect the outcome of your negotiation. If just three or four of these spark ideas that you haven't thought of, you'll gain a fair advantage.

Things People See

1. Clothing
2. Hair
3. Weight
4. Height
5. Shoes
6. Jewelry
7. Watch
8. Facial hair
9. Facial expression
10. Makeup
11. Attaché case or purse
12. Glasses
13. Fingernails
14. Neatness
15. Cleanliness
16. Teeth
17. Smile
18. Laugh
19. Eye contact
20. Stance
21. Tan
22. Handwriting
23. Spelling
24. Writing
25. Business card
26. Stationery
27. Advertising
28. Brochure
29. Your car
30. Your office building
31. Your office
32. Office decor
33. Things on your desk
34. Your house or apartment
35. Your neighborhood
36. Bumper stickers
37. Body language
38. Physical grace
39. Manners
40. Nervous habits

Things People Sense

41. Nervousness
42. Relaxation
43. Handshake
44. Touching
45. Attitude
46. Warmth
47. Assertiveness
48. Meek
49. Realistic
50. Weird
51. Bogus
52. Nerdy
53. Introvert
54. Extrovert
55. Sincerity
56. Affectations
57. Believability
58. Punctuality
59. Use of the language
60. Accent, or lack of
61. Voice volume
62. Being succinct
63. Being verbose
64. Gift for being clear
65. Or obtuse
66. Controlling
67. Type A behavior
68. Depressed
69. Frenetic
70. Tasteful in what you say
71. Tasteful in how you dress
72. Liberal

73. Conservative
74. Gullible
75. Decisiveness
76. Indecisiveness
77. How open you are
78. Or how guarded
79. Leadership ability
80. Are you easily led?
81. Team player
82. Wide range of knowledge
83. Keep up with change
84. Religious
85. Helpful
86. Observant
87. Good memory
88. Inquisitive, ask good questions
89. Trying to impress
90. Uniqueness
91. Smile in your voice
92. Answering machine message
93. Messages left on other machines
94. Personal style
95. Listening
96. Sense of humor
97. Follow-up
98. Passion
99. Energy level
100. Everything that you say

■ JUST ASK FOR IT!

You don't always get what you want, but you'll almost always get what you expect and what you ask for. Guerrillas aren't afraid to ask and ask for everything possible.

➤ The Aladdin Factor

In their book, *The Aladdin Factor*,[2] Jack Canfield and Mark Victor Hansen write about the power of asking.

Ask the Right Person
Ask the person who is in a position to actually grant your request.

---

[2] Canfield, Jack, and Mark Victor Hansen. *The Aladdin Factor*. New York: Berkley, 1995.

Ask for the Right Things

Time	Equipment	Spare parts
Help	Support	Warranty
Information	Training	Cleaning
Material	Financing	Repairs
People	Recycling	Disposal
Space	Documentation	

Ask Three Times

Don't take "no" for an answer the first, or even the second time. You'll find that people will often relent on the third request.

Ask for More

Ask for more time, more money, more space, more equipment, more help. Make a list of everything you could possibly wish for in the negotiation, then ask for even more. Ask for more than you think they will agree to. Ask for more than you think is available. Ask for more than you think you deserve.

Ask for Less

Ask for less responsibility, less pressure, fewer hours. Ask to lighten your load.

Keep Asking Until They Say "No"

Keep asking for more and more and more until they say "no." Many people make the mistake of not testing the actual boundaries of the negotiation.

How to Find Out What They Want

Until you know what your counterpart wants, you'll never be successful getting what you want. Here's a series of weapons and tactics to get the information you need.

■ WHY LISTENING GIVES GUERRILLAS THE COMPETITIVE EDGE

Active listening gives you an advantage. You'll get better information, learn more, and make fewer mistakes. The person who wants something is responsible for the communication. If they misunderstand you, it's your fault: You haven't used a communication approach that connects. If they're not listening, it's your problem: You must manage their motivation and allow for times when they'll stop listening in order to have an internal dialogue.

➤ How Well Do You Listen?

When talking with a person, do you:

	Usually	Sometimes	Seldom
1. Prepare yourself physically by facing the speaker and making sure you can hear?	☐	☐	☐
2. Maintain eye contact with the speaker?	☐	☐	☐

	Usually	Sometimes	Seldom
3. Assume what the speaker has to say is worthwhile regardless of their dress or appearance?	☐	☐	☐
4. Listen primarily for ideas and underlying feelings?	☐	☐	☐
5. Encourage the speaker to continue by using verbal signals like "Uh-huh," "I see," and "I understand"?	☐	☐	☐
6. Keep your mind on what the speaker is saying?	☐	☐	☐
7. Encourage the speaker to elaborate when you hear a statement that you believe is incorrect?	☐	☐	☐
8. Use gestures like smiling, nodding your head, and leaning forward in your chair to encourage the speaker to elaborate?	☐	☐	☐
9. Paraphrase and demonstrate your understanding of what you've heard?	☐	☐	☐
10. Make a conscious effort to evaluate the logic and credibility of what you hear?	☐	☐	☐

➤ Scoring

Give yourself 10 points for each answer of Usually; 5 points for each answer of Sometimes; 0 for each answer of Seldom.

90+	You're a very good listener.
75–89	Not bad, but could improve.
74 or less	You definitely need work on your listening skills

➤ Stop Guessing

Guessing at what they want will destroy you. You don't know what they need until they tell you. Asking the right questions and digging out the right information gives you an advantage. The only information you can use with confidence is the information they tell you. Illustrate this by taking notes and referring to what they said throughout the negotiation. Discuss their wants and you'll increase the sense of collaboration.

➤ Head Their Direction

When you know what they want, you can start the discussion in a direction they're heading. Ride the horse in the direction that it's going. Once you're on the horse, you can change directions by asking new questions and introducing new information. When you're asking nonthreatening questions and actively listening, your counterpart has nothing to defend.

➤ Drive the Conversation

The listener controls the conversation. The listener can decide what to ask next. The person asking the questions is determining the direction of the conversation. You can guide your counterpart's train of thought with your comments and questions.

➤ Get to Your Goal Faster

Focus on the solution and you'll naturally focus on the task that gets you there. When you do this based on what they've told you, your ideas are accepted and acted upon without resistance.

➤ What's Missing?

People make the best possible choice given the information available. Add new information and they can make a new choice. If you can't come to resolution, either you or they are missing something. So ask the question: "I'm confused. What information am I missing? What am I misunderstanding?"

➤ Misunderstandings

Misunderstanding occurs when there's missing information, or both sides have different information. For example, Mark filled his car with gas, and because of the long line of cars waiting, he pulled away from the pump and parked in front of the store. Before walking inside to pay, he wrote down the mileage and the amount pumped in his travel log. After waiting in line for a few minutes, it was his turn to pay.

> The clerk said, "That will be $17.03."
>
> "Excuse me? I put in $9.06," replied Mark.
>
> "What pump were you using?"
>
> "Number three."
>
> "That will be $17.03!" the clerk snapped, consulting his control panel.
>
> "I just wrote in my log that I pumped $9.06. I took that number right off the pump," countered Mark.
>
> "Well, sir, you owe me $17.03." It was getting nasty.
>
> "I don't think so." Mark had forgotten to say, "I'm confused" to neutralize the conflict.
>
> "Well, sir, you do," the clerk insisted.
>
> Just then, another clerk said, "What's the matter? Her colleague explained the situation. She replied, "I just had someone pay $17.03 at that pump."
>
> What happened was another customer used the pump during the wait and Mark's total had been cleared before he could pay.
>
> When there's conflict, say, "I'm confused. What are we missing? What do you know that I don't, and what do I know that you don't? What could cause this?"

■ THE PHYSIOLOGY OF LISTENING

Listening is comprised of three steps: hearing, understanding, and remembering.

➤ Listening

You have to hear your counterpart clearly. This means conducting your negotiation in a quiet location free from distractions.

If this means you have to reschedule or relocate the negotiation, do so. If you notice that your counterpart seems to have a difficult time hearing, move closer or speak louder. Ten percent of the population has faulty hearing.

➤ Guerrilla Listening

Active listening is intense, hard work. You are both thinking, there's no mental loafing going on. Guerrilla's listen selfishly: "What can I learn? What can I get out of this conversation that I can use? How can I get what I want?"

➤ Staying Focused

You can't afford the luxury of letting your thoughts wander. Here's how to recapture your focus:

Let It Go
Guerrillas prepare mentally for their negotiating session. Tell yourself, "There's plenty of time later to think about other things." If a thought pops up, remind yourself that you can think about that later.

Make a Quick Note
If you simply can't keep an intruding thought away, make the briefest note to remind yourself to consider the point later. You can then return to listening to your counterpart.

Take Notes
We gave you more details on this in Chapter 2. Remember that when you take notes, you'll stay focused.

➤ Understanding

People don't *feel* understood until they *know* that you understand. People check for understanding by observing feedback, so give your counterpart verbal attends, such as "Uh-huh. Oh? I see." Use nonverbal attends, as well. These include gestures such as head nods, leaning forward, or hand gestures that let them know you're listening.

Understanding is extracting meaning from the conversation. The meaning that you understand should be as close as possible to what your counterpart actually intends. Words transmit meaning, yet subtle changes in interpretation occur between people and can shift over time. Meaning changes with tonal inflection and word usage. Meaning is built by past feelings, images, and associations of words. We judge meaning by our standards. Guerrillas double check meaning whenever they are even slightly uncertain.

➤ Remembering

The final phase of listening requires accurately remembering what was said, in context.

Recall

There's a difference between recall and remembering. Recall retrieves memories that are there but not available unless prompted. You probably won't remember the name of your third-grade teacher unless someone reminds you. A classic example is having the word on the tip of your tongue. You know you know it, but you can't quite remember it right now.

Remembering

Remembering is what you know actively, without thinking. Examples include your name, phone number, address, or names of close friends. Guerrillas never rely on remembering alone. Instead, take notes to prompt recall, recording the slightest detail that may be useful. Then use your notes to prompt your counterpart's recall.

■ UNDERSTANDING BARRIERS CREATED BY THE LISTENER

The listener frequently creates barriers to understanding. Some of these barriers are unintentional, whereas others are the result of bias or past experience.

➤ Attitude

Negative expectations sabotage listening. When you say to yourself, "I've always had a problem listening," or "I'm lousy at remembering names," or "They just don't listen to me!" you unconsciously limit your abilities in these areas. If you must think this way, at least add the tag phrase, ". . . but I'm getting better at it."

Better yet, guerrillas create positive expectations. "I'm better than most at listening" or, "Although I don't remember every name, I do remember the names of people who I think are important" or, "People listen to me because I have something to say that they'll find useful."

➤ Distractions

Perhaps you're distracted. Noise may bother you. Music in the background helps some people relax, whereas it annoys others. If that happens to you, ask that the noise be eliminated, or move to a new location. Simply say, "I'm sorry, but that music is interfering with my concentration. I'd appreciate it if we could please turn it off."

➤ Interruptions

Interruptions disrupt the listening process, too. People walk by the open door, an assistant asks a question, the phone rings incessantly. Guerrillas will preempt these interruptions. "May I close the door? I have a few things I need to tell you." "Can we go to a place where we won't be interrupted? I want to give you my undivided attention." If the phone continues to ring, stand and leave the room. If they wave you to sit back down, respond with, "No, I want to give you your privacy. Just let me know when you're through." This sends the message loud and clear that you think their privacy is important, and subtly indicates that you will not tolerate phone interruptions. Better yet, select a neutral territory where there will be no interruptions, such as a conference room, training room, or an off-site location at a hotel or conference center.

➤ Personal Tics

Certain personal habits can be distracting. Constant throat clearing or other verbal (ahh . . .) habits may annoy. Tics such as finger tapping or fiddling with pens, twisting paper clips, or shuffling papers will distract you from listening. If these are an issue for you, cut back on the coffee and relax. If your counterpart has them, do your best to ignore the tics and focus on what they're saying.

➤ Health

Illness can impair your ability to listen. If you have a bad cold or the flu, you'll be less than your best. Viral infections and medications can decrease mental acuity. Others may not appreciate being exposed to someone with a bad cold or flu. Delay the meeting, or bring along a colleague to make sure that you get all the details. You may choose to let your counterpart know that you're not as sharp as usual, and to forgive, in advance, any lapse or misunderstanding.

➤ Family Issues

Personal problems can interfere with listening. If you just got bad news about your health, or if you were just served with divorce papers, you'll probably have a hard time concentrating on what your counterpart has to say. It might be wise to delay the negotiation until you can devote your undivided attention.

➤ Unresponsive Counterpart

If your counterpart has a poker face, offering no verbal or non-verbal feedback, you can be distracted from listening accurately. In this case, guerrillas actively ask for feedback. "Does that make sense?" "Have you experienced that?"

➤ Timing

When are you at your best? When are your bad times? Are you a morning person? Guerrillas identify when they are and aren't at their peak, emotionally and physically. If you're not a morning person you may wish to shift negotiations to the afternoon. Or you may wish to schedule negotiations immediately after a vacation when you may be more refreshed.

➤ Pressure

Perhaps you're feeling pressured by other deadlines. Those deadlines prevent you from paying full attention to the negotiation at hand. Guerrillas will delay. "I'm on a deadline, and that pressure means I probably won't be able to listen. Can we reschedule this for later?" Or perhaps you're being pressured to agree to an outcome you can't support. Guerrillas will acknowledge the pressure: "I understand your position, yet I can't agree with it. Can we agree to disagree on this point?"

➤ Speed of Thought

People think three to six times more rapidly than they speak. Normal speech clips along at an average of 150 words per minute. Thought screams along at 500 to 600 words per minute.[1] It's easy to complete their sentence mentally and ignore what they actually say. Or you may be thinking about the clever reply you'll be making while they're talking. This may cause you to miss important information.

Guerrillas slow down their thinking to match their counterpart. Focus on what they're saying and the underlying meaning and how that's important to you. Taking notes helps.

➤ Need to Speak

Some people feel compelled to perpetually pitch their position. Like a carnival barker bullying suckers into the sideshow, all they can do is talk, talk, talk. These people think that they can force their position by filibuster. This tactic fails in anything more than a simple impulse-buying transaction. Put aside your need to speak, and focus on your ability to understand.

➤ Delivery versus Content

Boring speakers create barriers to understanding. There are three classes of speakers. There are the *great delivery, low content* speakers, like the convention keynoters who captivate you with

---

[1] Anastasi, Thomas E., Jr. *Listen! Techniques for Improving Communication Skills.* Boston: CBI Publishing, 1982, p. 31.

their presence but give you only three ideas in an hour. Guerrillas listen critically for the actual idea and refuse to be swayed by the emotionally charged stories during a negotiation.

Then there are the *great content, lousy delivery* speakers, like the egghead professor presenting a paper at a conference. They know far more than they have time to tell, and sometimes get sidetracked with tangential points. Guerrillas counter this type of speaker by listening skillfully and clarifying key points.

The most difficult type of speaker to listen to is the *poor delivery, low content, no organization* speaker who's bluffing their way through. You may be tempted to dismiss them as useless. Guerrillas remember that they are still the customer. Here's a great opportunity to hone your listening skills.

➤ What If . . .

Sometimes we mentally play "what if . . ." games, evaluating the discussion or creating scenarios and playing them through to outcomes. Although this can be a valuable technique for understanding potential solutions, it's a barrier to listening if you're "what if-ing" during the conversation.

If you notice that you've disconnected, stop and make a note of the scenario and then refocus and reconnect with your counterpart. You can resume with, "I'm sorry, something you said triggered a thought and I missed your last sentence. Would you please repeat that?"

➤ Complexity

Perhaps you're overwhelmed by the complexity of the issues. Or you approach a difficult situation with a negative prediction, "I can't possibly understand this!" Guerrillas never allow complexity to deter them. Say, "I'm confused," or "I'm sorry, I missed part of that," or "Could you say that another way?"

If necessary, bring along an expert who can explain things to you and be your advocate when you face a complex situation.

➤ Misstatement

When your counterpart makes a misstatement, you have the choice of ignoring it and assuming that you know what they meant and possibly be wrong, or you can verify what you heard. They say, "That's $3,100," when you think they mean $31,000.

Guerrillas take the blame for misunderstanding the misstatement. "I'm sorry, I thought I heard you say thirty-one hundred?" and let them correct themselves. "Oh, I'm sorry. That's thirty-one *thousand*." Use this approach and you'll get the right answer without annoying your counterpart.

■ UNDERSTANDING BARRIERS CREATED BY THE SPEAKER

The speaker can create barriers to understanding, often unconsciously. Guerrillas are aware of these barriers and use certain tactics to get the information they need.

➤ Ambiguous Statements

A statement could have several meanings. For example, what percentage of time do each of these words refer to?

Often	Seldom
Always	A lot
Sometimes	Almost always
Never	Rarely
Usually	Frequently
Most of the time	Quite often
Occasionally	

You'll find few people who will agree on the precision of these words. When your counterpart says that they'll reach a decision "soon," most salespeople will assume that means this week, or at least this quota period, whereas the counterpart may be thinking six months. If you're working with the government, they may be thinking *years*.

Guerrillas double check any ambiguous statement with the *about-face* strategy. Play back the word you're uncertain of. "Soon? When you say 'soon,' exactly when will that be? Could you be more precise?"

➤ Assumption

Where there is a lack of information, certain personality types will leap to conclusions. Some assumptions will be correct; others will be meaningless. Certain assumptions are wrong and can even be disastrous. If any single assumption can be proven wrong, all other assumptions must be considered doubtful until proven otherwise. Guerrillas gain a fair advantage by challenging assumptions that could materially alter the outcome of the negotiation.

➤ Non Sequitur

Literally meaning "no connection," guerrillas are on guard for non sequiturs, where the conclusion does not follow from the counterpart's premises or evidence. "I want a discount because you're too expensive," is a classic example.

Guerrillas counter by asking for clarification. "I'm sorry. I don't understand how those two things are related. Can you help me understand your viewpoint? What's the connection?"

➤ Incorrect Interpretation

Another common barrier to listening and a variation of non sequitur is where "this action means that outcome." "He slammed the door, so I know he's angry." It's possible that the wind blew the door shut. Guerrillas test the interpretation, "How does this mean that?" "You slammed the door. Does that mean you're angry?"

➤ Deletion

When your counterpart accidentally or intentionally deletes parts of the meaning, understanding is compromised. They may ignore certain points that don't support their position or insist on incomplete data that does. You may not be getting the whole story. Guerrillas ask for all the information they need to understand what's going on. They keep asking, "What's missing?" "What else?" "And then what?"

➤ Generalization

When your counterpart takes one or several examples of a situation, and claims that it's always that way, they make a generalization. People tend to remember outstanding items. When a salesperson hears complaints from some prospects, they tend to generalize and say, "Everyone is complaining about this." Other examples: Your counterpart says, "I always get three quotations," or "I'll never do business with them again." Generalizations are common and easy to make. They're a lazy way to state an opinion or hold a position without solid evidence.

Guerrillas counter generalizations by asking for more information or finding a case where the generalization isn't true. "Has there ever been a time when you have . . . ?" or "What percentage of the time does that really happen?"

➤ Unspecified Pronouns

Sometimes your counterpart will use pronouns in the conversation without specifying who is being referred to. They speak of he, she, they, them, those, and it, and you have no idea who they're talking about. "They" is probably the most commonly used unspecified pronoun. "They said . . ." or the frequently quoted, "They won't let me."

Also watch out for "it." "Well, I took care of it." or "It's too expensive."

Guerrillas will insist on clarifying who exactly the pronoun refers to. "When you say, 'they've been complaining lately,' *who* exactly are you referring to?"

➤ Comparisons

When your counterpart uses language such as, "fewer complaints," or "more leads," or "better communication," check to see what the words *fewer, more,* or *better* actually mean.

A guerrilla manager was hearing a complaint from her employees that "our E-mail newsletter is creating lots of complaints from our customers." Her first response was, "What do you mean by 'lots'?" She asked her employees to identify each person who complained and discovered that there were just *five* people who complained every time the newsletter went out. She took them off the mailing list, and now employees say, "No one complains about our E-mail list."

➤ Inconsistent

When your counterpart says one thing and the documentation says another, there's a barrier until the inconsistency is resolved. Sometimes the inconsistency is accidental, other times it's intentionally misleading. Guerrillas counter by asking for clarification: "I'm confused . . ."

➤ Judgment

Judgmental statements can create a barrier. Your counterpart may say, "You don't understand the concept," evaluating your ability to understand. Guerrillas will counter by challenging the judgment, asking for facts to support the counterpart's claim. "How do you know whether I understand or not?"

➤ Distortion

When your counterpart distorts the facts to support their position, there's a barrier to understanding. When an employee says, "The company demoralizes me," they distort the facts by claiming that the company has an effect on them, when it's likely that a personality conflict is causing the demoralization. Another common distortion used by parents is, "You make me angry." In fact, the child doesn't make them angry; a particular action by the child makes them angry.

Because people use distortions so frequently, and they are not challenged, they're easy to gloss over them. Guerrillas test distortions by getting more information. "How is it possible that the company demoralizes you?" Or, "How do I make you angry?

■ CREATING RAPPORT

Solid rapport permits both parties to achieve their desired outcome. Rapport occurs when you and your counterpart have mutual trust and a positive relationship.

Moving from agreement to agreement is easier than moving from disagreement to agreement. Guerrillas begin by finding common ground, no matter how insignificant. A solid relationship is built on shared interests, beliefs, and values. Everyone experiences the world using a unique system based on experience, values, and beliefs. Although your counterpart may have a completely different set of values, their values are just as valid as yours. When your view of the world and theirs are in conflict, rapport is difficult to achieve.

➤ You Are Responsible for Rapport

The person who wants something is responsible for developing the rapport. If you want to have rapport, you have to understand your counterpart's point of view. If you want to reach agreement, you have to be understanding and supportive.

For example, if you want to do business in the Orient, you must have business cards printed in your native language and in the language of the company with which you wish to trade. All things being equal, the vendor who can work within their counterpart's culture, and can meet their special needs will get the business.

The person with the most flexibly in understanding situations and the broadest choice of behavior has the greatest chance of success.

➤ Four Basic Needs All People Share

Everyone you work with has these basic psychological requirements. Meet their needs and you'll gain an advantage.

The Need to Feel Welcome
You'll get rapport started when you make your counterpart feel welcome. Acknowledge them as soon as possible. Shake their hand. Give them a warm greeting.

The Need to Feel Comfortable
You'll increase rapport when your prospect is comfortable physically and psychologically. Show hospitality by providing coffee, water, and other refreshment. Offer them seating. Offer

them use of the telephone. Ask them about the temperature of the room.

The Need to Feel Important

Rapport is lost when one feels unimportant. Look at your counterpart when they're speaking to you. Take notes to let them know that their ideas are important to you. Go first class when bringing in refreshments.

The Need to Feel Understood

Rapport is the sharing of understanding. Use the magic phrase, "I understand" appropriately, and you'll connect with your counterpart.

➤ How to Test Rapport

You know you've achieved rapport when your counterpart matches your behavior. Look for matching in posture, gesture, voice, limb movements, positioning. If your counterpart mismatches you, that means they've moved into a mismatch mode and dropped out of rapport. It's time to stop and check what happened to lose the rapport.

Sales trainers often tell their students to create rapport by matching and mirroring the counterpart. Guerrillas refuse to do this for two reasons: (1) it doesn't work with about 30 percent of your counterparts; (2) it eliminates a key guerrilla tool for detecting rapport—are they matching you? Then you're in rapport!

➤ Body Language

Signal	Possible Meaning
1. Folded arms	Defensive, no compromise. Could be cold, or wish to rest their arms.
2. Hands covering mouth	Insecure, not sure of what is being said.
3. Tugging at ear/nose/ throat	Impatient, usually wants to interrupt.

4. Fingers of both hands touching	Supremely confident.
5. Tightly clenched hands, wringing hands, excessive perspiration, rocking/ swaying	Nervous to varying degrees.
6. Feet and/or body pointing toward exit	Ready to leave.
7. Hands supporting head when leaning back	Thinking, unsure of position, stalling.
8. Hands to face	Evaluating, listening.
9. Clenched hands, locked ankles	Nervous or upset.
10. Legs comfortable and arms open	Interested and involved.
11. Avoiding eye contact	Ill at ease (this can be cultural).

■ CONVINCER STRATEGIES

People become convinced by a number of means. Some people have to hear the information, others must read the information, while others have to discuss ideas before they can make a decision. Some people have to think things through and others have to test the ideas.

No matter how you are convinced, it's likely that your counterpart will need to be convinced a *different* way. Guerrillas give their counterparts whatever they need to decide, whether it's documents to read, a presentation to watch, time to think, time to experiment, or time to talk about it.

➤ A Rewarded Behavior Tends to Be Repeated

Positive reinforcement of a behavior leads to an increase in the frequency of that behavior in the future. Conversely, negative reinforcement of a behavior tends to discourage that behavior. But negative reinforcement is less effective in changing behavior than positive reinforcement.

One can learn a lot by watching animals in training, a child learning a new skill, or an executive negotiating the first few weeks of a new position. In every case, new behavior is quickly learned and reinforced with small, often subtle rewards. For a dog, a tidbit for a trick; for a child, a hug and a smile for trying to walk; for an executive, access to information for following corporate protocol. Positive reinforcement creates successful motivation.

➤ Free Stuff

Guerrillas will find things that they can give their counterpart with no strings attached to create rapport and foster goodwill. Giving a gift opens many doors. However, not everyone will accept your gift. You can prove that by going around your office and offering people a piece of gum or a mint. Some will accept, some will refuse, and some will wonder, "What's the catch?" Your counterpart may or may not respond to a free offer. If they think that you're trying to create an unfair obligation by offering them something for nothing, they may resist.

■ HOW YOUR COUNTERPART COMMUNICATES

Have you ever noticed how often conflict arises between technical people and the marketing people, between salespeople and management? That's because people process information differently. People have different styles of communicating, just as they have preferences for styles of clothing or styles of music.

Observe how people process information and how you can switch communication modes so your message connects and they understand your viewpoint. Keep in mind that there is no judgment in any of these communication styles. Each style is important to accomplish specific tasks, and the most successful people can recognize and adapt to their counterpart's preferred communication approach. People tend to move along the communication-style continuum in response to the task at hand. Like tuning in a radio, your discussion must be structured to align with your counterpart, so they can hear and understand your message.

We'll look at six categories of communication style:

➤ General versus Specific

The first of these categories describes your prospect's *need for information and detail*. What is their need for explanation and tolerance for specifics? You can think of this as a continuum that ranges from the *general* communicator at one extreme, to the *specific* communicator at the other.

General. . . . . Specific

Your prospects can fall anywhere along this scale; some have already made up their mind and would rather not be confused with the facts, while others need lots of information in order to make a decision.

Test yourself; you may be a *Specific* communicator if right now, without looking, you know exactly how much money you have in your checking account. On the other hand, if you haven't balanced your checkbook since 1973, or perhaps you rely on the ATM method (when the automatic teller machine stops giving you cash, you know you're overdrawn), then you are more likely to be a *General* communicator. This spectrum is easy to recognize. Pay attention to the level of detail that a person uses in their conversation.

You can recognize the *General* communicators because these people are most comfortable talking in sweeping generalities. They prefer the big picture, the overview, the executive summary. They are impatient with minutia. Getting any real information from *General* communicators can be like pulling teeth. They are notorious for making assumptions, because in the absence of hard data they will fill in the details based on their general understanding. If conclusion jumping were an Olympic event, these people would be gold medalists. *Generals* have a tendency to think big, without considering the potentially limiting practical details. They have big dreams and big goals. They think long-term, and may have a 10-year plan and a 5-year plan, but they don't have plans for lunch.

The opposite extreme of this scale is the *Specific* communicator. You can recognize this style by their high capacity for, and need for detail, and their very precise style of communication. Their conversation is peppered with particular references such as place names, proper nouns, dates, times, statistics, percentages, quantities, or distances. They have a tendency to think in the short term, the close-up, and have difficulty understanding the big picture or seeing the overview. With this counterpart you have to be extremely accurate because *Specifics* are alert to the tiniest omission or contradiction, and you'd better be right on time!

Be very careful when dealing with *Specifics* because the intent of their communication can get lost in all this "detail fog."

Communicate

To communicate with the *General* communicator, be direct. One of the most frequent mistakes negotiators make is overloading this counterpart with irrelevant detail. Start with the bottom line. If they need more information, *Generals* will ask for it.

To communicate with the *Specific* communicator, be thorough, complete, and precise. They need all of the salient facts and then some. Explain your reasoning and the evidence that supports it before drawing a conclusion. Show them how you will perform in exact terms, using dollars, percentages, and dates.

Persuade

To persuade the *General,* summarize using charts, graphs, or maps. For *Generals,* a picture is worth a thousand words, and the more concisely you present your case, the easier it is for them to understand.

To persuade the *Specifics,* break your proposition down into incremental commitments. These people hate to make decisions, especially big decisions, so give them a series of small decisions to make.

Motivate

To motivate the *General,* align your proposal with their long-term plan. Show them how it fits into the big picture. These people enjoy making decisions, especially big decisions. To motivate the *Specific,* include all the supporting documentation you can get your hands on: computer printouts, brochures, specifications, everything. The specific may not read it all, but they have an emotional need to feel that they're getting the whole story.

Where on the line between *General* to *Specific* do you see your own communication style? Place an X there. If you're a *General,* anywhere close will do. If you're a *Specific,* be as accurate as you can.

Motivating Both General and Specific Communicators

You run into problems when you put a *Specific* communicator and a *General* communicator together. The *General* will simply stop listening and daydream if their need for detail is exceeded.

The opposite is true for the *Specific;* unless they have every bit of information filled in, they have trouble arriving at a conclusion.

For a mixed audience, communicate with stories and rules of thumb that appeal to the *General,* and also deliver detailed how-to instructions for the *Specifics.*

If you're creating a written proposal, the executive summary is for the *Generals;* the rest of the proposal is for the *Specifics.*

➤ Match versus Mismatch

This dimension of communication looks at whether people sort information for *similarities* or for *differences;* they tend to either *match* or *mismatch. Matchers* look for common ground and search for alignment of their experiences and values when working with others. They tend to ignore misalignments. Conversely, *Mismatchers* look for what is different or out of match with their experience and values. They identify misalignment, ignoring where there is a similarity.

Match. . . . . Mismatch

We are all born *Matchers,* and later in life, about a third of us are trained to become *Mismatchers. Matchers* make friends easily because they're looking for ways to connect and find common ground. *Mismatchers* are good at troubleshooting and fixing things. They're looking for what's not correct, so sometimes they tend to be critical—the devil's advocate.

Matchers make good salespeople, because they are terrific at delivering customer service, and they are politically savvy. *Mismatchers* are excellent at keeping the world in order; they are our police, engineers, software programmers, accountants, doctors, and pilots. Police officers aren't concerned with people who obey the law; they only worry about those who break the law. Accountants don't notice the numbers that are correct; they notice the numbers that are incorrect. Doctors don't concern themselves with healthy people; they concern themselves with with those who are sick. Software programmers look for the bugs, not the code that's running well.

Matching and Mirroring Sometimes Won't Work
Many sales trainers teach salespeople to match and mirror their prospects to create rapport. The problem is that when you

match and mirror a *Mismatcher,* they'll un-match you, so the salesperson thinks that there's no rapport, so they re-match, and the prospect will un-match again. Both people feel frustrated because their needs are not met. Because matching and mirroring techniques are inappropriate with *Mismatchers,* you can use matching and mirroring to test for rapport. If they match and mirror you, you have rapport. If not, they may just be in mismatch mode.

Perhaps you've dealt with a person who argues with you. You think, "There's no way they'll ever do business with me." And then at the end of the conversation, they surprise you by saying, "Okay, let's go with it." You almost fall off your chair. You were working with a *Mismatcher.*

Communicate

The best way to communicate with a *Matcher* is to search for common ground. Look for areas of similar interest or any kind of connection from people you both know, to liking the same sports, or rooting for the same teams. Communicate with a *Mismatcher* by debating the issues. If they don't debate an issue, consider it settled. No discussion is good news. They live by the rule of "If there's a problem, I'll let you know."

Persuade

Persuade *Matchers* by building consensus. Check each important item with them to make sure that you are both in agreement on the issues. *Matchers* will go over all the points, to "touch all the bases," making sure there is a match before proceeding. When most of the issues are in accord, they're ready to make a decision.

Persuade *Mismatchers* by validating your evidence with authoritative proof. Use third-party references that they respect. You can ask *Mismatchers:* "How will you know what's right?" and they'll likely tell you what evidence they'll need.

Motivate

Motivate *Matchers* by inviting them along. Use phrases such as, "I invite you to join the growing ranks of successful people who work with our company." Motivate *Mismatchers* with a preponderance of proof. They are motivated when they see sufficient evidence. They will then be compelled to move forward to a new position.

What style are you? Place an X where you consider yourself on the *Match–Mismatch* continuum. You might be a *Matcher* if you avoid conflict at all costs. You might be a *Mismatcher* if you're always right, and you can always prove it. You might be a *Matcher* if it's easy for you to make friends. You might be a *Mismatcher* if you are good at troubleshooting problems.

Motivating Groups with Both Match and Mismatch Styles

To make your message compelling for a mixed group, use examples that illustrate that you do business with companies like theirs. "We help companies *just like you* solve their biggest challenges." Use lots of social proof, using your counterpart to confirm your ideas with polls and discussion.

Suspend your judgment when people argue with you; they may be in *Mismatch* mode. You can temporarily suspend their judgment, too. Here's how. When processing sentences containing the word *but,* our brains diminish or negate what comes before the *but,* and accepts what comes after as fact. So using a double negative along with *but* temporarily suspends a *Mismatcher*'s judgment. The formula is "I don't know if . . . or not, but . . ."

"I don't know if you've thought of this or not, but . . ." "I don't know if you've had this experience or not, but . . ." "I don't know if this will work for you or not, but . . ." "You may not be interested in this, but . . ." "This probably isn't going to make sense to you, but . . ." Or the one that will really get them listening, "I don't know if I should tell you this or not, but . . ."

Another safe way out is, "I could be wrong, but . . ." Benjamin Franklin introduced this method in the eighteenth century, and it still works well today. If they disagree, you can say, "I thought I might be wrong."

Use this script as a preamble to presentations when you know you're negotiating with *Mismatchers:* "I know that you're a skeptical, critical thinker. And that's good, because it avoids errors and traps. A critical thinker decides by comparing new information with past experience. Yet the ideas I have for you are *so* new, I'd be surprised if you have anything to compare them with. So I suggest that you sit back, relax, and first listen all the way through before coming up with questions or making a judgment."

➤ Options versus Procedures

This dimension of communication describes the *need for order and structure*. How your counterpart organizes their world will be a reflection of how they tackle problems. By matching the process they use, you are more likely to arrive at a favorable outcome.

Options. . . . . Procedures

Think in terms of a scale with *Options* at one end, and *Procedures* at the other. Test yourself. If you prefer to do things step-by-step, in routine, repetitive procedures, then you may be a *Procedural* communicator. You keep a neat desk, taking out one file folder at a time, working on it until you're finished, then putting it carefully away. You are upset with messes.

On the other hand, if you have the messy desk, piled high with books, papers, and file folders, 14 different projects underway all at the same time, it's likely you are an *Options* communicator. If some well-meaning colleague cleaned your desk for you, you'd have to kill them. (In some states, this is justifiable homicide.)

You can recognize an *Options* communicator as soon as you talk to one. This counterpart is talking on the phone, writing a letter, eating a snack, and carrying on a conversation—all at the same time! These folks are often good at handling multiple demands and simultaneous tasks. They organize their work as a set of alternatives. They are notorious for starting projects and not finishing, so you have to follow up carefully on any commitments they make.

The *Procedural* communicator, on the other hand, organizes tasks sequentially, or as a checklist. They'll often numerate their conversations, starting with item number one, and discussing it until it's resolved. Then and only then will they move on to item number two. If you interrupt them by changing the subject, they become stressed, and they may have to start all over again to regain their train of thought. They'll say things like, "Look, I can only do one thing at a time!"

People who do sequential, repetitive tasks tend to be *Procedural* communicators as well. Generally speaking, the higher you go in an organizational hierarchy, the more *Options* the style of communication.

Communicate

To communicate with the *Options* prospect, be flexible. This counterpart may interrupt you with questions or comments, and you must give them free rein in the conversation and follow their lead. Be prepared to follow them on a joy ride around the issues. A carefully planned discussion is of particular value here, even if you don't follow it sequentially, because like a road map, it helps you steer the conversation to the desired destination.

With *Procedurals,* there is one right way to do everything—their way—and any deviation violates their need for order and correctness. To communicate with these people, stay on track and enumerate your carefully prepared presentation step-by-step. If you digress, use an, "as I was saying . . ." transition to get back into your outline. It helps if you can give your counterpart a copy of your notes. Give them an agenda in advance so they can check off each issue as you cover it.

Persuade

To persuade the *Options* counterpart, spell out an array of alternatives, outlining the advantages and disadvantages of each. This person must see the alternatives in order to make a choice.

To persuade the *Procedural,* structure your case as the only logical choice, given the evidence. If you can lead the *Procedural* to a logical conclusion, based on the facts, it's easy for them to accept with your deal.

Motivate

To motivate *Options,* give them a set of alternatives to choose from, and ask them to make a choice. Be careful not to give them too many possibilities, particularly if they are also a *General* communicator. You can overload them with too many alternatives.

To motivate the *Procedural,* use a demonstration or show before-and-after pictures. If they follow some structured routine, find out exactly what it is. If they order on a regular schedule, make sure you call on exactly the same day each month to take their order. Whatever you do, be consistent.

Where on the line from *Options* to *Procedures* do you see your own communication style? Place an X there. If you're an *Options,* only one X please. If you're procedural, you may have to evaluate that for a moment. But you should place the X before proceeding to the next section of this chapter.

Motivating Both Options and Procedural People

You run into problems when you put an *Options* communicator and a *Procedural* communicator together. *Options* will jump from point to point, whereas *Procedurals* will want to stick to the agenda. The good news is that *Options* will often go along with the procedure, because it's an option.

To make your presentation compelling to a mixed group, provide open space for the *Options* to write notes. Offer fill-in-the-blank sections for *Procedurals,* and most important, stay on track and on schedule.

➤ Internal versus External

The next style is locus of motivation. From what point does their motivation come from? Where does your counterpart *look for evidence to confirm that they have made the right choices?* People differ in the strategies they use to maintain their motivation. Do they look for it internally or do they look for it externally?

Internal. . . . . External

Some people look within themselves for *Internal* confirmation of their decision making, whereas others look to the *External* world for praise and feedback. This distinction will help you communicate in a way that will build powerful motivation.

You can find out how people are motivated by the way they answer such questions as, "How do you know when what you are doing is working?" or "How do you know when what you have bought is doing a good job for you?" You might ask a prospect, "Based on your experience, how do you know when you've found the right vendor?"

Test yourself: You might be *Externally* motivated if you work your butt off for a year to earn a $35 plaque at the sales meeting. Externally motivated people will decorate their offices with trophies, awards, and mounted animals.

Someone who is *Internally* motivated references their gut reaction, their conscience, or their intuition to validate their decision making. They base their choices on factors inside themselves, a vision, a feeling, or a voice inside their head. If you're thinking, "What voice? I don't have a voice inside my head," *that's* the voice we're talking about.

Internals know they've done a good job when they feel that they've done their best. You can recognize *Internally* motivated people because they're less interested in what other people think or do. They tend to be independent thinkers—not as interested in what you've done for others, but more interested in what you can do for them. They make choices based on personal goals, ethics, and morals.

An *Internally* motivated counterpart might respond to the question, "How do you know . . . ?" by saying, "You just know when it's right. You get a feeling when you first talk with them. Are they knowledgeable? Is the company's reputation solid? If I'm going to spend 5 or 10 years with a vendor, the relationship has to be comfortable." This person might be interested in the same vendor as the *Externally* motivated counterpart, but for very different reasons.

Externally motivated people tend to respond to the question, "How do you know . . . ?" by saying something like, "I want a vendor who won't embarrass me if something goes wrong." These people are fixing their frame of reference externally, on the outside world, depending on what others might say or feel about their choice. *Externally* motivated people are motivated to "look good" or do things because other people tell them they should. They seek acceptance, and a guerrilla delivers tangible proof of acceptance with testimonial letters, certificates of appreciation, plaques, and award ceremonies.

Most salespeople are *Externally* motivated. Sales positions attract *Externally* motivated people—they're motivated by quotas and rewarded with commissions and sales contests. Salespeople will work tirelessly for a pat on the back. They tend to quit working hard once they've reached their quota. *Externally* motivated managers insist that commission is the only way to motivate a salesperson. They're right as long as they hire only *Externally* motivated people.

Communicate

Internally motivated counterparts may be motivated independently of what's going on in the real world. These people really don't care what you or what anyone else thinks. Communicate with the *Internal* person by asking questions, and listening actively to the answers.

Conversely, people who are *Externally* motivated are dependent on your input, statistics, and testimonials; they have to have that input in order to make a decision. They want you to tell them about your product, make suggestions, perhaps even prescribe a particular course of action. They expect you to use *external* forms of proof, including third-party references, testimonial letters, demonstrations, and referrals.

Persuade

Persuade the *Internal* communicator by soliciting their advice, asking for their opinions, feelings, and values. "What do you think of this capability?" Use questions to help them access their own *Internal* judgment, because that's the scale they'll use for weighing the evidence and for making the decision. They become uneasy when you try to overwhelm them with rave reviews. Not only do they ignore it, they resent it. In sales, you can't "close" an *Internally* motivated person. Them must close themselves.

Persuade the *Externally* motivated prospect by appealing to what other people are going to think. You could make comments like, "This is the most popular product on the market," and "I can just see your colleagues green with envy when you take delivery." To convince the *External*, tell your story and offer third-party testimonials.

Motivate

Motivate the *Internal* communicator by aligning with their personal vision, by saying, "Well, I'm sure that you understand your company's needs better than I do, and I'm really counting on your feedback as we discuss different options. I'd like to help you, yet ultimately you have to live with your decision." Effective motivators are based on things that *Internally* motivated people are already committed to. Make it easy for them to follow their inclination. A powerful motivator could be the offer of a donation to a favorite charity in their name.

Motivate the *External* person by providing constant praise, especially public recognition. They want you to say, "You are a very savvy customer. Most of my clients aren't nearly as knowl-edgeable." Send them a Customer of the Month Award.

Where are you on the *Internal* versus *External* motivation continuum? Place an X where you most often find yourself. If you're internally motivated, you'll know it. If you're exter-nally motivated, you might have to ask someone to confirm that for you.

Managing Both Internal and External Motivation

Most people are a blend of *Internal* and *External* motivation, which is why you have to ask for their feedback *and* offer opin-ions and testimonials. To make your message compelling for a mixed audience, tell *your* success stories that appeal to *Inter-nally* motivated people. Tell *others* success stories that appeal to *Externally* motivated people. To cover both styles, tell them what's in it for them and what's in it for others.

You will be successful when you realize that you may be negotiating with both *Internally* and *Externally* motivated peo-ple. The secret is to offer a choice. Offer outcomes that attract either or both styles of motivation.

For *Externally* motivated people, discuss rewards and recog-nition, prizes with their names on them, public proclamations, certificates, and plaques. They like trips to exotic places and meeting celebrities.

For *Internally* motivated people, discuss ways that they can develop themselves or help others. Offer them outcomes that are culturally or socially significant. They tend to respond to ecological and humanitarian issues. They respond to doing the right thing.

➤ Proactive versus Reactive

Another dimension to watch for is your prospects' *level of ini-tiative.* How well do they deal with change? Do they take the ini-tiative to make things happen, or do they wait for others to get things started?

Proactive. . . . . Reactive

Proactive counterparts like to be in control and make things happen. They tend to act impulsively. They have a bias for experimentation over analysis, and tend to act first and ask questions later. *Reactive* counterparts prefer that someone else to do the driving and take them along for the ride. They prefer analysis over experimentation, and tend to ask questions rather than act. Test yourself: What do you do when you approach a yellow traffic light? *Reactives* stop. *Proactives* gun it!

Proactives want to take the lead, to be in control, and in some cases, may resist the initiative of others, including you. Inaction makes them uncomfortable. They prefer to try out your suggestion, but if it doesn't work the way they expect it to the first time, that's enough; they're ready to deal with someone else. They have a bias for products that are "new," "improved," "state-of-the-art," and "leading-edge." They hate to be kept waiting. You may be *Proactive* if you've ever found yourself standing in front of the microwave saying, "Come on! COME ON!!!"

At the other end of the scale are the *Reactives*. These people are not motivated to start things, but instead rely on the initiatives of others, so guerrillas assume leadership role by making suggestions and recommendations. *Reactives* have a bias for products that are "proven," "old-fashioned," and "guaranteed." *Reactives* are afraid to rock the boat; they prefer the status quo and may be resistant to change. You may be *Reactive* if you are still waiting for them to work the bugs out of color TV.

Communicate

Communicate with the *Proactive* by following their lead, and treat everything as if it were their idea. These people are go-getters. If you promise to send a document, brochure, or catalog, get it out the same day.

Communicate with *Reactives* by advising, spelling out the solution, and taking small initiatives. Also keep in mind that these prospects resist change, so describe your product in terms of "progression," "evolution," and "improvement," rather than "new," "revolutionary," or "breakthrough."

Persuade

Persuade the *Proactive* by offering something that they can say "yes" to. Fill out the order blank or write up the contract in advance.

Persuade the *Reactive* by soliciting the opinions and recommendations of others. Be prepared to prescribe a specific solution or get others involved. Be prepared to offer *Reactives* all of the facts, figures, and test results, and take the initiative to offer demonstrations, do a trial run, or get the ball rolling in some other way.

Motivate

Motivate the *Proactive* by initiating, and expedite everything. Once they've made up their mind, they want it delivered yesterday. With *Proactives,* any actions on your part will be well received. They respect people of like mind and are happy to push things along. Be careful if you meet a *Proactive* who is also *Externally* motivated; they may make commitments they can't keep.

Motivate the *Reactive* by pushing gently, and involving others. Go over their head for approval if necessary. They may interpret your initiative as being pushy, but they *will* react to it, either positively or negatively. They require constant attention, checking back, and prodding along, or the momentum of the sale will be lost.

Where on the line from *Proactive* to *Reactive* do you see your own communication style? Place an X there. If you're *Proactive,* you've already placed the X before reading the instructions. If you're *Reactive,* you've been waiting for the instruction to place the X now.

Motivating Both Proactive and Reactive People

Make your message compelling to a mixed audience; remember that *Proactives* love audience interaction and *Reactives* love to be entertained. Include lots of opportunity to discuss the issues, and offer breaks from the action with simple but enjoyable activities.

➤ Toward versus Away-From

Another communication style involves how people view their objectives and goals. Some people move *toward* an objective, whereas others move *away from* a threat penalty. Some people seek pleasure; others seek to avoid pain.

Toward. . . . . Away From

Toward communicators are motivated to move toward a desired outcome. They seek a pleasant objective. They want to be included. They live their lives according to their priorities. If you make your program a priority, they'll respond. If you talk to these people about avoiding pain, your message won't connect. Instead, speak in terms of benefits that they and those they care about will receive, and they'll take notice. They respond to offers such as "Think of the personal satisfaction you'll feel." or "Your family will love you for this."

Toward people climb mountains because getting there is worth the effort. They talk about what they gain, achieve, or now have because of their past efforts.

Many sales trainers teach people to find the prospect's pain and sell to that pain. However, many of the people you'll negotiate with are motivated *Toward* dreams, not pain. If you seek out and make them feel their pain, you'll be much less successful than if you seek out their dreams.

Away-from communicators want to get rid of something, or want to exclude things. These people go through life managing one crisis after another. They run from fire to fire. *Away-from* people talk about problems, what they want to get rid of or avoid. They don't want to do anything that is troublesome or difficult. To connect with *Away-from* people, talk about what they'll avoid, what will happen if they don't act, or what headaches they'll eliminate when they do act. They respond to offers such as: "You'll never again have the drudgery of cleaning your office," or "Get away from it all."

A colleague asked a prospective client who is an *Away-from* style: "What do you want to <u>not</u> happen?" He responded with, "I want to <u>stop not getting</u> business."

Notice that parents often motivate their children with *Away-from* phrases.

"Don't run with that stick! You'll put your eye out!"
"You're misbehaving! Do you want a spanking?"
"I'll send you to your room if you don't eat your vegetables!"

Parents may wish to also try *Toward* phrases,

"Walk with that stick! I want you to be safe!"
"When you behave, you'll get to play with your friends."
"There's dessert when you finish your vegetables."

In negotiations, if you use a value proposition, "If you're not with the program, you'll be left in the dust," you're using an

Away-from phrase. To appeal to a counterpart with a *Toward* style, use, "When you're with this program, you'll take advantage of a great opportunity."

You can tell the style of a person's motivation by their physical actions and by the words they use. Physical *Away-from* signals include shaking their head no, closing their hand, crossing arms, and pushing *Away-from* the table. Physical *Toward* signs are open hands, inclusive gestures, nodding their head yes, and pointing at things.

The words in Figure 9.1 will help you identify whether their motivation direction is *Away-from,* and Figure 9.2 indicates whether their motivation direction is *Toward.*

Communicate

Communicate with *Toward* people by discussing the potential positive outcomes with them. Talk about how they'll achieve their goals, get what they want, let others have what they want. Discuss how you'll get them where they want to go.

Communicate with *Away-from* people by talking about how they'll avoid potential negative outcomes, how they'll avoid going out of business, how they'll stop not having customers, how they'll avoid embarrassment. Show them how you'll help them avoid what they fear.

Persuade

Persuade *Toward* people by proving to them the return on their investment, both financially and emotionally. Show them that it's worthwhile to make a decision in your favor.

Persuade *Away-from* people by discussing the cost of not moving forward. Illustrate how waiting will be too costly, and not making a decision will make their situation worse than it is now.

Motivate

Motivate *Toward* people by showing them how pleasant it will be to work with you. Illustrate that you'll be an absolute pleasure to do business with.

Motivate *Away-from* people by showing them how you'll help them avoid pain, how other choices will be more painful. They really look at the hassle factor of changing vendors, so make it more painful to stay than to change.

Where on the line between *Toward* to *Away from* do you see your own communication style? Place an X there.

Abate
Avoid
Avoid the trap
Consequence
Consider the risk factor
Count the cost
Decline
Decrease
Deny
Deprive oneself
Diminish
Discard
Disclaim
Dismiss
Dispose of
Do without
Don't
Don't want
Drop
Dump
Eliminate
Escape
Except
Exclude
Fight back
Forgo
Get rid of
Give a wide berth
Go without
Grudge

Have no heart for
Have no stomach for
Hold off
Keep a safe distance
Keep clear of
Keep off
Keep out
Leave nothing to chance
Lessen
Live to fight another day
Make less
Minimize
Mitigate
Not allow
Not have to
Not like the look of
Pass up
Problem
Prohibit
Push
Refuse
Scrape through
Shut the door
Side-effect
Stand aloof
Survive
Turn away
Turn down
Turn one's back on
Unload

Figure 9.1 Away-From Phrases.

Accommodate	Find room for
Accomplishment	Get hold of
Achieve	Goal
Admit	Grasp
Advance	Have
Adventure	Hit the jackpot
Affinity	Include
Aim	Lead
Ambition	Objective
Appeal	Open arms
Arrive	Outcome
Aspiration	Payoff
Attraction	Performance
Attractiveness	Possess
Be successful	Progress
Break through	Prosper
Breakthrough	Pull
Collect	Qualify
Come out on top	Receive
Comprehend	Reclaim
Desire	Regain
Destination	Score
Dream	Succeed
Embrace	Take in
End	Want
Enjoy	What I want

Figure 9.2 Toward Phrases.

Managing Both Toward and Away-From Personalities

To be successful, offer messages that cover both motivation styles. Discuss the advantages of moving forward, the value of the proposition, the cost of letting things remain as they are, and the price of being left behind. "When you choose to work with us, you'll get exactly what you've asked for, and you'll avoid the headaches associated with a company that can't deliver on its promises."

Chapter

Controlling
the Negotiation

The person asking the questions controls the direction of the negotiation. By asking the right questions, you gain an advantage and guide your counterpart to consider your position in a new way. Questions that let them discover data and precedence to support your position will be more convincing than your most persuasive presentation. You gain an advantage when you ask the right questions in the right order.

■ QUESTIONS WITH LIMITED POWER

Avoid these questions that decrease your power.

➤ Closed Questions

These are questions that can be answered by a limited set of responses. The answer could be yes or no. "Do you want red or blue?" Asking these questions reflects your agenda, not theirs, and can limit your potential outcome as much as it limits their choice. Use closed questions only if you are in agreement, and you're helping them make a choice.

➤ Leading and Trap Questions

Leading questions suggest that you already know the answer. Questions that begin with *don't you,* or *shouldn't you,* presuppose need. "You need this, don't you?" This approach is time worn and smacks of pushy and manipulative tactics.

226

Negotiators often use trap questions such as, "If I can meet your needs, *will* you agree?" The logical answer is yes, but it places their counterpart in a defensive position. There's no buy in, and they'll be listening to the proposal searching for reasons *not* to agree.

➤ *Why* Questions

Why questions force your counterpart to *dextify*—*de*fend, *ex*plain, and jus*tify* their position. Unless you wish to challenge them, pushing them off balance, avoid *why* questions. Replace them with these queries:

"What is it about . . . ?"
"How come . . . ?"
"What do you get when . . . ?"
"What is important about . . . ?"

■ POWER QUESTIONS

Here are categories of questions that take you where you want to go. Pick and choose depending on what you want to accomplish.

➤ Questions That Build Rapport

"Is this a good time for us to talk about this?"
"What has changed since we last spoke?"

➤ Questions to Find the Objective

"What do we need to talk about?"
"What's on your mind?"
"What do you wish to accomplish?"
"How will you know when we're successful?"

➤ Questions That Search for Facts

"Where . . ."—Environment
"What . . ."—Behavior
"How . . ."—Capabilities

"Who . . ."—Identity
"Who else . . ."—Purpose

➤ Clarification Questions

"What do you mean by . . . ?"
"What are you referring to?"
"Who are you referring to?"
"Can you give me an example?"
"I'm curious . . ."
"What would happen if . . . ?"
"Let me see if I understand you correctly."
"Are we on track?"
"How is that important?"
"How would you approach the problem?"

➤ Questions That Let Them Explore

"If you had to make a guess . . . ?"
"Suppose for a moment that you could . . . ?"
"What would happen if you did?"
"What else?"

➤ Questions That Discover Your Counterpart's Values

"What's important about . . . ?"
"How is that important . . . ?"

➤ Questions That Find Evidence

"How will you know when . . . ?"
"How do you know . . . ?"

➤ Questions That Find Causes

"What causes . . . ?"
"What makes you . . . ?"
"How come . . . ?"

➤ Questions That Find Effects

"What do you get?"
"What does that do?"
"What does that accomplish?"

➤ Questions That Increase Precision

"What do you mean by . . . ?"
"What are you referring to . . . ?"
"Who are you talking about . . . ?"
"How do you mean . . . ?"
"When does that happen . . . ?"
"How often does that happen . . . ?"
"Can you give me an example?"

➤ Questions That Find Obstacles

When they say, "I can't . . . ," explore their refusal by asking,
"What stops you from . . . ?"
"What helps you when . . . ?"
"What happens when . . . ?"
"What happens if you do . . . ?"
"What happens when you don't . . . ?"
"What would happen if you did?"
"I know you can't, but what would happen if you did?"

➤ Questions to Find Resources

"What do you need to . . . ?"
"What would you do first?"
"What do you need in order to . . . ?"

➤ Questions That Request Feedback

"What I'm hearing is . . ."
"It seems to me that . . ."
"If I understand you correctly . . ."

"What do you think?"

"How are we doing?"

"Are you getting what you need?"

"Are you getting what you expected?"

"Is there anything else?"

"What am I missing?"

"Let me get this right; are you saying . . . ?"

■ 37 MAGIC QUESTIONS

We've developed a list of the 37 most powerful questions guerrillas can ask. This list will automatically take a counterpart all the way through the critical parts of the negotiating process. Your team members should memorize these until they can recall on demand, "What's question number 10?"

These questions really work magic. We've italicized the magic words in each question with an explanation of the strategy behind each one.

1. What is your main *objective?*
   When you understand what your counterpart is trying to achieve, you can align your proposal with their intent.

2. How do you *plan* to achieve that goal?
   You may already fit into their plan and not even know it. If you're part of their plan, your counterpart will close themselves.

3. What is the *biggest problem* you currently face?
   If you can help them solve their biggest problem, you will be a hero.

4. What *other* problems do you experience?
   You may not be able to solve their biggest problem, so find out what other problems they have that you can solve.

5. What are you doing *currently* to deal with this?

6. What is your strategy for the *future?*
   These two questions, together, give you an outline of the counterpart's current trajectory. These questions tend to accelerate the negotiation process.

7. What *other ideas* do you have?
   This fills in the blanks and lets you uncover their other ideas with which you can align.

8. What role do others play in *creating* this situation?
   Anyone who is contributing to the problem is a potential adversary. They'll probably want to maintain the status quo. Find out who they are.

9. Who else is *affected?*
   Anyone who is affected by the problem is a potential ally.

10. What are you using *now?*

11. What do you like *most* about it?

12. What do you like *least* about it?
    Always use these three as a group. Question 10 tells you about their past experiences, such as what they're buying, from whom, and for how much, revealing both the need and the budget. Question 11 gives you their critical buying criteria. A replacement vendor must be equivalent in these areas to even be considered. This also tells you the thought *process* they went through to purchase last time. Question 12 tells you where the competitor is vulnerable. If you can offer them everything they like most, and fix the things they like least, now they have a justification to change.

13. If you could have things any way you wanted, what would you *change?*
    People are naturally resistant to change. "Better the devil you know than one you don't." This question inoculates the issue of change. It also allows them to dream and explore possibilities. You can probably do about half of the things they request. There's something compelling about making a person's dream come true.

14. How will this *affect* the present situation?
    This question brings the dream to reality. When they do change, how close will it be to what they really want?

15. What would *motivate* you to change?
    This question creates the rationale they will use to justify the change, reducing their resistance later.

16. Do you have a *preference?*
If they do, you need to know what it is, and what it's based on.

17. What has been your *experience?*
If they have had an unfavorable experience with the competitor, you may be able to exploit it. If they've had an unfavorable experience with your company, you'd better fix it.

18. How do you *know?*
Sometimes they really don't know. You want to know where they got their information. Be very careful not to speak in an accusatory tone.

19. Is there *anything else* you'd like to see?
This open-ended question encourages them to brainstorm additional options and may reveal additional opportunities for the guerrilla.

20. How much would it be *worth* to you to solve this problem?

21. What would it *cost,* ultimately, if things remained as they are?
These two questions set up the *cost justification* for the investment you'll ask them to make. Question 20 tells you the most they should be willing to pay; question 21 tells you the least they should be willing to pay. If they didn't have a budget before, they have a budget range now. Always ask both questions because some people are motivated *Toward* some positive outcome or reward, whereas others are motivated *Away-from* some consequence or penalty. Whichever question they answer in most detail reveals the strategy you should pursue when preparing a return-on-investment presentation.

22. Are you working within a *budget?*
If so, they should reveal it here. If not, you have the necessary data to create one. A budget is the best indicator of commitment.

23. How do you plan to *finance* it?
Where is the money going to come from? Can you offer alternative financing?

24. What *alternatives* have you considered?
Don't be naive. They're talking to the competition. It is perfectly appropriate to ask a counterpart who you're competing with. You'll know how to present your offering in the best light against that competitor.

25. What benefit would you *personally* realize as a result?
People do things for their reasons, no matter how good your reasons might be.

26. How would *others* benefit?
The answer to this question creates a justification for what may ultimately be a selfish decision.

27. How can I *help?*
This is easily the most powerful question in the book.

28. Is there anything I've *overlooked?*
This gives you a chance to tie up any loose ends that might tangle and trip you up later on.

29. Are there any *questions* you'd like to ask?
Encourage your counterpart to get all their questions answered here and now.

30. What do you see as the *next step?*
The counterpart will tell you what you need to do to advance the negotiation: write up an order, check on a specification, make a presentation to a committee, or nothing.

31. Who else, *besides yourself,* will be involved in making the decision?
Even if you're meeting with the custodian, always assume they may be a behind-the-scenes influence. Even if you think you've found the decision maker, keep asking this question of everyone else.

32. On a scale of 1 to 10, how confident do you feel about doing business with us? *What would it take* to get that up to a 10?
This two-part question will tell you exactly what incremental evidence they need, and what form of proof they will require. If they say, "8," say, "What would it take to get to a 9?" If they say "10," proceed to closing the deal.

33. Are you working against a particular *deadline?*

34. How *soon* would you like to start?

35. *When* would you like to take delivery?
These are all time-frame questions. Remember, if they're not motivated by some time frame, they probably will not be motivated to conclude the negotiation, at least not for a while.

36. When should we get together to discuss this *again?*
It's likely that you won't be able to close the deal on the first contact, or even the second or third. Let them define the time frame for the next meeting. Their response is the best indication of their motivation to move forward.

37. Is there *anything else* you'd like me to take care of?
We leave far too much money on the table because we do not ask this simple parting question.

■ HOW TO ANSWER THEIR QUESTIONS

Sooner or later your counterpart will be asking you questions. Brainstorm likely tough questions and have your answers ready. Well prepared is well armed. Guerrillas use these guidelines to gain an advantage.

➤ Think First

The first rule of Guerrilla Negotiating is to think, and then think again before responding. Many negotiations have been sabotaged by a blurted answer.

➤ Understand Why

Why are they asking that question? What's their motive for asking? Not all questions deserve answers. Some are designed to provoke or throw you off balance. Until you clearly understand the question, don't answer.

➤ Partial Answer

Answer just part of their question. If the question is really important, they'll keep asking until they get the necessary information.

➤ Answer Another

You can evade a question by actually answering a different question, one you want them to understand. Politicians are experts at this tactic. Say, "Let me clarify . . ." and off you go on your agenda.

➤ Let Them Interrupt

When your counterpart interrupts, you've just gotten a break from answering the question. If your answer is important, you can resume your answer with, "As I was saying before you interrupted . . ." You've just gained an advantage.

➤ The Truth

Your most powerful weapon is the truth. A truthful answer is last thing your counterpart expects from you. When you have a strong position, you can gain a guerrilla advantage by setting the ground rule that both sides are expected to always tell the truth. "If we discover that you're being less than truthful, we're done with this discussion."

➤ When You Don't Know the Answer

Not knowing the answer is okay. Unless you're under oath, you're not obligated to answer just because a question is asked. Acting confused will often work to your advantage. Peter Falk's character Colombo uses this confused approach to gain information that ultimately incriminates the suspect.

➤ When You Don't Want to Answer

Sometimes you don't want to answer their question. The answer may weaken your position, or you may not understand their question, or their question can have several answers, or you're just not ready to release that information. Here's a list of side steppers.

Stalls

"Repeat the question, please."

"I don't understand your question."

"Good question. What makes you ask?"
"How is that important?"
"Could you ask that question another way?"
"Before I answer . . ."
"I can't discuss that now, because . . ."

No Knowledge

"I don't recall."
"I don't remember."
"I don't really know."
"I've forgotten."

Limited Knowledge

"I don't have the entire story, but . . ."
"I don't know all the details."
"My knowledge is pretty sketchy."
"Sometimes it can be that way."
"I'm guessing that . . ."
"I could be wrong, but . . ."
"It appears to me that . . ."
"I don't have firsthand experience with that."

Change of Scope

"It varies because . . ."
"Could you be more specific?"
"There's many reasons why. What were you referring to specifically?"
"I think you're splitting hairs."
"In general . . ."

Different Tack

"That depends on . . ."
"I think that's an unfair characterization . . ."

"It depends on how you look at it."

"To be fair, you should know that . . ."

"It depends on your point of view."

"It depends on several factors . . ."

"That's another subject."

"No, it's not quite that way."

"I should clarify . . ."

"That's not a yes or no question because . . ."

"That's a good question because. . . ." (then answer a different question.)

"I don't want to argue with you."

"I think that you need to understand the background first."

I Won't Answer

"I can't agree with you."

"That's outside my authority."

"I can't comment on that."

"I'd rather not discuss that."

Gaining
the High Ground

■ FORMS OF PROOF

Support your position with as many forms of proof as necessary. The more documentation you have, the more weight your position caries. Consider using:

- ➤ Audio recordings
- ➤ Books
- ➤ Checks
- ➤ Contracts
- ➤ Correspondence
- ➤ Documents

- ➤ Film clips
- ➤ Magazines
- ➤ Newspapers
- ➤ Photographs
- ➤ Receipts
- ➤ Videotapes

People in our seminars often comment, "But what I sell is *different*. I sell a *service,* and because it's *intangible,* traditional presentation methods won't work. How do I adjust?"

Keep in mind that *all* products have *both* tangible and intangible aspects. An automobile is a *tangible* bundle of steel and glass and electronics, but it is also an *intangible* bundle of prestige, freedom, and safety.

➤ Make the Intangible Tangible

When selling a service, the challenge is to solidify the intangible aspects into tangible forms that the customer can see, touch, and feel. Use presentation aides like faxed information, your

Web site, or videoconferences for telephone negotiations, or props and charts for in-person meetings. Invite your counterpart to tour your office or plant where they can get close to the action. One of our clients, a linen service, brings customers into the cleaning plant where they can hear the noise of the machinery and feel the heat of the steam presses.

➤ Make the Tangible Intangible

The opposite is true when selling tangible products. Because the tangible aspects are somewhat self-evident, negotiators typically emphasize these features. The challenge is to get your counterpart to *feel* the intangible benefits associated with the tangible features.

The guerrilla tactic is to emphasize these *intangible* aspects in your presentation, through testimonials, test results, or consumer reports. "The heated leather seats in the car are more *comfortable* in the winter." Or, "This mutual fund will not only provide a generous rate of return, but will give you a sense of *security* as it builds equity for your retirement."

■ FACTORS AFFECTING RECALL

How you sequence your presentation will affect how your demands are received, and which parts of the conversation your counterpart is most likely to recall.[1]

➤ Primacy

Open with a bang. Adults tend to remember the *first* thing they hear. Plan the opening of your negotiation very carefully. We suggest that you script and memorize it. Present your biggest demand first, and in the most passionate terms. People with higher expectations get larger settlements. This sets the expectations of your counterpart.

Open the negotiation on a secondary issue. This gives you a psychological advantage because your counterpart will give additional weight to whatever demand you make *first*. Use this

---

[1] Rose, Colin. *Accelerated Learning*. New York: Dell, 1987.

tactic to misdirect their attention away from your major issue. If you are more concerned about terms, open the discussion by demanding that they cut their price. Later on, when you concede to pay the asking price, you are more likely to get the favorable terms you really wanted.

➤ Recency

People also remember the *last* thing they've heard, so plan your closing arguments just as carefully. Imagine that you're making your closing statement to a jury.

Take advantage of the light-at-the-end-of-the-tunnel effect. Your counterpart is more likely to concede items asked for at the end of the negotiation. Use the Nibbler approach, "Just one more thing . . .," to improve your settlement before you adjourn.

➤ Specificity

People remember comments that include specific references, (even if those references are unspecified, as in the preceding examples). Do not guess. Do not round. Ask for specific concessions using accurate, multi-decimal place numbers. Offering an interest rate of 7.14 percent is perceived to be less negotiable than an offer of 7 percent. Quote actual statistics to support your rationale. Instead of saying, "Office space in this area rents for around $10.00 a foot," be specific. "The average rent for office space within a six-block radius is $10.32 a foot."

➤ Uniqueness

People remember things that are unusual, outstanding, or new. Use the Ripley effect. If you've ever been in one of these "Believe It or Not" museums you've experienced how uniqueness reinforces memory. Unique features evoke the influence principle of scarcity.

> "We are the *only* vendor with a warehouse within a five-mile radius of your plant."
>
> "This is a *patented* process."

"Guerrilla Selling is a *trademarked* seminar."

"I'm the *only* CPA in town who makes house calls."

Make sure that your claims of uniqueness are not so outrageous as to be unbelievable.

➤ Contrast

Comparisons, when properly constructed, can turn a negotiating weakness into a strength, especially when combined with presuppositions, emotive directors, minimizers, claiming to know, and other credibility builders from this arsenal.

From A to Z

From bad to worse

From cradle to grave

From head to toe

From pillar to post

From start to finish

Notice the difference between these two identical negotiating positions:

"The location isn't great, but it's cheap." versus "You're probably thinking that the location of this property is less than ideal, especially when you compare it to the much more expensive space downtown."

Or: "Yes, we know that our competitor's price is lower." versus "We have no argument with those who sell for less. They know best what their product is worth."

Or: "Our quality is great, but you'll have to wait." versus "Because of our production backlog, you may be disappointed by our delivery schedule, but you'll be astounded by our quality."

"While we may not be able to _____, you'll be happy to discover that we can _____ better than anyone."

"Perhaps our price seems a bit high, especially if you're comparing it to a quick fix."

Instead of saying, "That repair won't last," try this: "I realize that if all you want is a quick fix, that could be a temporary solution. If you're looking for a headache-free alternative, this works for you."

Notice how this response was constructed.

"*I realize that* (claiming to know) if all you *want* (trance word) is a *quick fix* (idiom), that *could be* (minimizer) a *temporary* solution (temporal control). If you're *looking for* (imagination trigger) a *headache-free* (credibility builder) *alternative* (option generator), *this works* for you." (embedded command)

➤ Gradient Comparison

You can greatly enhance the effectiveness of these weapons by combining them with a scratch-pad presentation that compares alternatives along a gradient.

For example, a painting contractor is negotiating a bid to paint a client's house, and the prospect complains that he is too expensive. Taking out a pad of paper, the painting contractor says, "Let me put this in perspective." Then he draws a line diagonally across the length of the pad from left bottom to top right. (See Figure 11.1.)

"At the cheap end of the scale you have the fly-by-nights," he says, writing it at the bottom of the gradient. "These guys typically work out of the trunk of their car. They *get by* with the cheapest tools and materials they can. Their office consists of an answering machine and a P.O. box. Because their overhead is so low, they can underbid everyone else *just to get the work.* Usually, they are not bonded or insured, so if they're injured on the

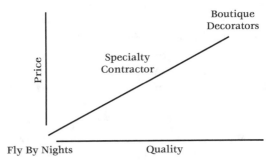

Figure 11.1 A painting contractor uses gradient comparison to help his customer understand the price.

job, you could be liable for tens of thousands of dollars. They may or may not show up on a particular day, and if they skip out, they're impossible to track down. But *if all you want* is a really cheap quote, they can give you that.

"At the expensive end of the scale you have the boutique decorators," he says, using the persuasive principle of *contrast* and writing it at the top of the gradient. "These people have a downtown boutique stocked with books of wallpaper, paint chips, fabric, and copies of *Architectural Digest*. The have rich references, a receptionist, and a custom van. They will show up on the job in spotless white uniforms. They use the very best materials and equipment, and they take their dear sweet time. If you *don't care* how long it takes or how much it costs, these are the people to use.

"In our case, we're a specialty contractor, and we would fall *more or less* in the middle of the scale. Our office is in the industrial park, right next door to our suppliers. Our painters are insured and bonded, so you *don't worry* about being liable if someone fell off a scaffold. We are big enough to afford a fleet of trucks, and equip our painters with the *best* tools and equipment. Because we have multiple jobs going on at any one time, we can move people around to *meet your deadline*. If there is a problem, all of our work is *guaranteed,* and *based on what you've told me so far,* that's what you really want."

"Now," he asks, putting the pen down, "does our quote *make sense to you?*"

■ 10 WAYS TO MAKE YOUR PRESENTATION IRRESISTIBLE

1. Discuss *specific* benefits your counterpart gains that would allow them to meet the needs they've discussed. People do things for *their* reasons, not yours. You might have 100 good reasons why they should agree with you; their decision will hinge on the three or four reasons that they consider important. Present *proof* that you can fulfill these few criteria, and you can safely ignore everything else.

2. Show *exclusive* or superior features. Don't waste time on basics. Discuss what your competitor can't do, but only

if it's important to your counterpart. Use the magic word *only.* "We are the *only* supplier that has a warehouse within same-day shipping radius of your plant."

3. Project that you are *dependable* and your company is a *reliable* vendor. This is done with with a professional attitude and a positive approach to negotiating. Negative remarks about your competition imply you don't really have a superior product and destroy your credibility.

4. Position what you offer as having the *right price.* Make sure your counterpart understands the value you provide for the price you ask. And that doesn't mean the *lowest* price (see Chapter 7).

5. Demonstrate that the time is right to decide *now.* Do this through special this-week-only pricing or promotions, or by immediately solving one of your counterpart's problems.

6. Use *proof statements,* based on your notes, to match your benefits to your counterpart's needs. "You mentioned that saving time is important to you. With this new technology, our product takes less time to do the job than what you're using now, thereby saving you hundreds of dollars."

7. Support your case with *visual aids.* Guerrillas use their Web site or the fax machine to deliver instant visuals while on the phone. "I'll fax you a chart that shows your savings over the next three months." "Go to our Web site, and I'll talk you through our catalog to help you find exactly what you're looking for." Have samples, props, charts, graphs, photos, and documents to support your position for in-person meetings.

8. Present an *emotional appeal.* Emotion puts the motion in motivation. Explain not only the features and advantages, but also put the prospect in the picture. Demonstrate how they will personally benefit. Put them in the action. Help them imagine themselves using the product, benefiting from it, and enjoying it.

9. Dramatize with *success stories.* These are especially effective when they're from your counterpart's indus-

try or location. "Widgets Inc. has slashed its production costs by 10 percent with this product."

10. Include a *demonstration.* If a picture's worth a thousand words, then a demonstration's worth a thousand pictures. Arrange for a demonstration. Have them come to your location, visit their home or office, or send them a videotape.

Chapter 12

How to Keep the Deal Together

Many deals come apart at the seams after the negotiation has closed. If the deal doesn't stick, why bother negotiating? Guerrillas ensure that the deal stays together by using these tactics.

■ HAVE THEM FILL OUT THE PAPERWORK

If they fill in the blanks or prepare the contracts, they will have a greater investment in the outcome and will be less likely to back out. You're using the influence principle of consistency. Once they write it themselves, they'll defend it.

■ CELEBRATORY LUNCH OR DINNER

Celebrate the successful conclusion of the negotiation by going out for a meal, and/or drinks. Breaking bread together helps cement the deal. This works well when you arrange to pick up the check in advance.

■ SEND THEM A THANK-YOU GIFT

Express your appreciation for their cooperation and constructive participation in the negotiation. A small token, such as a bouquet of flowers, a bottle of wine, or an autographed book does a lot to reinforce the relationship.

■ SEND THEIR BOSS A CONGRATULATORY LETTER

Congratulate them on having such an effective negotiator on their team. The word will get back to your counterpart.

■ SEND THEIR SECRETARY A CONGRATULATORY/THANK-YOU FAX

Thank them for any behind-the-scenes support they may have provided. The more people who have a stake in the outcome, the more likely the organization will follow through and deliver.

■ CALL TWO DAYS LATER TO FOLLOW UP

Check to see if there were any additional issues that surfaced after the negotiation. Deal with these matters immediately.

■ BE RESPONSIVE AND RESPONSIBLE

Keep up your end of the bargain by acting immediately. Ship the product, prepare the documents, or deposit the required funds in escrow immediately.

■ THANK-YOU NOTES

When you talk with someone particularly interesting, write a personal follow-up note. Let your prospect know that more information will follow in the mail, or that you'll be in touch soon.

The added contact of a personal note will take you miles ahead of your competition.

Use the guerrilla THANKS approach:

T—Today! Write your thank-you letter the same day if at all possible, and get it in the mail. The only thing worse than receiving a late thank-you note is receiving none at all. An E-mail thank-you note is inexpensive, easy to get out, and arrives instantaneously.

H—Handwritten. In today's world of word-processed every-thing, a handwritten note stands out in a stack of mail. It will probably be the first piece read. A barely legible scrawled sentence has more impact than a typewritten page. The exception: same-day E-mail.

A—Active. Make your note active. Don't start out, "Dear John"; say, "It was great to speak with you today, John!"

N—Next Step. Remind them what is scheduled to happen next. "I'm really looking forward to seeing the installation of your new equipment. Sincerely, Mary." Make sure your reader knows what to anticipate, what date to check, and when to expect action.

K—Keep It Short. You only need 25 words or so. A few sentences are enough to make the point and the impression. Write the note in 90 seconds or less.

S—Specific. Be very specific on why you're writing the note. For example, "I kept thinking about what you need and I believe I have an answer. I'll call Monday with my idea." You can be certain that your call will be taken.

■ SHADOWING THE DEAL

Negotiating an acceptable agreement is only the first step. Now you will have to track the deal all the way through your organization to make certain that they deliver what you promised, and that your counterpart does the same. Don't be surprised if, in the process, things change, and you find yourself right back in the negotiating arena once again. Fortunately, this time, you're better prepared and better armed than ever. After all, you're a guerrilla!

■ POSTMORTEM

Get together with your team and carefully analyze the outcome of the negotiation. How did it proceed? Did you follow your plan? Did you compensate for your counterpart's motivation? Did you adapt your presentation to their preferred forms of proof and communication style? Did you ask for what you wanted? Did you get it? If not, why not? Did you fall into any of the common negotiation traps, such as split the difference? What would you do differently next time?

Guerrillas make every negotiation a learning experience. When you do, you'll be a leader in your field.

Appendix

■ WORLD WIDE WEB RESEARCH RESOURCES

http://www.fuld.com/body.html

Fuld & Company presents a Competitive Intelligence Guide to pulling together information and creating intelligence on your counterpart. They serve more than half of the Fortune 500 companies.

➤ **http://www.montague.com/scip/scipweb.html**

The Society of Competitive Intelligence Professionals Web site offers ideas and resources for corporate intelligence.

➤ **http://www.indigo-net.com/intel.html**

An electronic version of *Intelligence Newsletter.* You can read about worldwide corporate and political intelligence. The headlines are free. There is a small charge to read the articles.

➤ **http://www.marketingtools.com**

The on-line version of *American Demographics* magazine. You can search archives of demographics.

➤ **http://www.businesswire.com**
http://www.prnewswire.com

Read corporate media releases including links to corporate Web sites on these competing services.

➤ **http://www.dnb.com**

For a few dollars run a background report on U.S. companies. Includes history, operations, management, and recent news.

➤ **http://www.hoovers.com**

Hoover's Business Profiles offers detailed profiles on thousands of companies, worldwide. They include sales figures, employee counts, and product summaries.

➤ **http://www.inquisit.com**

Inquisit is a subscription-based personal intelligence service that lets you track customers, competitors, markets, technologies (or almost anything that impacts your job or business), and then delivers it to you via E-mail, pager, or cell phone. The service lets you create your own "personal agents" that monitor more than 600 content sources and search for breaking information. Subscriptions are a small monthly charge. A free trial is available.

➤ **http://www.findsvp.com**

FIND/SVP consultants are a resource for executives who want to keep informed and stay ahead of the competition. From quick consulting to in-depth studies and custom analysis, their specialists can find the answers you need.

➤ **http://www.dialog.com**

The Dialog Corporation offers one of the most comprehensive, and most authoritative, sources of online information available.

➤ **http://www.lexis-nexis.com**

The LEXIS-NEXIS service contains more than one trillion characters and approximately one billion documents in more than 7,300 databases. It adds 9.5 million documents each week.

➤ International Resources

http://www.profnet.org/intermar.html offers a list of international marketing resources listed by country.
http://www.geocities.com/Athens/Forum/8363/ delivers ideas for managing cross-cultural issues.
http://www.webofculture.com specializes in dealing with cultural issues.

Bibliography

■ BOOKS

Acuff, Frank L. *How to Negotiate Anything With Anyone, Anywhere Around the World.* New York: AMACOM Books, 1997.

Aherman, Sandy. *25 Role Plays for Negotiation Skill.* Amherst, MA: Human Resource Development Press, 1997.

Albrecht, Karl and Ron Zemke. *Service America!* Homewood, IL: Dow Jones-Irwin, 1985.

Albrecht, Karl and Steve. *Added Value Negotiating: The Breakthrough Method for Building Balanced Deals.* Homewood, IL: Irwin Professional Publications, 1993.

Anderson, Kare. *Getting What You Want: How to Reach Agreement and Resolve Conflict Every Time.* New York: Plume, 1994.

Aubuchon, Norbert. *The Anatomy of Persuasion: How to Persuade Others to Act on Your Ideas, Accept Your Proposals, Buy Your Products or Services, Hire You, Promote You.* New York, AMACOM Books, 1997.

Bandler, Richard, and John Grinder. *Reframing.* Boulder, CO: Real People Press, 1979.

Bassham, Lanny. *With Winning in Mind.* Wilsonville, OR: BookPartners, Inc., 1995. 1-800-879-5079.

Bazerman, Max H. and Neale, Margaret A. *Negotiating Rationally.* New York: Free Press, 1993.

Belasco, James A. *Teaching the Elephant to Dance.* New York: Crown, 1990.

Beckwith, Harry. *Selling the Invisible.* New York: Warner Books, 1997.

Burg, Bob. *Endless Referrals: Network Your Everyday Contacts into Sales.* New York: McGraw-Hill, 1998.

Berne, Eric. *Games People Play.* New York: Ballantine, 1964.

Bettger, Frank. *How I Raised Myself from Failure to Success In Selling.* Englewood Cliffs, NJ: Prentice-Hall, 1975.

Brodow, Ed. *Negotiate with Confidence.* Washington, DC: AMI Press, 1996.

Canfield, Jack, and Mark Victor Hansen. *The Aladdin Factor.* New York: Berkley, 1995

Cates, Bill. *Unlimited Referrals.* Wheaton, MD: Thunder Hill Press, 1996.

Cathcart, Jim. *Relationship Selling.* New York: Perigee Books, 1990.

Chapman, Jack. *Negotiating Your Salary: How to Make $1,000 a Minute.* Seattle, WA: Ten Speed Press, 1996.

Charvet, Shelle Rose. *Words that Change Minds.* Dubuque, IA: Kendall/Hunt, 1997.

Cialdini, Robert B. *Influence: The Psychology of Persuasion.* New York: Quill, 1993.

Cohen, Herb. *You Can Negotiate Anything.* New York: Bantam Books, 1989.

Covey, Stephen R. *The Seven Habits of Highly Effective People.* New York: Simon & Schuster, 1989.

Dawson, Roger. *Secrets of Power Negotiating.* Franklin Lakes, NJ: Career Press, 1995.

Dawson, Roger. *Secrets of Power Persuasion.* New York: Prentice Hall, 1992.

Diener, Marc. *Deal Power: 6 Foolproof Steps to Making Deals of Any Size.* New York: Henry Holt, 1998.

Dolan, John Patrick. *Negotiate Like the Pros.* New York: Perigee, 1992.

Donaldson, Michael C., and Mimi. *Negotiating for Dummies.* Foster City, CA: IDG Books, 1996.

Farber, Donald C. *Common Sense Negotiation: The Art of Winning Gracefully.* Seattle, WA: Bay Press, 1996.

Fisher, Roger, and Danny Ertel. *Getting Ready to Negotiate: The Getting to Yes Workbook.* New York: Penguin, 1995.

Fisher, Roger, et al. *Beyond Machiavelli: Tools for Coping with Conflict.* New York: Penguin, 1996.

Fleming, Peter. *Negotiating a Better Deal.* Stamford, CT: International Thompson Business Press, 1997.

Fleming, Peter. *Successful Negotiating.* Hauppauge, NY: Barron's Educational Series, 1997.

Fuller, George. *The Manager's Negotiating Answer Book.* Englewood Cliffs, NJ: Prentice Hall, 1995.

Gerber, Michael E. *The E Myth.* Cambridge, MA: Ballinger, 1986.

Gitomer, Jeffrey. *The Sales Bible.* New York: William Morrow, 1994.

Gross, T. Scott. *How to Get What You Want from Almost Anybody.* New York: Mastermedia, 1992.

Hartman, George M. *How to Negotiate a Raise Without Losing Your Job.* Hauppauge, NY: Barron's Educational Series, 1997.

Helps, Vanessa. *Negotiating: Everybody Wins.* London: BBC Publications, 1995.

Ilich, John, and Robert K. Heady. *The Complete Idiot's Guide to Winning Through Negotiation.* New York: MacMillan, 1996.

Jandt, Fred Edmund. *Win–Win Negotiating: Turning Conflict into Agreement.* New York: John Wiley & Sons, 1987.

Karrass, Chester L. *Give and Take: The Complete Guide to Negotiating Strategies and Tactics.* New York: Thomas Y. Crowell, 1995.

Karrass, Chester L. *The Negotiating Game: How to Get What You Want.* New York: HarperBusiness, 1994.

Karrass, Gary. *Negotiate to Close: How to Make More Successful Deals.* New York: Simon & Schuster, 1987.

Kellar, Robert E. *Sales Negotiation Skills that Sell.* New York: AMACOM, 1996.

Kennedy, Daniel S., and Scott Degarmo. *How to Succeed in Business by Breaking All the Rules.* New York: Dutton, 1997.

Kennedy, Daniel S., and Maxwell Maltz, M.D. *Zero-Resistance Selling.* Englewood Cliffs, NJ: Prentice-Hall, 1997.

Kennedy, Daniel S. *No B.S. Business Success.* Bellingham, WA: Self-Counsel Press, 1998.

Kennedy, Gavin. *The New Negotiating Edge: How to Use Negotiating Styles and Strategies to Get the Results and Relationships.* London: Nicholas Brealey, 1998.

Knight, Sue. *NPL at Work.* London: Nicholas Brealey Publishing, 1995.

Kozicki, Stephen. *Creative Negotiating: Proven Techniques for Getting What You Want from Any Negotiation.* Holbrook, MA: Adams Publishing, 1998.

Kublin, Michael. *International Negotiating: A Primer for American Business Professionals.* Binghamton, NY: Haworth Press, 1995.

Laborde, Gene Z. *Influencing with Integrity.* New York: Sintony, Inc., 1984.

Lax, David A., and James K. Sebinius. *The Manager as Negotiator: Bargaining for Cooperation and Competitive Gain.* New York: Free Press, 1986.

LeBoeuf, Michael. *The Greatest Management Principle in the World.* New York: Berkley, 1985.

Lebow, Richard Ned. *The Art of Bargaining.* Baltimore, MD: John Hopkins University Press, 1996.

Levinson, Jay Conrad. *Get What You Deserve. How to Guerrilla Market Yourself.* New York: Avon Books, 1997.

Levinson, Jay Conrad, Bill Gallagher, and Orvel Ray Wilson. *Guerrilla Selling—Unconventional Weapons and Tactics for Increasing Your Sales.* Boston: Houghton Mifflin, 1992.

Levinson, Jay Conrad, Mark S.A. Smith, and Orvel Ray Wilson. *Guerrilla TeleSelling: New Unconventional Weapons and Tactics to Get the Business When You Can't Be There in Person.* New York: John Wiley & Sons, 1998.

Levinson, Jay Conrad, Mark S.A. Smith, and Orvel Ray Wilson. *Guerrilla Trade Show Selling: New Unconventional Weapons and Tactics to Meet More People, Get More Leads, and Close More Sales.* New York: John Wiley & Sons, 1997.
Levinson, Jay Conrad, and Seth Godin. *Guerrilla Marketing Handbook.* Boston: Houghton Mifflin, 1994.
Levinson, Jay Conrad. *Guerrilla Advertising: Cost-Effective Tactics for Small-Business Success.* Boston: Houghton Mifflin, 1994
——. *Guerrilla Marketing Attack: New Strategies, Tactics & Weapons for Winning Big Profits from Your Small Business.* Boston: Houghton Mifflin, 1987.
——. *Guerrilla Marketing Excellence: 50 Golden Rules for Small Business Success.* Boston: Houghton Mifflin, 1993.
——. *Guerrilla Marketing for the Home Based Business.* Boston: Houghton Mifflin, 1996.
——. *Guerrilla Marketing Third Edition.* Boston: Houghton Mifflin, 1998.
——. *Guerrilla Marketing Weapons: 100 Affordable Marketing Methods for Maximizing Profits from Your Small Business.* New York: Plume, 1990.
——. *Guerrilla Marketing With Technology.* New York: Addison-Wesley, 1997.
——. *The Way of the Guerrilla: Achieving Success and Balance as an Entrepreneur in the 21st Century.* Boston: Houghton Mifflin, 1997.
Lewicki, Roy J., et al. *Essentials of Negotiation.* 1997.
——. *Think Before You Speak: The Complete Guide to Strategic Negotiation.* New York: John Wiley & Sons, 1996.
Mackay, Harvey. *Beware the Naked Man Who Offers You His Shirt.* New York: Ivy Books, 1990.
——. *Swim with the Sharks Without Being Eaten Alive.* New York: Ivy Books, 1988.
Maddux, Robert B. *Successful Negotiation: Effective "Win–Win" Strategies and Tactics.* Menlo Park, CA: Crisp Publications, 1995.
Mattock, John, et al. *How to Be a Better . . . Negotiator.* Dover, NH: Kogan Page, Ltd., 1997.
McCormack, Mark H. *On Negotiating.* Newstar Press, 1997.
Moore, David C. *Government Contract Negotiations: A Practical Guide for Small Business.* New York: John Wiley & Sons, 1996.
Morrison, Terri, et al. *Kiss, Bow, or Shake Hands: How to Do Business in Sixty Countries.* Holbrook, MA: Bob Adams, Inc. 1994.
Nelson, Noelle C. *Winning! Using Lawyers' Courtroom Techniques to Get Your Way in Everyday Situations.* Englewood Cliffs, NJ: Prentice-Hall, 1997.

Nierenberg, Gerard I. *Do it Right the First Time: A Short Guide to Learning from Your Most Memorable Errors, Mistakes, and Blunders.* New York: John Wiley & Sons, 1996.

Onaitis, Susan. *Negotiate Like the Big Guys: How to Establish Fees, Reach Agreements, Finalize Contracts, While Building Long-Term Business Relationships.* 1998.

Patterson, James G. *How to Become a Better Negotiator.* New York: AMACOM, 1996.

Peoples, David. *Presentations Plus: David Peoples' Proven Techniques.* New York: John Wiley & Sons, 1988.

Rinke, Wolf J. *The 6 Success Strategies for Winning at Life, Love and Business.* Deerfield, FL: Health Communications, 1996.

Riso, Don Richard. *Personality Types.* Boston: Houghton Mifflin, 1987.

Roane, Susan. *How to Work a Room.* New York: Warner Books, 1988.

Rose, Colin, *Accelerated Learning,* New York: Dell, 1987.

Robinson, Colin. *Effective Negotiating.* Dover, NH: Kogan Page Ltd., 1997.

Rutherford, Robert D. *The 25 Most Common Mistakes Made in Negotiating . . . and What You Can Do About Them.* Boulder, CO: Rutherford Group. 1997.

Salacuse, Jeswald W. *Making Global Deals.* New York: Times Books, 1992.

Schaffzin, Nicholas Reid, *Don't Be a Chump!: Negotiating Skills You Need.* New York: Random House, 1995.

Schoonmaker, Alan N. *Negotiate to Win: Gaining the Psychological Edge.* Englewood Cliffs, NJ: Prentice-Hall, 1989.

Schwartz, David. *The Magic of Thinking Big.* Englewood Cliffs, NJ: Prentice-Hall, 1965.

Shapiro, Ronald, and Mark Jankowski. *The Power of Nice: How to Negotiate So Everyone Wins—Especially You!* New York: John Wiley & Sons, 1998.

Simon, Mary B. *Negotiate Your Job Offer: A Step-By-Step Guide to a Win-Win Situation.* New York: John Wiley & Sons, 1997.

Skopec, Eric W., and Laree S. Kiely. *Everything's Negotiable When You Know How to Play the Game.* New York: AMACOM, 1994.

Slutsky, Jeff. *How to Get Clients.* New York: Warner Books, 1992.

Slutsky, Jeff. *Streetfighting.* Englewood Cliffs, NJ: Prentice-Hall, 1984.

Spence, Gerry. *How to Argue and Win Every Time.* New York: St. Martin's, 1996.

Steinmetz, Lawrence L. *How to Sell at Prices Higher than Your Competitors.* Boulder: Horizon Publications, 1994. (800) 323-2835

Pearson, Ginny. *Successful Negotiating: Letting the Other Person Have Your Way.* Franklin Lakes, NJ: Career Press, 1998.

Toffler, Alvin. *Future Shock.* New York: Random House, 1970.

——. *Powershift.* New York: Bantam, 1990.

Udall, Sheila, and Jean-Marie Hiltrop. *The Essence of Negotiation.* Englewood Cliffs, NJ: Prentice Hall, 1995.

Ury, William, and Roger Fisher. *Getting to Yes: Negotiating Agreement Without Giving In.* New York: Penguin, 1991.

Ury, William. *Getting Past No: Negotiating Your Way from Confrontation to Cooperation.* New York: Bantam, 1993.

Walker, Michael A., and George L. Harris. *Negotiations: Six Steps to Success.* Englewood Cliffs, NJ: Prentice Hall, 1995.

Zeckhauser, Richard J. (Ed.), et al. *Wise Choices: Decisions, Games, and Negotiations.* Boston: Harvard Business School Press, 1996.

■ AUDIOTAPES[1]

Dolan, John Patrick. *Negotiate Like the Pros.* Boulder, CO: CareerTrack Publications, 1990.

Nierenberg, Gerard I. *The Art of Negotiating,* Audio Cassette, Los Angeles: Dove Books Audio, 1996.

Wilson, Orvel Ray. *Guerrilla Selling—Live!* Boulder, CO: The Guerrilla Group, Inc, 1996. (800-247-9145)

■ VIDEO TRAINING MATERIALS

Wilson, Orvel Ray. *Guerrilla Selling—Live!* Boulder, CO: The Guerrilla Group, Inc., 1996.

---

[1] To order audio and video materials call CareerTrack Publications (800-334-1018, or, in Colorado, 303-447-2323) or Nightingale-Conant Corporation (800-323-5552).

Index

About the Authors

■ JAY CONRAD LEVINSON

As an author, speaker, workshop leader, and owner of a successful marketing firm, Jay personifies the true entrepreneur. Before embarking on his life of writing and public speaking, he was a vice president and creative director at one of the largest advertising agencies in the world. With an award-winning career in advertising and a nationally syndicated column, Jay has authored 25 books, including the best-selling marketing book ever, *Guerrilla Marketing* (Boston: Houghton Mifflin, 1984) with more than 800,000 copies sold. His work has been translated into 37 languages. He is also coauthor of *Guerrilla Selling: Unconventional Weapons and Tactics for Increasing Your Sales* (with Bill Gallagher, Ph.D., and Orvel Ray Wilson, CSP, Houghton Mifflin) and *Guerrilla Trade Show Selling* (with Orvel Ray Wilson and Mark S.A. Smith, John Wiley & Sons. The books have led to a rapidly growing newsletter, *The Guerrilla Marketing Newsletter,* two successful audiotapes, a videotape, columns on marketing in 12 national publications, and presentations at major conventions throughout North America.

He served as senior VP and creative director for the world's largest advertising agency, J. Walter Thompson, and sat on the board of directors at Leo Burnett Advertising in the United States and Europe. His work has won major awards worldwide, in virtually every marketing media, including direct mail, television, radio, and magazines. Current clients include Fortune 500 companies, and start-ups that want to be.

Levinson's small business expertise has also been demonstrated in his *Earning Money Without a Job, 555 Ways to Earn Extra Money* (Holt, Rinehart & Winston, 1979 and 1982), and *Quit Your Job!* (Dodd, Mead, 1987).

He has been married 41 years, has one child, and lives north of San Francisco.

■ MARK S. A. SMITH

An internationally renowned speaker and writer on sales, Mark has been producing and delivering seminars on sales topics since 1982. He is one of The Guerrilla Group's highest-rated speakers. His clients demand his return year after year to deliver new and innovative training and keynote speeches at their sales events. His repeat clients include IBM, Raytheon Aircraft, AT&T Capital, Goodkind & O'Dea, igus, Association of Incentive Manufacturers, Meeting Professionals International, Meridian VAT Reclaim, and Bankers Life Insurance.

He has published more than 300 articles on various sales and marketing topics. He is coauthor of *Guerrilla Trade Show Selling* (with Orvel Ray Wilson and Jay Levinson, John Wiley & Sons, 1997) and *Guerrilla TeleSelling* (with Orvel Ray Wilson and Jay Levinson, John Wiley & Sons, 1998).

Although he graduated with a degree in electrical engineering, he went straight into sales support for Hewlett-Packard. Based in Amsterdam for three years, he was European product manager. Later he was worldwide sales manager for a high-tech software company, growing sales by 600 percent over four years, primarily with teleselling efforts and trade shows.

Mark has served as president of the Colorado chapter of the National Speakers Association.

■ ORVEL RAY WILSON, CSP

An internationally acclaimed author and standing-ovation speaker on sales, marketing, and management, Wilson's speaking career, launched in 1980, has taken him to more than 1,000 cities in the United States, Australia, Canada, England, Germany, and the Soviet Union. His content-packed programs are entertaining, motivating, and memorable. He is the coauthor of the runaway best-selling book, *Guerrilla Selling: Unconventional Weapons and Tactics for Increasing Your Sales,* with Bill Gallagher and Jay Conrad Levinson, (Houghton Mifflin, 1992) and *Guerrilla Trade Show Selling: Unconventional Weapons and Tactics to Meet More People, Get More Leads, and Close More Sales,* with Mark S. A. Smith (John Wiley & Sons, 1997).

Already in its ninth printing, *Guerrilla Selling* has since been published in German, Korean, and Romanian. It was featured as "one of the 10 most important business books of the decade" in the July 1994 issue of *Selling* magazine. His articles appear regularly in dozens of industry and trade magazines.

He started his career early, selling garden seeds door-to-door when he was 12 years old, and he founded his first company at 19. More than 25 years of real-world sales experience spans the range from encyclopedias to advertising, from automobiles to computers. He's taught closing techniques to Xerox field reps, and job search skills to Indochinese refugees.

In 1980, he founded the Boulder Sales Training Institute, and his client list has since grown to include industry leaders like Apple Computer, Century 21, and CellularOne. He has taught in the management development programs for the University of Colorado and the University of Denver, and has created innovative business courses for Harbridge House, the University of Toledo, the Spring Institute for International Studies, and Australia's Canberra College of Advanced Education. He has even pioneered workshops on capitalism for the Tyumen School of Management in the Russian Republic.

Recognized as a leader by his peers as well, Orvel Ray served as president of the Colorado Chapter of the National Speakers Association in 1986, and served two additional terms on their board of directors. In 1997, the National Speakers Association bestowed upon him the highest earned award in the speaking profession, the Certified Speaking Professional, an honor held by fewer than 300 of all professional speakers worldwide.

He's led hundreds of large-audience seminars and on-site workshops, including "How to Give Exceptional Customer Service," "Managing Multiple Demands," "Taking Control of Your Workday," "Effective Collection Strategies," "Power Presentation Skills," and "Dealing with Difficult People." He has also collaborated with best-selling authors to develop seminar versions of *Guerrilla Marketing* by Jay Conrad Levinson, *The Time Trap* by Alec McKenzie, and *Don't Do, Delegate!* by Jack Kelly and John Jenks. He is also the author of four audiotape albums and several videos, including *The Art of Persuasion—A Win/Win Approach*, *Selling Smart* (CareerTrack Publications, 1988), *Guerrilla Selling—Live!*, and *Guerrilla Selling in Action*. All enjoy international distribution.

Orvel Ray is president of The Guerrilla Group, Inc., an international training and consulting firm serving clients worldwide.

About the Guerrilla Group Inc

■ INCREASE YOUR SALES NOW

Make your sales force exceptional at:

- ➤ Guerrilla Negotiating
- ➤ Guerrilla Selling
- ➤ Guerrilla TeleSelling
- ➤ Guerrilla Trade Show Selling
- ➤ Customer Service Excellence
- ➤ Managing Multiple Demands
- ➤ Guerrilla Marketing

We coach companies how to increase sales with the unconventional weapons and tactics of Guerrilla Selling and Guerrilla Marketing. Call The Guerrilla Group today at 800-247-9145 to find out how we can do this for your people.

You can expect fully-customized on-site training programs and seminars in formats ranging from a 30-minute keynote to a multi-day boot camp, from sales interventions to long-term consulting.

Our clients tell us that they choose us because we deliver the "how-to-do-it" as well as the "what-to-do" to win the business. Call today for more information.

■ THE GUERRILLA GROUP inc

947 Walnut Street
Boulder, CO 80302
800-247-9145
http://www.guerrillagroup.com
postmaster@guerrillagroup.com